Welfare Reform
in
West Virginia

Welfare Reform in West Virginia

by

Robert Jay Dilger
Eleanor H. Blakely • Melissa Latimer
Barry L. Locke • F. Carson Mencken
L. Christopher Plein • Lucinda A. Potter
David Williams

West Virginia University Press
Morgantown 2004

West Virginia University Press, Morgantown 26506
© 2004 by West Virginia University Press

All rights reserved

First edition published 2004 by West Virginia University Press
Printed in the United States of America

10 09 08 07 06 05 04   9 8 7 6 5 4 3 2 1

ISBN 0-937058-82-3 (alk. paper)

Library of Congress Cataloguing-in-Publication Data

West Virginia University Press.
Welfare Reform in West Virginia / Robert Jay Dilger, Eleanor H. Blakely, Melissa Latimer, Barry L. Locke, F. Carson Mencken, L. Christopher Plein, Lucinda A. Potter, David Williams.
328 p. 23 cm.

1. Public Welfare—United States. 2. Public Welfare—West Virginia. 3. Social Service—United States. 4. West Virginia—Economic Conditions. 5. Welfare recipients—Employment—West Virginia. 6. Social work with the unemployed—West Virginia. I. Title. II. Dilger, Robert Jay. III. Blakely, Eleanor H. IV. Latimer, Melissa. V. Locke, Barry L. VI. Mencken, F. Carson. VII. Plein, L. Christopher. VIII. Potter, Lucinda A. IX. Williams, David.
IN PROCESS

Library of Congress Control Number: 2004106782

Cover photo by Neal Newfield, WVU Social Work
Cover map by WV State GIS Technical Center/US Geologic Survey
Printed in USA by Bookmasters

Table of Contents

Acknowledgments vii

Chapter 1: Studying Welfare Reform in West Virginia 1
    Robert Jay Dilger

Chapter 2: Setting the Socioeconomic Context for Welfare Reform in Appalachia 23
    Melissa Latimer

Chapter 3: Cash Assistance and Social Welfare Policy in the United States: The Political and Institutional Context 55
    Robert Jay Dilger

Chapter 4: Managing Welfare Reform in West Virginia: Lessons Learned 107
    L. Christopher Plein and David Williams

Chapter 5: Implementing Reform in West Virginia: The Evolution of Field Level Administration 137
    L. Christopher Plein

Chapter 6: Welfare Reform's Consequences for West Virginia's Safety Net System 163
    L. Christopher Plein

Chapter 7: Training Opportunities and Outcomes for WV WORKS Recipients 209
    Melissa Latimer

Chapter 8: Is Work the Solution? 237
    Lucinda A. Potter

Table of Contents

Chapter 9: The Most At-Risk, Disadvantaged Populations in West Virginia 261
Robert Jay Dilger

Chapter 10: WV WORKS Recipients' Orientations About the Future: Does Place Matter?... 287
F. Carson Mencken

Chapter 11: Lessons From the Mountain State............................ 303
Eleanor H. Blakely, Robert Jay Dilger and Barry L. Locke

About the Authors 317

Index 321

Acknowledgments

This work is an outcome of a long-term collaboration between West Virginia University and the West Virginia Department of Health and Human Resources. Special appreciation is extended to the Department's officers and staff who worked closely with the authors on several research projects involving WV WORKS recipients. The authors also wish to extend a special thank-you to the thousands of West Virginians who shared their WV WORKS experiences with us. This book would not have been possible without their contribution.

The opinions and conclusions expressed in this book are solely those of the authors and should not be considered to represent the views of any agency or individual within West Virginia state government, or the United States Libarary of Congress.

Robert Jay Dilger
Eleanor H. Blakely
Melissa Latimer
Barry L. Locke
F. Carson Mencken
L. Christopher Plein
Lucinda A. Potter
David Williams

Chapter 1

Studying Welfare Reform in West Virginia

ROBERT JAY DILGER

Cash assistance for the poor, what people commonly refer to as welfare, has been one of the most talked about and criticized intergovernmental programs in American political history. Elected officials, federal, state, and local government administrators, scholars, and political pundits have quarreled over the program's structure, its goals, who it should serve, what, if anything, recipients should do in exchange for receiving benefits, and if the program has been a success or a failure. These differences are rooted in long-standing, fundamental disagreements concerning government's role in American society and the best means to help the poor leave and stay off welfare (Washington Research Council 1998). In recent years, the debate has focused on the efficacy of the human capital development strategy (i.e., focusing on education and job training programs) versus the workforce attachment strategy (i.e., focusing on immediate job placement) to help recipients leave, and stay off, welfare.

Given the often acrimonious and partisan debate that has taken place over welfare legislation in recent years, it may seem surprising that the federal government's cash assistance program for the poor enjoyed relatively widespread support when it was created in 1935, and it continued to enjoy bipartisan political support for many years. Initially, cash assistance for the poor (called Aid to Dependent Children (ADC) until 1962, Aid to Families With Dependent Children (AFDC) from 1962 to 1995, and Temporary Assistance for Needy Families (TANF) since 1996) provided funding to serve the needs of children under age 16 who were orphaned or in households with only one adult female caretaker present.[1] In 1940, program eligibility was extended to older children and, in 1950, to the child's mother or other female caretaker. The extension of program eligibility to adults altered the nature of the debate concerning the program's future. American political culture, molded by the Protestant work ethic and "liberal" values of individualism, personal responsibility, the importance of work, and a general distrust of collectivism and centralized government, ran counter to the notion of providing governmental assistance to adults, especially able-bodied adults, without receiving some form of "payment" in return (Hofstadter 1948; Leiby 1978; Reid 1995). Initially, welfare mothers "earned" their benefits by providing children ". . . the physical and affectionate guardianship necessary . . . [to] rear them into citizens capable of contributing to society" (Garfinkel and McLanahan 1986, 102). However, as structural changes in the American economy led to increased numbers of women entering the workforce, many began to question why welfare mothers were not required to earn their benefits through work. Also, the extension of program eligibility to unemployed fathers in two-parent families, as a state option in 1962 and mandated in 1990, led to increased debate concerning what able-bodied adult recipients should be expected to do to earn their benefits and, related to that debate, the most appropriate means to ensure that their stay on cash assistance was as brief as possible.

Congressional debate concerning welfare's future and the best means to help recipients to become economically self-sufficient has always had ideological and partisan overtones. Historically, congressional members aligned with the political "right" have attempted to (1) contain program costs by targeting resources to the "truly" needy, (2) provide states maximum programmatic flexibility to encourage experimentation, innovation, and cross-state learning, and (3) focus resources on the workforce attachment strategy as the best means to help recipients leave welfare and become economically self-sufficient. Those aligned with the political "left" have attempted to (1) expand eligibility to enable a greater percentage of those with incomes below the national poverty line to participate in the program, (2) impose national minimum standards on states to increase benefit levels, expand program eligibility, and equalize recipient treatment nationwide, and (3) focus resources on the human capital development strategy as the best means to help recipients leave welfare and become economically self-sufficient.

Congressional debate concerning welfare's future became increasingly partisan following the enactment of legislation in 1967, advocated by those aligned with the political "left," that required states to disregard one-third (plus $30) of an applicant's income when determining program eligibility. Ironically, this income disregard rule was designed to encourage recipients to work. At that time, welfare recipients were automatically enrolled in Medicaid. Many recipients worried that if they went to work they would not only lose their cash assistance, but their medical benefits as well. Although those aligned with the political "right" valued work, the income disregard rule led to a dramatic increase in program enrollment over the next four years, from 5 million recipients in 1967 to 10.2 million recipients in 1971. As the program grew in both size (increasing to 14.2 million recipients in 1994) and cost ($27 billion in 1994, $15 billion from the federal government and $12 billion from the states), opposition to the program from fiscal conservatives in both major political parties, but especially from within the Republican Party, became more widespread. In addition, noting that a large number of welfare recipients (approximately 15%) received cash assistance for many years, several scholars and others associated with the political "right" argued that the poor had become so accustomed to receiving government handouts that they had forgotten how to take personal responsibility for their own futures. They were convinced that cash assistance and related social-welfare programs (Medicaid, Food Stamps, public housing, etc.) were creating an enduring culture of poverty, where government assistance was likened to an addictive narcotic. Worse, recipients were passing these "un-American" values to their children, creating a vicious, intergenerational cycle of poverty (Murray 1984; 1986). Specifically, they complained that welfare and related government support programs (1) discouraged work by providing benefits equivalent to, or better than, entry-level jobs, (2) encouraged sloth by providing benefits to "non-deserving," able-bodied adults capable of working, (3) encouraged immoral behavior by increasing benefits for each additional child, even if the child was born out-of-wedlock, and (4) discouraged marriage by counting the husband's income when determining program eligibility. Moreover, they argued that despite spending tens of billions of dollars on welfare and other government support programs each year, there was little improvement in the national poverty rate. To address these deficiencies, they advocated a major program overhaul, with an increased emphasis on the work attachment strategy to assist recipients to escape poverty, and additional programmatic flexibility to allow states to experiment and learn from each other's successes and failures.

Those advocating the human capital development strategy for assisting recipients in making the transition off welfare disagreed. They argued that most recipients want to work, lead a decent, moral life, and do whatever is necessary to ensure that their children have a better life than their own. However, many of them were victims of unfortunate circumstances largely beyond their control. These include poor educational systems, racial and gender discrimination, structural flaws in the economic system, and physical and emotional disabilities. As a result, government had an obligation to provide these individuals with the economic resources necessary to survive while they received the help necessary (primarily education and job training assistance) to compete for decent paying jobs in the private marketplace. To prove their point about recipient motives, they noted that the vast majority of recipients received cash assistance for only a year or two, and that most of those who were on cash assistance for longer periods of time had legitimate reasons for not working, such as a physical or mental disability (U.S. ACIR 1980; Ellwood and Summers 1986; Nathan et al. 1980; Nathan 1983).

A New Direction

Although various work-related provisions have been part of the cash assistance program since 1960 (see Chapters 3 and 8 for additional details), the human capital development strategy generally prevailed until 1996. At that time, a host of political and cultural circumstances converged creating the conditions necessary for the work attachment strategy to achieve prominence (see Chapter 3 for details). In 1996, President Bill Clinton, after twice vetoing welfare reform legislation emphasizing the work attachment strategy earlier in his presidency, fulfilled his 1992 presidential campaign promise to "end welfare as we know it" by signing into law the six-year, $110 billion *Personal Responsibility and Work Opportunity Reconciliation Act of 1996*.

The 1996 welfare reform law was based on the assumption that most adult recipients are not victims of unfortunate circumstances or forces largely beyond their control. Instead, recipients are seen as being responsible for their own circumstances, and, therefore, responsible for changing them. The law emphasized the work attachment strategy and contained numerous provisions (especially a new 60-month maximum limit on the receipt of benefits and the imposition of mandatory state work participation rates and fiscal sanctions for noncompliance) that, collectively, were designed to force recipients and state welfare bureaucracies to "change their ways." Importantly, it also "de-linked" cash assistance from Medicaid. The result was a dramatic decline in welfare caseloads nationwide and in West Virginia.

Nationally, TANF enrollment fell from 11.4 million in January 1997 to 9.1 million in January 1998. Enrollment continued to decline, falling to 7.4 million in January 1999 and 6.2 million in January 2000. The reductions were even more dramatic in West Virginia. In January 1997, there were 98,690 West Virginians on welfare. By January 1998, that number had been cut almost in half, to 51,348. A year later, the figure was 32,161, and by January 2000 there were 28,850 West Virginians receiving cash assistance (DHHS 2000).

TANF's dramatic enrollment drop, both nationally and in West Virginia, was viewed initially by many policymakers as an indication that the 1996 welfare reform law was working. The reductions, it seemed, clearly indicated that the law was meeting one of its stated goals, stemming the rising tide of welfare dependency. At first, it was assumed that TANF enrollment declined because the law's provisions encouraged welfare recipients to find work at a time when the national economy was booming, and jobs, especially entry-level jobs, were relatively plentiful. However, a closer examination of state welfare agency data revealed that, nationwide, fewer than half of the recipients who left welfare were employed. In West Virginia, fewer than one-third of those who left welfare following the new law's enactment entered the workforce (Fischer 1998; WV WORKS 1998). Policymakers and academics across the nation, and in West Virginia, began to ask questions, such as:

- "What is happening to these people?"

- "If many leavers (those who had left TANF) are not finding employment, what are they doing, how are they getting by, and why did they leave?"

- "Were former recipients on the way to economic self-sufficiency, or were they likely to return to TANF during the next recession?"

- "Now that each state's allotment of federal funding is fixed, if leavers return in large numbers, will states have the resources and/or the political will to use their own money to assist them?"

- "Were the dramatic caseload reductions following the 1996 reforms an indication that welfare reform was helping the poor escape poverty or an indication that many recipients had decided that they would rather "go it alone" than deal with the social stigma of being on welfare and dealing with the program's work and other requirements?"

West Virginia's Welfare Leavers

In 1999, West Virginia's Department of Health and Human Resources (DHHR) provided funding to the authors of this book to design, administer, and interpret a comprehensive statewide survey of West Virginians who left WV WORKS (the title of West Virginia's TANF program) during 1998. The study's primary objectives were to provide:

- Information concerning why the respondents left WV WORKS,
- A profile of their current economic and social well-being,
- An indication of how welfare reform affected their behavior and prospects for economic self-sufficiency,
- Their assessment of their experiences with DHHR's programs.

Because the federal government does not require states to provide detailed reports on the status of their former welfare recipients, the only systematic data available about welfare leavers was from research efforts states initiated to meet their own information needs (GAO 1999). Fortunately, the National Conference of State Legislatures (NCSL) kept track of these efforts and served as a central repository for information concerning those who have left welfare since the *Personal Responsibility and Work Opportunity Reconciliation Act of 1996* went into effect. To date, NCSL has obtained information from thirty states and the District of Columbia that have conducted or sponsored studies of their state's welfare leavers, creating a national database for making comparisons. Also, in 1997 the Urban Institute released its *National Survey of America's Families* (Loprest 1999). This comprehensive survey of American families in thirteen states also provided a great deal of information concerning the poor and near poor in the United States that can be used for making comparisons.

Most of these state studies were based upon telephone interviews with former recipients. The authors also considered using a telephone survey. However, DHHR officials were reluctant to provide their welfare leavers' telephone numbers to non-Department personnel. Also, given the transient nature of welfare leavers, the reliability of the Department's list of leavers' telephone numbers was suspect. As a result, DHHR asked the authors to conduct a mail survey. This turned out to be a fortuitous decision for two reasons. First, welfare leavers tend to move fairly often. When they move, they often change their telephone number. This reduces the reliability of welfare leaver telephone lists and raises concerns over the validity of survey results drawn from such lists. Mail surveys, on the other hand, can compensate for welfare leavers' transient nature by making use of the U.S. Postal Service's address correction service. Although some of the West Virginia welfare leaver mail surveys were rerouted more than once (one survey was rerouted four times before being returned to the authors as undeliverable), the U.S. Postal Service's address correction service guaranteed that nearly all of the mail surveys would eventually find their way to the welfare leaver. Second, and importantly, it was later discovered that almost half of West Virginia's current welfare recipients do not have access to a working telephone. This suggests that using telephone surveys to assess the views of West Virginia's poor and near poor populations may suffer serious validity problems.

The ten-page, eighty-question WV WORKS leaver survey was developed in close consultation with DHHR officials. It was mailed to 1,900 randomly selected WV WORKS leavers in July 1999. To encourage a high response rate, respondents were guaranteed anonymity and informed that DHHR had agreed to use the aggregate survey results to improve the program. Also, because response rates to mail surveys are often low, especially when the survey population has relatively low income and educational levels, respondents were offered $15 to complete the survey. These strategies worked. Half of the surveys (962) were completed and returned. The respondents' demographic characteristics were compared to the demographic characteristics of WV WORKS' adult recipients to make certain that the survey respondents were representative of the survey population. Their characteristics were very similar to the population of WV WORKS adult recipients in all respects, including gender, age, marital status, location, and ethnicity. The survey results were presented to DHHR officials in December 1999 and to two state legislative committees in January 2000 (Dilger et al. 1999).

The WV WORKS leaver survey results contained both good and bad news. The good news was that most of the respondents who left the program in 1998 were still off the program when they completed the survey in 1999, more than half of the respondents (54.3%) were employed, and, as a group, their assessment of their future and their children's future was relatively positive. Also, the respondents' answers, especially to open-ended questions concerning what they would do to improve their personal and family's well-being, suggested that they are a remarkably resilient group who are trying to improve their lives and their children's lives. Most of them were struggling financially, yet, as a group, they maintained a relatively positive outlook on life.

The bad news was that many of the respondents were experiencing severe financial difficulties. Most of the respondents (82.9%) had a total annual household income of $10,000 or less, and many experienced times when they did not have enough money to buy food, go to the doctor, or buy medicine. Also, 8 percent of the respondents reported that their financial situation was much worse since leaving WV WORKS/TANF, and 13.5 percent reported that their future looked very poor. The situation of those reporting that they are now much worse off since leaving WV WORKS/TANF was best represented by the following response to the open-ended question: "If there was one thing you could do to improve your family's well-being, what would it be?" The respondent wrote: "I need a miracle."

WV WORKS' Current Recipients

West Virginia's DHHR officials subsequently cited the authors' WV WORKS leaver study's research findings as one of the reasons they decided to increase funding for various support services for WV WORKS' recipients and to provide additional transitional benefits for WV WORKS leavers. They also provided the authors additional funding to administer a comprehensive statewide survey of WV

WORKS recipients enrolled in the program during 2000. The second study's primary objectives were to provide:

- The recipients' assessments of their experiences with WV WORKS, DHHR's personnel and services, and other government assistance programs,
- Information concerning their work experiences and job readiness,
- Their assessment of their experiences with vocational, educational, and job training programs,
- Information concerning their childcare needs and arrangements, and their assessment of what should be done to meet those needs,
- A profile of their current economic and social well-being,
- An indication of how welfare reform has affected their behavior and their prospects for economic self-sufficiency,
- Information concerning their knowledge of WV WORKS' rules and regulations, and of other governmental programs available to assist them,
- Their assessment of what the state should do to improve their social and economic well-being, including recommended changes to WV WORKS.

The ten-page, seventy-nine question WV WORKS recipient survey was developed in consultation with DHHR officials and mailed to 2,100 randomly selected WV WORKS recipients in August 2000. Respondents were guaranteed anonymity and informed that DHHR would use the aggregate survey results to improve the program. Respondents were also offered $15 as an inducement to complete the survey. Fifty-seven percent of the surveys (1,206) were completed and returned. The respondents' demographic characteristics were then compared to the demographic characteristics of WV WORKS adult recipients to ensure that the survey respondents were representative of the survey population. The respondents' demographic characteristics were very similar to the population of WV WORKS adult recipients in all respects, including gender, age, marital status, location, and ethnicity.

The WV WORKS recipient survey results were presented to DHHR officials in June 2001 (Dilger et al. 2001). Again, like the WV WORKS leaver survey, the WV WORKS recipient survey contained both good and bad news. The good news was that most of the respondents were relatively satisfied with how DHHR personnel treated them, the help DHHR provided helping them obtain other benefits, and with their overall experience with their caseworker. However, many respondents reported that they did not have the knowledge necessary to make an informed judgment about a wide range of issues and available services. For example, although DHHR provided recipients with information about all of the following, most of the respondents (71%) reported that they did not know how many months of eligibility they had left in the program. Less than half of the respondents reported that they had enough information about educational options (48%), transportation reimbursements (37%), job training options (36.9%), supportive services (clothing needed for work, car repair, etc.) (35.8%), childcare support or subsidies (35.3%), the federal earned income tax credit (26.8%), WV WORKS dental and vision benefits (26.1%), transitional Medicaid benefits (26%), and the employer health insurance buy-in program (15.5%).

The survey also revealed that nearly two-thirds (65.1%) of the respondents had an annual household income below $5,000, and more than half of the respondents reported that while they were on WV WORKS they had experienced times when they did not have enough money to get glasses (55.6%), buy food (52.9%), buy medicine (52%), and go to the dentist (51%). In addition, many respondents reported that their personal and financial futures look poor or very poor. Yet, as a group, respondents were relatively optimistic concerning their children's future, and nearly two-thirds reported that they did not expect to be on WV WORKS next year.

A statistical analysis of the survey results disclosed that respondents lacking a General Educational Development credential (GED) or high school degree (39.6% of respondents), are over age thirty (48.3%), reside in an economically distressed county (defined by the Appalachian Regional Commission) (56.5%), or have applied for and received AFDC/TANF benefits more than three times in their lifetime (48.7%) had the most difficult time coping both financially and socially. These groups are at high risk of not being able to make the transition from WV WORKS to economic self-sufficiency.

For a number of reasons, including political pressure to spend TANF funds that had been set aside in case of an economic downturn, West Virginia's DHHR officials subsequently increased recipient cash assistance payments and funding for existing support services. DHHR also later contracted with various nonprofit organizations to implement several new support service programs (see Chapter 4 for details). These expenditures alleviated the most dire economic pressures WV WORKS recipients faced and expanded opportunities for recipients to prepare for, find, and retain employment. However, in 2002, DHHR reluctantly reduced funding for many support programs as they spent down their TANF funds and state revenue tightened as the national and state economy weakened. One hundred and seven support services contracts with local nonprofit organizations were canceled, reducing expenditures by approximately $27 million a year. The cuts eliminated 521 jobs in the nonprofit sector and affected a variety of programs, including child protective services, truancy diversion, domestic violence prevention, assistance for the homeless, and several welfare-to-work projects (Kabler 2002).

The Next Logical Step for the Research

The authors' WV WORKS leaver and WV WORKS recipient surveys provide one of the most comprehensive data sets available in the United States regarding recipient and former recipient perspectives about and experiences with welfare reform within a single state. The authors' previous reports concerning these surveys provide an excellent overview of recipient and leaver perspectives on welfare reform in West Virginia (Dilger et al. 1999; Dilger et al. 2001). This book extends the analysis begun in these previous reports. It utilizes the survey data, as well as information garnered from studies about welfare reform in other states and interviews and personal interactions with key policymakers, both in West Virginia and in other states, to more fully describe, explain, and assess West

Virginia's experiences with welfare reform. The results of the analysis are then used to reach conclusions and recommend policy concerning welfare reform in general, and specifically for welfare reform in rural areas and in areas experiencing economic hardship.

Why a Book about West Virginia?

Studying West Virginia's experiences with welfare reform is, obviously, of great interest to West Virginia's policymakers, administrators, scholars, advocates, and recipients. Learning about how welfare reform policy was implemented and discovering its effect on recipients can help West Virginians determine how to best design and implement more effective welfare policies in the future. However, at first glance, it might be assumed that West Virginia's experiences with welfare reform might be of only marginal interest to policymakers, administrators, scholars, advocates, and welfare recipients in other states. West Virginia, after all, is a relatively small, rural, "post-industrial" state, with just 1.8 million people. It has one of the oldest populations in the nation, and because the state's population is overwhelmingly white, with relatively few members of minority groups, in many respects it is not representative of the nation. In social science terms, it is difficult to generalize West Virginia's experiences to the nation as a whole. However, while West Virginia is obviously not a microcosm of the nation, its experience with welfare reform is of interest to non-West Virginians for several reasons.

First, and perhaps most importantly, studying welfare reform in a predominately rural state like West Virginia is of interest nationally because most welfare reform research has focused on urban areas, even though more than one-third of welfare recipients reside in rural areas. As a result, this book contributes to the growing literature about welfare reform's effect on welfare recipients residing in rural areas. To date, that literature suggests that welfare recipients from rural areas face several unique challenges leaving and staying off welfare. Rural residents, for example, tend to be less educated and less likely to pursue a college degree than their urban counterparts (Gibbs et al. 1998). This suggests that welfare recipients from rural areas may be less prepared for the transition to work than urban recipients (Cook and Dagata 1997; RUPRI 1998). Rural recipients also face more challenging labor market conditions. Job opportunities, especially full-time jobs paying more than minimum wages, are more difficult to find in rural areas than in urban areas (Parker and Whitener 1997; Besser 1998; Findeis and Jensen 1998; JCPR 2000; Weber and Duncan 2000). Also, rural communities have lower population densities than urban ones, thus it costs more to provide services. There are also fewer job opportunities for welfare recipients in rural areas and a longer daily commute to the work place (RUPRI 1998; Weber and Duncan 2000). Rural residents also tend to have access to fewer available resources and support programs (such as public transportation, childcare facilities, job training programs, healthcare facilities, and affordable housing) than urban residents to help them make the transition from welfare to work (Emlen 1991; Hofferth et al. 1990; Rucker 1994; Whitener 1997; CTAA 1998; JCPR 2000; Weber and Duncan 2000). Rural communities also tend to have fewer nonprofit resource organizations available to help residents deal with issues that serve as a deterrent to work, such as domestic violence situations and alcoholism (RUPRI 1998). They are also more likely to be subject to persistent poverty, a condition that can lead to a sense of hopelessness (RUPRI 1998).

Another reason West Virginia's experience with welfare reform might be of interest to non-West Virginians is that although most of the state is rural, it also contains several urban areas. This provides an opportunity to compare and contrast the perspectives and experiences of welfare recipients and leavers from urban areas to those from rural areas. Also, given West Virginia's relatively anemic economic status (the state's per capita income and labor force participation rates are typically among the very lowest in the nation), it serves as a potential harbinger of things to come in other states during recessionary times. This is an especially important consideration because many of welfare reform's critics argue that the true test of welfare reform's efficacy will come during a recession.

The authors' working relationship with West Virginia's Department of Health and Human Resources also provides a unique opportunity to examine, in-depth, welfare reform's effect on institutions as well as individuals. As a result, this book offers a more comprehensive assessment of administrative responses to significant policy change than is found in most other studies. Finally, the book adds to the literature about intergovernmental relations by offering a case study of West Virginia's response to the changes in federal rules and requirements brought about by the *Personal Responsibility and Work Opportunity Reconciliation Act of 1996*.

The Organization of the Book

In Chapter 2, Melissa Latimer extends the argument presented earlier in this chapter that place matters, both when examining welfare reform's implementation and its effect on recipient behavior and their prospects for achieving economic independence. She notes that several studies have demonstrated that welfare recipients residing in rural areas face several unique barriers to achieving economic independence. Latimer then provides an in-depth portrait of West Virginia's socioeconomic characteristics. She demonstrates that West Virginians have experienced multiple socioeconomic hardships for many years and that these hardships make West Virginia an especially interesting place for testing welfare reform's efficacy in helping recipients leave and stay off welfare. She argues that achieving economic self-sufficiency in a predominantly rural state that lacks extensive support systems and suffers from a persistently weak economy is a daunting task and that federal policymakers should consider place when imposing fiscal sanctions for noncompliance with federal requirements, such as recipient workforce participation rates.

In Chapter 3, Robert Jay Dilger establishes the political and institutional context for studying welfare reform in West Virginia by providing an overview of the development of welfare policy in the United States and in West Virginia. He discusses the different approaches that have been offered to help recipients leave and stay off welfare, the political and cultural changes that led to the adoption of the *Personal Responsibility and Work Opportunity Reconciliation Act of 1996* and its emphasis on the work attachment strategy to reduce adult welfare dependency, and the major changes the legislation has brought about. He then examines West Virginia's response to the new rules and regulations, as well as to the additional programmatic flexibility the 1996 law imposed.

L. Christopher Plein and David Williams provide a detailed and comprehensive analysis of West Virginia's implementation of welfare reform, called WV WORKS, in Chapter 4. They examine front line procedures and practices as well as case management techniques, compare those procedures, practices, and techniques with those other states employ, and present several lessons that can be learned from West Virginia's experience implementing welfare reform.

In Chapter 5, Plein extends the analysis presented in Chapter 4 by focusing on implementation strategies West Virginia's "street level" administrators employed. He examines how they dealt with several unexpected implementation problems, such as difficulties in coordinating job placement and training activities, increasing caseload differentials between Family Support Specialists and Income Maintenance workers, and a programmatic disconnect when clients left the welfare rolls. He then presents a list of remaining challenges and recommendations for addressing them.

Plein assesses the interrelationship of social-welfare programs in Chapter 6, focusing on the effect TANF's "de-linking" of cash assistance, Medicaid, and Food Stamps had on WV WORKS recipients. He notes that, at first, when recipients left WV WORKS, many of them also left Medicaid, Food Stamps, and other support programs, even though they were eligible to receive benefits from those programs. DHHR later instituted several administrative reforms in an effort to maintain contact with WV WORKS leavers and inform them about their eligibility for benefits under these other support programs, especially Medicaid and Food Stamp benefits.

In Chapter 7, Latimer uses data from the WV WORKS leaver study to examine the effect of different types of job and educational training programs on welfare recipients in West Virginia. She uses logistic regression analysis to determine the extent to which labor market, household, and individual demographic characteristics affect

(1) access to educational, vocational, and job training programs, (2) completion of educational, vocational, and job training programs, (3) the types of skills learned in these programs, and (4) recipients' assessments of these programs' usefulness. She then assesses WV WORKS' effectiveness in promoting job preparation for adult recipients.

In Chapter 8, Lucinda Potter uses the authors' welfare leaver data to analyze the important question: "Is Work the Solution?" She begins her analysis by discussing the historical precedents underlying the current emphasis on requiring recipients to work in exchange for benefits. She also examines the ongoing debate concerning the efficacy of work-first, education-first, and training-first strategies to assist welfare recipients to leave and stay off welfare and escape poverty. She then uses logistic regression analysis to determine the influence of having paid employment (the work attachment strategy), at least a high school degree or GED (education-first strategy), completing a job training program (training-first strategy), local economic conditions, and the receipt of various support services (childcare, transportation, and post-welfare support services) on WV WORKS leavers' (1) ability to leave and remain off welfare, (2) household income, (3) expectations concerning future household income, and (4) their assessment of their well-being.

Dilger then examines the experiences and perspectives of West Virginia's most at-risk populations in Chapter 9. He begins by explaining why it is useful to differentiate among recipients, discusses different ways that have been used to define at-risk populations, and notes which factors the national literature suggests should be used to define who is most at-risk of being unable to make the transition from government assistance to economic self-sufficiency. Dilger then uses the authors' WV WORKS 2000 survey data to compare and contrast the responses of West Virginia's most at-risk populations with those of other WV WORKS recipients to determine if their perspectives and experiences are significantly different from those of other recipients. He concludes with a description of what is currently being done, both in other states and in West Virginia, to address the needs of welfare's most at-risk populations and offers several policy recommendations based upon his analysis.

In Chapter 10, Carson Mencken examines the effect place (local economic conditions) and the recipients' relationship with their caseworker and administrative agency (in this case, DHHR) have on WV WORKS recipients' attitudes and opinions concerning their future. Previous research has demonstrated that people's attitudes and opinions concerning their future affect their behavior. People with fatalistic attitudes about the future generally withdraw from life and are less successful than others in a variety of ways, including obtaining and retaining employment. Mencken utilizes the data in the WV WORKS 2000 survey to determine if place (local economic conditions) and the recipients' relationship with their caseworker and DHHR affect recipients' future orientations. His findings are important because the *Personal Responsibility and Work Opportunity Reconciliation Act of 1996* is predicated on the assumption that people should take responsibility for their own well-being and that place is not a mitigating factor. For example, mandated work participation quotas are the same nationwide, regardless of the state's economic circumstances. If place matters, then an argument can be presented that mandatory work participation rates and other rules, regulations, and sanctions should not be uniform throughout the nation.

The book concludes with a chapter by Eleanor Blakely, Robert Jay Dilger, and Barry Locke that summarizes the key findings from the authors' WV WORKS leaver and WV WORKS recipient studies as well as each of the book's previous chapters. They then discuss key issues affecting welfare policy in the United States and, based on the analysis of West Virginia's experience with welfare reform, provide policy recommendations for improving the welfare system and creating greater opportunities for welfare recipients to escape poverty.

Notes

1. Many political science, public administration, and social work sources erroneously indicate that ADC was renamed AFDC in 1950 when the adult relative or caretaker of eligible children in the home (implemented as a female relative or caretaker) was made eligible for assistance.

References

Besser, Terry. 1998. "Employment in Small Towns." *Rural Development Perspectives* 3(2): 31-39.

Cook, Peggy and Elizabeth Dagata. 1997. "Welfare Reform Legislation Poses Opportunities and Challenges for Rural America." *Rural Conditions and Trends* 8(1): 32-41.

Community Transportation Association of America (CTAA). 1998. "Mobility: Key to Welfare Reform." Washington, D.C.: Community Transportation Association of America.

Dilger, Robert Jay, Eleanor Blakely, Karen V.H. Dorton, Melissa Latimer, Barry Locke, Carson Mencken, L. Christopher Plein, Lucinda A. Potter, David Williams, and Dong Pil Yoon. 1999. *West Virginia Works Case Closure Study*. Morgantown, WV: West Virginia University Institute for Public Affairs. Reprinted in *The West Virginia Public Affairs Reporter* 17:1 (Winter 2000): 2-15.

Dilger, Robert Jay, Eleanor Blakely, Melissa Latimer, Barry Locke, Carson Mencken, L. Christopher Plein, Lucinda A. Potter, and David Williams. 2001. *WV WORKS 2000: The Recipients' Perspective*. Morgantown, WV: West Virginia University Institute for Public Affairs. Reprinted in *The West Virginia Public Affairs Reporter* 18:3 (Summer 2001): 2-19.

Ellwood, David T. and Laurence H. Summers. 1986. "Is welfare really the problem?" *The Public Interest* 83 (Spring): 57-76.

Emlen, Arthur C. 1991. "Rural Child Care Policy: Does Oregon Have One?" Working Paper, Corvallis OR: Rural Policy Research Group. April.

Findeis, Jill and Leif Jensen. 1998. "Employment Opportunities in Rural Areas: Implications for Poverty in a Changing Policy Environment." Paper presented at the Annual Meeting of the American Agricultural Economics Association. Salt Lake City, Utah.

Fischer, Karin. 1998. "Officials say state welfare program has been reduced by two-thirds." *Charleston Daily Mail*, September 14, 1A.

Garfinkel, Irwin and Sara McLanahan. 1986. *Single Mothers and Their Children: A New American Dilemma*. Washington, D.C.: Urban Institute Press. Cited in Jeffrey Grogger, Lynn A. Karoly and Jacob Alex Klerman. 2002. *Consequences of Welfare Reform: A Research Synthesis*. Washington, D.C.: U.S. Department of Health and Human Services, The Administration for Children and Families.

Gibbs, Robert M., Paul L. Swaim, and Ruy Teixeira. 1998. *Rural Education and Training in the New Economy: The Myth of the Rural Skills Gap*. Ames, IA: Iowa State University Press.

Hofstadter, Richard. 1948. *The American Political Tradition*. New York: Vintage Books.

Hofferth, Sandra L., April Brayfield, Sharon Deich, and Pamela Holcomb. 1990. *National Child Care Survey, 1990*. Urban Institute Report 91-5. Washington, D.C.: The Urban Institute Press.

Joint Center on Poverty Research (JCPR). 2000. "Rural Dimensions of Welfare Reform." Conference. Washington, D.C., May 4-5. Program Findings. http://www.jcpr.org/conferences/ruralbriefing.html#selectfindings.

Kabler, Phil. 2002. "Deficit forces cuts in welfare: Hundreds of state social services employees to be laid off as well." *The Charleston Gazette*. May 21, 1A, 11A.

Leiby, James. 1978. *A History of Social Welfare and Social Work in the United States*. New York: Columbia University Press.

Loprest, Pamela. 1999. "How Families That Left Welfare Are Doing: A National Picture." Washington, D.C.: Urban Institute.

Murray, Charles. 1984. *Losing Ground*. New York: Basic Books.

———. 1986. "No, welfare Isn't really the Problem." *The Public Interest* 84 (Summer): 3-11.

Nathan, Richard. 1983. *The Administrative Presidency*. New York: John Wiley and Sons.

Nathan, Richard, Robert R. Carlson, and Paul H. O'Neill. 1980. "Welfare Reform: Federalism or Federalization." *Common Sense* (Winter): 1-30.

Parker, Timothy and Leslie Whitener. 1997. "Minimum Wage Legislation: Rural Workers Will Benefit More Than Urban Workers From Increase in Minimum Wage." *Rural Conditions and Trends* 8(1): 48-52.

Reid, P. Nelson. 1995. "Social Welfare History." *Encyclopedia of Social Work.* 19th Edition. Ed. Richard Edwards. Washington, D.C.: National Association of Social Workers Press.

Rucker, George. 1994. *Status Report on Public Transportation in Rural America, 1994.* Washington, D.C.: Rural Transit Assistance Program, Federal Transit Administration.

Rural Policy Research Institute (RUPRI). 1998. *Welfare Reform in Rural Areas.* Washington, D.C.: Rural Policy Research Institute.

U.S. Advisory Commission on Intergovernmental Relations (U.S. ACIR). 1980. *Public Assistance: The Growth of a Federal Function.* Washington, D.C.: U.S. Advisory Commission on Intergovernmental Relations.

U.S. Department of Health and Human Services (DHHS). 2000. "State by State Welfare Caseloads since 1993 (Recipients)." Washington, D.C.: U.S. Department of Health and Human Services, August 8, 2000. http://www.acf.dhhs.gov/news/stats/caseload.htm.

U.S. General Accounting Office (GAO). 1999. *Welfare Reform: Information on Former Recipients' Status.* Washington, D.C.: U.S. Government Printing Office. GAO/HEHS-99-48. April.

Washington Research Council.1998. *Catching Up on Welfare Reform.* Washington, D.C.:Washington Research Council.

Weber, Bruce and Greg Duncan. 2000. "Welfare Reform and Food Assistance in Rural America." Congressional Research Briefing on Welfare Reform and Rural Poverty. Washington, D.C., June 21. http://www.jcpr.org/conferences/rural-summary.pdf.

Whitener, Leslie. 1997. "Rural Housing Conditions Improve but Affordability Continues To Be a Problem." *Rural Conditions and Trends* 8(2): 70-74.

WV WORKS. 1998. "Caseload By County." Charleston, WV: West Virginia Department of Health and Human Resources. http://www.wvwelfarereform.org/Statistical%20Information.html (link no longer maintained).

Chapter 2

Setting the Socioeconomic Context for Welfare Reform in Appalachia

MELISSA LATIMER

The previous chapter provided a historical framework for understanding how national trends and conditions, as well as historic trends and conditions in West Virginia, shaped the state's development and implementation of welfare reform. This chapter extends that discussion by focusing on the key socioeconomic conditions that have influenced the state's response to the adoption of the *Personal Responsibility and Work Opportunity Reconciliation Act of 1996*.

The Significance of Geographic Space: Place Matters

One of the most significant changes in recent sociological research has been a refocusing on the importance of geographic space for understanding economic change and social inequality (Lobao 1990,1993). Central to this perspective are the nation's spatial and historical patterns of uneven economic development. By incorporating measures of geographic space in their analyses, researchers have shown that the distribution, causes, and consequences of inequality vary "across both time and space" (Tomaskovic-Devey 1987, 56).

According to Colclough and Tolbert (1993, 153), "Each location has its own history, economy, population composition, and traditions that affect the economic inequalities . . ." Thus, an area's physical, historical, social, and political characteristics, as well as the combination of these factors, influence the unique social relations that develop within that area (Colclough and Tolbert 1993; Lobao 1993). In addition, the structural characteristics of a region, state, and/or local labor market area affect the economic opportunities and limitations of individuals and institutions within that area in terms of jobs, income, potential economic bases, transportation and communication systems, levels of economic well-being, and development and implementation of welfare programs (Colclough and Tolbert 1993; Lobao 1993; Lichter 1989; Ollenburger et al. 1989; Rank and Hirschl 1988; Singelmann and Deseran 1993; Tickamyer and Latimer 1993).

The *Personal Responsibility and Work Opportunity Reconciliation Act of 1996* reinforces the importance of place-specific analyses by passing on increased control, cost, and responsibility for welfare program design and operation to individual states. Thus, one of the keys to understanding the dynamics and effects of welfare reform on low-income adults and their families in any community in the United States is to document and analyze the geographic, economic, and demographic characteristics of the places in which they live.

West Virginia is an interesting place to study welfare reform because it is a predominantly rural state located in the heart of the Appalachian region. The Appalachian Regional Commission (ARC) has defined the Appalachian region to include more than 410 counties across thirteen states, ranging from northeastern Mississippi to southern New York (ARC 2003). Historically, a variety of criteria have been used to define this region, including (1) its physical characteristics (i.e., mountainous topography), (2) its economic base (i.e., bituminous coal mining and anthracite resources, timbering, and agriculture), (3) chronic economic problems (i.e., low incomes and high unemployment and underemployment), and even (4) the labor force's characteristics (i.e., white Anglo-Saxon heritage and generations of native born Americans) (People's Appalachian Research Collective 1991).

Considerable progress has been made in the Appalachian region since President Kennedy focused his, and the nation's, attention on the plight of the people living in this region. In fact, Billings and

Setting the Socioeconomic Context for Welfare Reform

Tickamyer (1993, 7) argue that the "War on Poverty" that targeted this region in the 1960s "brought the region to the state of the rest of the nation of twenty years earlier." Current data indicate that some of the early socioeconomic patterns "discovered" in this region persist today (Isserman 1996). Overall, the Appalachian region still has lower educational levels, population increases, labor force participation rates, incomes, and per capita incomes than the rest of the nation. The unemployment, underemployment, and poverty rates for the region continue to be higher than those of the rest of the nation (ARC 2003).

Although the predominant pattern has been to lump together the entire Appalachian region and present it as a unified whole (Billings and Tickamyer 1993), there is a great deal of diversity within and between the Southern, Central, and Northern parts of the region (Billings 1974; Couto 1994; Ergood and Kuhre 1991; Isserman and Rephann 1993; Mencken 1996, 1997). For example, places that were over-concentrated in extractive or production industries, such as mining and manufacturing in Central Appalachia (where nine of West Virginia's fifty-five counties are located), were negatively affected by the late 1970s recession and increased international competition (Falk and Lyson 1988; Murdock et al. 1993).

Isserman (1996) argues that to still talk about the Appalachian region as a place apart from the rest of the nation is problematic when looking at data from the whole region, but not when focusing on Central Appalachia, which lacks a metropolitan area with 250,000 people or more. In fact, only 15 percent of the people living in Central Appalachia reside in a metropolitan area compared to 60-65 percent of the population in Northern and Southern Appalachia (Isserman 1996). In addition, Central Appalachia's per capita income is 67 percent of the nation's, 11 percentage points lower than Northern and Southern Appalachia, and its poverty rate is twice that of Northern or Southern Appalachian counties (Couto 1994). The non-metropolitan poverty rate in Central Appalachia in 1990 was 24 percent and the metropolitan rate was 15 percent, lower than the 36 percent and 20 percent rates found there during the 1970s but still 5-10 percent higher than the rest of the nation (Isserman 1996). In 1980, only 13.5 percent of the adults in Central Appalachia had some education beyond high school, compared to 19 percent in North and South Appalachia (Couto 1994). In 1990, 51 percent of nonmetropolitan and 65 percent of metropolitan adults in Central Appalachia had completed their high school degree (Isserman 1996).

Billings and Tickamyer (1993, 9) argue that despite the clear variation and diversity within the region, "many Appalachian development issues are rural problems." In fact, "Two-hundred-and-ninety of Appalachia's counties were classified as non-metropolitan in 1993" (McLaughlin, Lichter, and Matthews 1999, 1). Like the states clustered in Central Appalachia, West Virginia's lack of urbanization has significant adverse economic implications for its people.

The Economic Consequences of Rural Location: Putting West Virginia into Context

As stated earlier, the labor markets in which people live shape the economic opportunities that are available to both workers and their families. Employment opportunities in rural areas are significantly different from those in urban areas, and these differences make labor force participation and higher earnings more difficult for the rural poor. Regardless of the indicators used to measure size and place, researchers have consistently found that individuals in rural locations (particularly in the South) fare worse in terms of occupational segregation (Cho and Ogunwole 1989; Goudy et al. 1986; Stafford and Fossett 1989) and economic hardship (Duncan 1992; Gorham 1992; Jensen and Tienda 1989; Pfeffer 1993; Ross and Morrissey 1986; Tickamyer and Latimer 1993; Tickamyer and Tickamyer 1988) than individuals in urban areas. Researchers have specifically documented the high rates of unemployment and underemployment rural workers face (Findeis et al. 2001; Lichter 1987). They have also consistently documented that rural areas have higher rates of poverty and more areas with persistent poverty than urban areas (Findeis et al. 2001).

In 1990, West Virginia was one of the most rural states in the nation with 64 percent of its total population located in a rural area compared to 25 percent nationally (Hannah 1995). The rural residency rate in West Virginia declined to 54 percent by 2000, still well above the national average (Census 2000 Summary File 3). Economic data on West Virginia reflect the state's rural nature in terms of low labor force participation rates, high unemployment rates, low average incomes, and high poverty rates.

West Virginia's Labor Force Participation Rates

In 1980, 1990, and 2000 West Virginia's labor force participation rates for both women and men were among the lowest in the country (Hannah 1995; Census 2000 Summary File 3). For example, in 2000, nationwide, 59.7 percent of individuals age sixteen years or older were in the labor force, compared to 50.4 percent in West Virginia (Census 2000 Summary File 3). Nationally, 54 percent of all women age sixteen and older were in the labor force, compared to just 44.4 percent in West Virginia (56.8% of West Virginia men were in the labor force in 2000) (Census 2000 Summary File 3). In addition, a much larger percentage of female workers than male workers in West Virginia were employed part-time (approximately 33% compared to 14% in 1990 and 29.6% versus 13.4% in 2000) or for only part of the year (44% of women worked for fewer than 48 weeks a year compared to 33% of men in 1990 and 36.5% of women in 2000 compared to 28.6% of men) (Hannah 1995; Census 2000 Summary File 3).

West Virginia's Unemployment Rate

Historically, West Virginia has always had one of the highest unemployment rates in the nation, and in 1990 it had the highest (9.6% compared to a national average of 6.3%) (Hannah 1995). West Virginia's unemployment rate has improved in recent years, partly because of economic growth in the Eastern Panhandle and in the Kanawha Valley, and partly due to the out-migration of people looking for work. In 2000, the state's unemployment rate stood at 5.5 percent compared to the national rate of 4 percent (Census 2000 Summary File 3). The unemployment rate in West Virginia for black men was 8.21 percent, 5.58 percent for black women, 4.75 percent for white men, and 3.0 percent for white women (Census 2000 Summary File 3). One possible reason that West Virginia women's unemployment rate is lower than men's (it was also lower in 1980 and in 1990) is that "women who do not have jobs may be more likely than men to drop out of the labor force entirely (e.g., to live at home, become full-time homemakers, go on public assistance) instead of taking actions required to meet the government definition of being officially 'unemployed'" (Hannah 1995, 39).

In 2003, West Virginia's unemployment rate ranged from a low of 3 percent in Monongalia county (where the state's land-grant institution, West Virginia University, is located) to 22 percent in Calhoun County. Thirteen of West Virginia's fifty-five counties had an unemployment rate below the national rate of 5.7 percent, and fourteen counties had unemployment rates in double digits. Given these statistics, it should not be surprising that a report from the ARC predicted that the majority of West Virginia counties (compared to other counties in the Appalachian Region) would face the greatest problems placing welfare recipients in jobs (Bischak 1997).

West Virginia's Average Incomes

In 1990, West Virginia's median income ($20,795 compared to $30,056), median family income ($25,602 compared to $35,225), and per capita income ($10,520 versus $14,420) were all below the national average (Census 1990 Summary File 3). In 2000, significant income gaps still existed between West Virginia and the rest of the nation. For example, West Virginia's median income for households was $29,696, compared to $41,994 nationally. Also, West Virginia's median family income was $36,484, compared to $50,046 nationally. Finally, West Virginia's per capita income was approximately $5,000 lower than the national rate ($16,477 versus $21,587) (Census 2000 Summary File 3).

According to Hannah (1995, 41), "In 1990, full-time women workers in West Virginia earned 58 cents for every dollar earned by a full-time male worker - two cents less than in 1980." By 2000, full-time, year-round women workers earned 68 cents for every dollar earned by comparable male workers ($21,154 versus $27,194). The national rate was 73 cents per dollar. In addition, more than one-third (approximately 36%) of West Virginia women and one-fifth (20%) of West Virginia men sixteen years or older with earnings in 1999 had incomes of less than $10,000 (Census 2000 Summary File 3). However, within the state, there is considerable variation in the income gap between women and men. For example, in 1990, full-time, year-round women workers in Calhoun County earned 69 cents for every dollar men earned while women in Tyler County earned just 39 cents per dollar earned by men (Hannah 1995).

West Virginia's Poverty Rate

State income deficits translate into unprecedented poverty rates in West Virginia. According to Hannah (1995, 45), "West Virginia historically has had a higher rate of poverty than the United States as a whole; however, this gap widened considerably during the 1980s." In fact, the percentage of West Virginia families living in poverty increased from 12 percent in 1979, to 16 percent in 1989, and to 17.9 percent in 2000 (compared to 12.4% nationally in 2000) (Hannah 1995; Census 2000 Summary File 3). In addition, 15.5 percent of West Virginia households had incomes of less than $10,000 in 1999, compared to 9.5 percent nationally. Female-headed households (especially those headed by African American women) had the highest poverty levels of any family type in West Virginia (62.8% of female headed households with children under five in West Virginia were poor compared to the national rate of 46.4%). Female headed households with related children under eighteen years old make up a larger percentage of the total poor black population in West Virginia, 59.5 percent compared to 31 percent of white female headed households (Census 2000 Summary File 3).

In addition, America's Second Harvest (ASH) (2002) reports that 9 percent of all households in West Virginia are food insecure and 3.1 percent are food insecure with hunger. Approximately 24 percent of the state's children receive Food Stamps, and nearly 30 percent receive reduced price or free lunches through the National School Lunch Program (ASH 2002; Child Welfare League of America 2001).

Melissa Latimer

Understanding The Rural Context: Barriers to Employment and Economic Self-Sufficiency in West Virginia

Rural areas are not densely populated and lack economic diversity (Tickamyer and Duncan 1990). Thus, rural labor markets constrain the employment opportunities of low income adults by providing fewer actual employment opportunities. In addition, rural labor markets constrain employment opportunities for low income adults by restricting those employment opportunities to temporary, seasonal, low-paying service jobs. Service industries, nondurable manufacturing sectors (i.e., periphery and secondary sector jobs), construction, and agriculture dominate rural areas, and these sectors offer low-wage, low-security employment.

Population Density and Composition

West Virginia, like many other rural states, has a low population density with no large city within its borders (Dilger and Witt 1994). According to the 2000 Census, there are 114 people per square mile in the Appalachian region, but only 75 people per square mile in West Virginia. In addition, between 1980 and 1990 West Virginia's population declined 8 percent (Hawley 1994). While the nation experienced 13.2 percent population growth between 1990 and 2000, West Virginia's population grew only 0.8 percent (Census 2000 Summary File 3).

West Virginia also reflects rural socioeconomic patterns in terms of the age structure, race, and the marital status of its population. West Virginia, like other states in the Appalachian region, has a large elderly population. In Appalachia, "the youngest age groups are a declining share of the population and the older age groups are increasing. There also is a loss in the share of those of early working and middle age" (McLaughlin et al. 1999, 2). The Rural Sociological Society Task Force (RSS) (1993) found that the elderly constitute a larger percent of the poor population in rural areas than in urban areas.

In 1990, 15 percent of West Virginia's population was 65 years old or older. In 2000, this rate increased slightly to 15.3 percent, compared to 12.4 percent nationally. West Virginia's median age increased from 35.4 in 1990 to 38.9 in 2000, the highest in the nation. According to Hawley (1994, 50), "West Virginia has a larger share of its population in every age group older than age 35 than does the remainder of the nation." It is not surprising that 33.9 percent of West Virginia residents receive income from Social Security, and 22 percent have retirement income. The national figures for these incomes are 25.7 percent and 16.7 percent respectively (Census 2000 Summary File 3). West Virginia's lagging economy has been cited as the cause for an unusually large out-migration of 20 to 30 year olds during the 1990s and limited in-migration of workers from other states (Hawley 1994).

In 1996, whites made up 90 percent and blacks almost 8 percent of Appalachia's population (McLaughlin et al. 1999). In 2000, 95 percent of West Virginians were white, compared to 96.2 percent in 1990 and 75 percent nationally in 2000. African-Americans constitute the state's largest ethnic minority (3.1% in 1990 and 3.2% in 2000) (Census 2000 Summary File 3). The RSS Task Force (1993) found that the rural poor are more likely to be white (73% white) than the urban poor (56% white). This pattern is also true in West Virginia.

A larger percent of West Virginia families are married than the rest of the nation. Married couples constituted 59 percent of West Virginia's households in 1990 and 54 percent in 2000 (Census 2000 Summary File 3). The RSS Task Force (1993) found that, nationally, the rural poor are more likely to be married, two-parent families than the urban poor (44% compared to 27%). The same pattern is found in West Virginia. Married couples made up approximately 54 percent of the total poor white population in the state in 2000 (Census 2000 Summary File 3).

Work disability is a prevalent health problem in rural Appalachia (Burkett 1994). Between 1990 and 1996, the number of Supplemental Security Income (SSI) cases in the Appalachian coal region increased more rapidly (37.5%) than the national rate (26%) (Latimer and Mencken 2003). Coal mining is dangerous work and has a high worker injury rate. However, these data show a marked increase in disability rates during a period of increased mine safety and decreased mining employment. It is possible that disability benefits have become a de facto income maintenance strategy in depressed regions of Appalachia, as unemployed workers are placed on disability (Latimer and Mencken 2003).

The disability patterns found in West Virginia are very similar to those found throughout the Appalachian region. All fifty-five counties in West Virginia have a county work disability percent that is above the mean for the United States. Eighteen of West Virginia's counties are part of the national 20 percent of counties with the highest rates of worker disability (Burkett 1994). In 2000, 22.8 percent of West Virginia's population five years and older had a disability. The national rate was 17.5 percent. Approximately 7 percent (6.9%) of West Virginians, compared to 4.4 percent nationally, received SSI benefits in 2000 (Census 2000 Summary File 3).

Economic Diversity

West Virginia's economy lacks diversity and has no long-term pattern of real economic stability. The state has a long history of relying on goods-producing industries, such as mining, manufacturing, and construction. In fact, "Employment concentration in the service-producing industries has always been higher in the national economy than in West Virginia, but these differences have been declining over time" (Cushing 1994, 21). Unfortunately, "Employment in the goods-producing industries collapsed between 1979 and 1983, creating a ripple effect which resulted in employment losses in nearly every sector of the state's economy" (Cushing 1994, 20). Economic growth in the state since 1983 has been limited (Cushing 1994).

The Effect of Farm Based Economies

Farm-based economies offer jobs that are part-time and seasonal (Tickamyer and Duncan 1990). These farm-based jobs limit the labor force participation of women by expanding their workload (i.e., rural women are responsible for childcare, housework, and farm labor) and limiting their geographic mobility (due to land ownership, farm labor, and difficulties in commuting) (Tickamyer and Bokemeier 1989).

Only about 0.5 percent of West Virginia's labor force are

currently employed as farmers or farm managers (Census 2000 Summary Tape 3). It is the legacy of subsistence farming in West Virginia that has influenced the state's economic development. According to Billings and Tickamyer (1993), the dominance of subsistence-oriented farming in West Virginia prior to the 1900s shaped the specific narrow way in which West Virginia was integrated into the national economy. They argue that "subsistence agriculture failed to generate sufficient local capital for indigenous entrepreneurs to undertake the huge costs of developing an industrial infrastructure in Appalachia" (Billings and Tickamyer 1993, 19). As a consequence (1) industrialization centered on the rich coal and timber natural resources, (2) outside investors accumulated vast amounts of land and power and further exaggerated existing land shortages, (3) displaced low-income farmers created a readily available, exploitable labor pool, and (4) local elites were able to maintain old patterns of power and control due to prior land-owning patterns (Billings and Blee 2000; Billings and Tickamyer 1993).

According to Billings and Tickamyer (1993, 14), "Coal production is often identified as the definitive economic force behind Appalachian development problems, and data confirm that counties with large-scale coal production have the highest poverty and unemployment rates." Thus, the key to understanding West Virginia's economic history is to understand the booms and busts of the coal mining industry.

Resource Extraction Dependency

Rural areas are the primary location for resource extraction industries, which tend to be highly volatile and unstable, capital intensive, and dominated by white males. Firms in these industries typically do not invest in human capital (RSS Task Force 1993). In addition, these industries dominate the areas in which they are located and thus limit other employment opportunities (Tickamyer and Tickamyer 1988). Since 1980, areas with higher extractive industry employment have higher levels of poverty (Lichter and McLaughlin 1995), greater racial and gender inequality (Tickamyer and Latimer 1993; Tickamyer and Tickamyer 1988), and higher levels of underemployment and unemployment (Couto 1994; Jensen et al. 1999; Maggard 1994) than areas with low extractive employment.

While all extractive industries have faced severe economic problems in the last few decades (Gramling 1996; Lobao 1990; Nord and Luloff 1993), the effects of industrial restructuring have been very tough on the coal mining industry. This is particularly true in Appalachia's rural regions, which, historically, have employed nearly 75 percent of all coal miners, and where coal mining dependency led to record levels of unemployment and poverty, and significantly lower incomes in the 1980s (Billings and Tickamyer 1993; Couto 1994; Isserman 1996; Maggard 1994; Mencken 1997).

West Virginia's historic and ongoing economic dependence on the resource extraction industry, particularly coal mining, is unprecedented in the United States. As a consequence, the state's economic history mimics the boom and bust cycles of this industry. In 1940 "mining provided nearly 30 percent of all jobs in West Virginia, compared with just under 3 percent for the nation" (Cushing 1994, 21). The percentage dropped to 23 percent in 1950, 12 percent in 1960, and bottomed out at 9.7 percent in 1970 (Cushing 1994, 22). More than 1,600 mines were closed in West Virginia during the late 1970s through mid-1980s. The number of coal miners decreased in the state from 55,627 in 1980 to 28,876 in 1990 (Hawley 1994). However, even after 1983, coal mining continues to dominate the economies in mining dependent counties in West Virginia, Kentucky, and Virginia with more than 20 percent of all earnings coming from this industry (Latimer and Mencken 2003).

Despite the decline in the number of coal miners, the demand for Appalachian coal has remained strong. Hawley (1994) shows that the amount of West Virginia coal produced in 1990 was 40 percent higher than in 1980, despite a 47 percent decrease in the number of coal industry workers during this period. Moreover, during the 1980s more than 50 percent of all electricity produced in the United States was coal generated. West Virginia produced a record 187 million tons of coal in 1998 (Energy Statistics Source Book 1999). The simultaneous decline and continued dominance of coal in West Virginia in the late 1980s and 1990s indicates a lack of new and alternative industry development in the state (Latimer and Mencken 2003).

Mining employment reductions were not the product of decreased demand, but of a number of interrelated market factors that conjoined to displace workers in the industry. The first of these was economic restructuring. The national shift from manufacturing to services decreased the demand for coal to produce direct energy for factories (Dilger and Witt 1994). In fact, coal consumption by coke plants declined 59 percent between 1980 and 1998 (Energy Statistics Source Book 1999). Second, new environmental laws decreased the demand for high-sulfur content Appalachian coal (Dilger and Witt 1994). Extracting this type of coal is a labor-intensive process. Cleaner burning, low-sulfur coal is located near the surface, and mechanized capital intensive surface or strip mining is used to extract this coal.

The third, and perhaps the most important trend, is the further mechanization of the coal extraction process (Dilger and Witt 1994). Foreign competition accelerated the mechanization of many manufacturing processes in the United States. However, since 1980, 95 percent of all coal produced in the United States was consumed domestically, and only 0.8 percent of all coal consumed in the United States was imported (Energy Statistics Source Book 1999). Unlike manufacturing, where restructuring was a product of global competition, coal mining industry competition arose from domestic producers. Competition further accelerated cuts in production costs through mechanization, which increased the productivity of coal extraction, thus lowering the price per ton. Falling prices created even greater competition among coal suppliers. Competition shut down many of the less competitive mines that could not survive on small profit margins, particularly the underground mines that employed more workers (Latimer and Mencken 2003).

Sex Segregated Labor Market

The low wage employment found predominately in rural areas is compounded by the fact that neither the sex segregation of the labor market (Goudy et al. 1986) nor racial inequalities in income (Cho and Ogunwole 1989) have significantly decreased in rural areas. The national trend, in terms of occupational sex segmentation, is that women, particularly women of color, are still relegated and isolated in the periphery, secondary, and service sectors of the labor market (Bertaux 1991; Lorence 1992). Recent changes in the economy's structure (i.e., a decrease in high wage industry jobs) have increased competition for more limited employment opportunities, and therefore, led to an even greater confinement of women in lower paid sectors of the occupational structure. Technological innovations have eliminated many of the traditional jobs held by women (Tickamyer and Tickamyer 1988). In addition to offering lower hourly wages, these traditionally female sectors of the labor market provide less stability and security and fewer benefits and opportunities for advancement than traditionally male sectors.

In 1990, industrial and occupational sex segregation was greater in West Virginia than in the nation. Employed women were highly concentrated in retail trade, services, finance, insurance and real estate, and government industries, but were "underrepresented in all other sectors, most particularly mining and construction" (Hannah 1995, 28). Approximately 75 percent of West Virginia women worked in either service industries or retail trade. In terms of occupations, 43 percent of all employed women in West Virginia in 1990 "were heavily concentrated in technical, sales, and administrative support occupations" (Hannah 1995, 29). Twenty-one percent of all working West Virginia women were employed in a service occupation (primarily waitresses and nursing aides). The top five occupations for women were secretaries, elementary school teachers, cashiers, nursing aides and attendants, and registered nurses. Hannah (1995, 30) found that overall "Women in West Virginia were less involved in traditional male occupations than women nationally."

Occupational (and industrial) sex segregation is still strong in West Virginia. Although the percentage of West Virginia women in sales and service occupations has declined to 60.3 percent (in 2000), most women are still concentrated in these occupations. This percentage contrasts sharply with the 27.6 percent of West Virginia men in these occupations. Forty-seven percent of men work in construction, extraction, maintenance, production, transportation, and moving occupations, compared to just 6.6 percent of women in the state (Census 2000 Summary File 3).

Public Services and Infrastructure Development

Rural area's limited employment and income bases have a cumulative effect on the community context because low wages likewise lower the local tax base. This limited tax base affects the development, quality, cost, effectiveness, and availability of public services. The lower average median household incomes found in rural areas also limit money spent on educational, transportation, and other infrastructure resources (Zimmerman et al. 1999).

Over-dependence on the coal mining industry and the boom and bust cycles that accompany this industry affects local institutions, particularly local governments and their ability to raise revenue and provide local services (Gramling 1996; Johnson et al. 1995). Local governments rely mostly upon locally generated revenues to provide key infrastructure and social services. Data from 1972-1992 show that the Appalachian coal region per capita revenue rate was approximately 50 percent of the per capita rate for all local governments in the United States (Latimer and Mencken 2003).

General expenditure data reveal the same trend. Local governments in the Appalachian coal region spend significantly less per capita than the national per capita rate, and this gap remained consistent from 1972-1992. This pattern held on specific per capita spending on health services, highway spending, and police services. Local government spending in the Appalachian coal region appears to face tighter prioritizing than what is typical for a local government in the United States (Latimer and Mencken 2003).

Over-dependence and boom/bust cycles can also create problems for local government finances, particularly if revenue shortfalls create local government debt. Latimer and Mencken (2003) found that the Appalachian coal region had significantly lower general and long-term per capita debt than the rest of the nation for all years available. On the positive side, this indicates that local governments in this region were not saddled with huge debts following the coal bust of the early 1980s. However, the lack of general and long-term debt may also reflect their inability to pass bonds for capital and school improvement projects (Latimer and Mencken 2003).

West Virginia has a long history of low property tax revenues due to constitutional limits on taxation rates and below market property assessments (Reece 1994). As a consequence, "Local public service levels in many of West Virginia's localities are very low" (Reece 1994, 311). In fact, West Virginia's local public expenditures and taxes per capita are lower than the national average, and lower than surrounding states such as Maryland, Ohio, Pennsylvania, and Virginia (Reece 1994). Reece (1994, 311) argues further that, "Businesses and labor looking for high levels of police and fire protection, extensive public libraries, high levels of public water, sewer, sanitation, and other local public services will not find these in many West Virginia localities."

Transportation

A number of researchers (Dewees 1998; Maynard 1995; Zimmerman et al. 1999) have documented that transportation is a key intervening variable in welfare recipients' pursuit of economic self-sufficiency. Zimmerman et al. (1999, 10) state that "Transportation is necessary not only to get to and from a job, but transportation is also critical for accessing childcare, health care, and other activities such as purchasing food." Welfare recipients in rural areas have fewer public transportation resources and face longer commutes to employment opportunities than their urban counterparts. According to Zimmerman et al. (1999, 11), "Close to 40 percent of all rural residents live in areas with no form of public transportation. Another 28 percent of all rural residents live in areas with very low levels of service provision." Even though rural households have higher rates of private vehicle ownership than their urban counterparts, "Nearly 57 percent of the rural poor do not own a car" (Zimmerman et al. 1999, 11).

West Virginia has no county highway system. Only half of the state's highways are paved, and 60 percent of the highways that are paved have a fair to very poor sufficiency rating in terms of curves, grades, lane and shoulder widths, and number of lanes (Martinelli and Eck 1994). In addition, "3,000 of the state's 6,800 bridges need structural and/or geometric improvements" (Martinelli and Eck

Setting the Socioeconomic Context for Welfare Reform

1994, 196). According to Martinelli and Eck (1994), West Virginia's mountainous terrain, poor soil and drainage systems, severe freeze/thaw cycles, and the trucking industry's use of roads not designed to carry heavy loads make maintaining (not expanding) the highway system the state's current focus.

Health Care

Healthcare also influences low-income adults' ability to leave and stay off welfare, particularly those residing in rural areas. According to a recent report, there are fewer doctors and medical services in rural communities (Zimmerman et al. 1999). At the same time, jobs found predominantly in rural areas (i.e., coal mining, timbering, construction, and farming) are some of the most dangerous occupations in the nation. These jobs place their workers at the highest risk for employment related injuries. In addition, the over-concentration of small businesses in rural areas translates into decreased chances that workers and their families will receive employment-related health benefits (Zimmerman et al. 1999).

In 1990, approximately 16 percent of West Virginians had no health insurance. Twenty-five percent of those uninsured were children. In 1993, 38 percent of West Virginia women in their first trimester of pregnancy did not receive prenatal care. By the end of their pregnancy, almost all of them had received some type of prenatal care. The majority indicated that they had received "adequate care," and 25 percent rated their care as either "intermediate" or "inadequate." In 1994, fifty of West Virginia's fifty-five counties were considered medically underserved by the federal government's definition (Hannah 1995). The National Association of Community Health Centers recently reported that in West Virginia, 58.2 percent of the state's population is medically underserved, and 28.2 percent do not have a regular source of primary care. In addition, 17 percent of West Virginians currently do not have any kind of health insurance, and 16 percent receive Medicaid or some other form of public assistance healthcare (NACHC 2001).

Childcare

The availability, flexibility, cost, and quality of childcare also affect low-income parents' ability to leave and stay off welfare. Some researchers estimate that full-time minimum wage workers pay between 35 percent (for the lowest-priced provider) and 50 percent (for the average cost provider) of their total income on day care for their children (Handler and Hasenfeld 1997). According to Harris (1998, 9) childcare constraints "consistently show significant effects in slowing women's exit from welfare and in causing women to return to welfare." Koon (1997) found that AFDC recipients with fewer children and recipients who delayed child bearing were among the individuals most likely to find employment after participating in the JOBS program. Negotiating childcare and employment should be particularly difficult for rural parents given that there are fewer childcare providers in rural areas, childcare costs are higher in rural areas, and rural parents travel farther for their childcare than their urban counterparts (Zimmerman et al. 1999).

Approximately 45 percent of pre-school children and 54 percent of school-aged children in West Virginia need some type of childcare. Three West Virginia counties (Pocahontas, Tucker, and Webster) had no licensed childcare centers at all in 1995. According to Hannah (1995, 38), "In 18 counties, licensed childcare for children under 24 months was unavailable, and only 105 (36%) of the state's childcare centers accepted infants and toddlers." The cost of day care in West Virginia was, on average, $15 a day in childcare centers and $11 a day for family day care providers (Hannah 1995). Thus, for a working mom with one child, the average childcare costs in West Virginia ranged between $2,860 and $3,800 per year. This cost is particularly difficult for the 36 percent of adult West Virginia women in the labor force with incomes less than $10,000 in 2000.

Housing

According to Zimmerman et al. (1999), lower income rental housing is harder to find in rural than urban areas. The housing that is available is more likely to be lower quality (even to the point of being substandard) and to have a major housing problem (i.e., incomplete plumbing or kitchen, exposed wiring, etc.) than

Setting the Socioeconomic Context for Welfare Reform

housing located in urban areas. In 1995, a larger percent of rural welfare households paid more than 30 percent of their income on housing than non-welfare households (Zimmerman et al. 1999). The quality and cost of housing available to rural families not only affects their labor force participation (i.e., consistent or interrupted) and employment opportunities, but the long-term prospects for economic development in their communities. Research indicates that "without an adequate supply of affordable housing, attracting new residents or businesses is difficult" (Zimmerman et al. 1999, 10).

At first glance, West Virginia residents appear to be doing better than their national counterparts in terms of home ownership (75.2% compared to 66.2%). However, Census data reveals a fairly large gap in the median value of these owner-occupied housing units ($72,800 compared to $119,600) (Census 2000 Summary File 3). In addition, approximately 17 percent of these dwellings are mobile homes (compared to 7.6% nationally), and almost 41 percent of West Virginia's housing units (compared to 35% nationally) were built prior to 1941. Seven percent of West Virginia families (1.8% nationally) used either coal or wood as the fuel to heat their homes. One percent of these homes lacked complete plumbing facilities and 4.7 percent had no telephone service (compared to 0.6% and 2.4% nationally) (Census 2000 Summary File 3).

Although the majority of West Virginia homeowners (50.8%) pay less than 15 percent of their total household income on monthly homeowner costs, 28.3 percent of renters pay 35 percent or more of their total monthly household income on rent. A larger percent of the total vacant housing units in West Virginia are mobile homes (19%) than for the rest of the nation (13.4%). In addition, a larger percent of the vacant housing units in West Virginia were built prior to 1941 (32.5% versus 23.4%), lack complete plumbing facilities (16.6% versus 6.4%), and lack complete kitchen facilities (17.8% versus 7.7%) than in the rest of the nation (Census 2000 Summary File 3).

The Child Welfare League of America (CWLA 2001) conducted an analysis of the cost of housing in West Virginia. According to this study, a two-bedroom apartment in the state (in 1999) cost $417 per month. At this rental rate, minimum wage workers spend approximately 47 percent of their average monthly income on rent. The rate is even higher (68%) for a family of three receiving TANF monthly benefits and Food Stamps.

Deindustrialization and Economic Restructuring

Rural communities have been particularly hard hit by deindustrialization and economic restructuring. These national changes have led to a polarization between low and high paying jobs with the middle range jobs being slowly squeezed out. According to Zimmerman et al. (1999, 8), "Between 1969 and 1992, rural manufacturing employment dipped from 20.4 percent to 16.9 percent of total employment." Almost one-quarter of rural workers were employed in the service sector in 1996.

In West Virginia, "The restructuring of the economy away from goods-producing activity toward service-producing activity was more substantial than for the national economy, especially during the 1980s. In some sense, West Virginia's economy may have hit rock-bottom by the mid-1980s, with stability occurring when the economy could not really fall any farther" (Cushing 1994, 27). Between 1979 and 1983, West Virginia lost 73,000 jobs in the goods producing industry. The decline in these industries continued through the 1980s with mining jobs reduced by half, manufacturing jobs reduced by one-quarter, and construction jobs by one-third (Hawley 1994, 59). By 1990, the total employment in this industry bottomed out at its lowest level in fifty years (Cushing 1994, 20). In contrast, employment in the service industry in the state grew by 38.2 percent between 1980 and 1990 (Hawley 1994, 58).

The 2003 Bureau of Employment Programs data for the state indicates that employment in goods producing industries continued to decline (-5.5%) while employment in service producing industries grew (+5.6%). Approximately 47% of the jobs lost were in manufacturing; 22.1 percent were in trade, transportation, and utilities; 15.6 percent were in natural resources and mining; 9.1 percent were in construction; and 6.5 percent were in information. Forty-four percent of the job growth in the service industries occurred in professional and business services; 21.8 percent was in leisure and hospitality; 16.7 percent was in educational and health services; and 17.9 percent was in government, financial activity and other services. Employment in the service producing industries constituted an overwhelming 83.6 percent of the total nonfarm payroll in January 2003.

The majority of the service sector growth in rural areas has been in the service industry's low wage sector (Gorham 1992). This is also the case in West Virginia. The 1990 average annual salaries for jobs in the rapidly expanding wholesale/retail trade and services industries were between $10,000 and $15,000 less than the average salary for manufacturing jobs and between $22,000 and $26,000 less than the average salary for mining jobs (Hawley 1994). The 2001 average annual wages for workers still employed in mining and manufacturing were $50,081 and $38,215 respectively. The average annual wages for whole trade, retail trade, services were between $3,500 and $13,000 less than the average wages for manufacturing jobs and between $15,000 and $35,000 less than the average wages for mining jobs for this same time period. Probably the most telling statistic is that Wal-Mart Associates, Inc. is now the state's largest employer (http://www.state.wv.us/bep/).

As mentioned in the previous chapter, the higher paying jobs that have been created in recent years require education and training qualifications that few rural workers can meet (Deavers and Hoppe 1992; Tickamyer and Duncan 1990). For example, "From 1981 to 1986, rural workers were more likely to be displaced and experienced higher economic costs following displacement than their urban counterparts" (Zimmerman et al. 1999, 8). Both the working poor and involuntary part-time workers in rural areas had significantly greater difficulty finding adequate jobs in the 1990s than their counterparts in the 1970s (Zimmerman et al. 1999).

According to the occupational projections for West Virginia, ten (including the top seven) out of the fifteen occupations expected to have the largest percent growth between 2000 and 2010 are in the highly specialized computer industry. The specific occupations include computer support specialists, software engineers, desktop publishers, network and computer systems administrators, computer information and systems managers, and database administrators.

Education and Training

Increases in average educational levels significantly (1) decrease the probability of being poor (Bokemeier and Tickamyer 1985; McLaughlin and Sachs 1988; Tickamyer and Latimer 1993) or experiencing underemployment or economic hardship (Lichter 1989), (2) decrease sex differences in occupational achievement (Bokemeier and Tickamyer 1985), and (3) increase both women's and men's labor force participation rates (Ollenburger et al. 1989). Both Koon (1997) and Harris (1998) document the strong relationship between education and employment for welfare recipients. Harris (1998, 7) found that for welfare recipients, access to "education is more important than work experience in helping women leave welfare, helping women to leave welfare more quickly, and helping women stay off welfare once they leave." She specifically found that "a high school education reduced the chance that a woman would return to welfare by 39 percent, and an education beyond high school reduced the chance of welfare return by 41 percent, compared to those who drop out" (Harris 1998, 8).

In the post-industrial economy, workers must have higher levels of education and training than were previously required for middle income jobs (Tickamyer and Duncan 1990). These new employment qualifications are particularly problematic in rural areas where there are twice as many unskilled workers as in urban areas and where workers (especially minority workers) have low educational levels (Deavers and Hoppe 1992). Lichter and Costanzo (1987) found that educational differences between metro and nonmetro areas are largely responsible for differences in unemployment and underemployment. In addition, individuals in rural areas have fewer job training opportunities than their urban counterparts (Zimmerman et al. 1999).

Adults in the Appalachian coal region lag far behind the nation in educational attainment. Some counties have non-high school completion rates at least twice the national rate of 24 percent, and all Appalachian coal counties in 1990 had percentages of adults not graduating from high school higher than the national rate (Latimer and Mencken 2003). Educational deficits are one of the legacies of natural resource dependency. These industries employ large proportions of non-high school graduates, and when the jobs leave, the more educated people move away. Those with the least skills and education are often those left behind (Latimer and Mencken 2003).

Overall, women in the United States currently have higher average educational attainment than men. West Virginia women do not have this educational advantage over their male counterparts. In 1990, 66 percent of West Virginians twenty-five years or older had at least a high school degree (Census 2000 Summary File 3). In addition, West Virginia had the lowest percentage (12.3%) of college graduates over age twenty-five in the nation. Fourteen percent of West Virginia males (compared to 23% nationally) and 11 percent of West Virginia females (compared to 18% nationally) had at least a bachelor's degree (Hannah 1995). In 2000, the state's overall high school completion rate reached 75 percent, and the college completion rate improved slightly to 14.8 percent. Sex differences in educational attainment continued, with 16 percent of males and 14 percent of females with at least a bachelor's degree (Census 2000 Summary File 3).

Making the Case: Why Study West Virginia

It is clear from the previous discussion that place matters. There are substantial differences in the geography, economic conditions, and demographic characteristics of rural and urban communities. These differences make labor force participation and higher earnings more difficult for the rural poor. Yet, the majority of existing poverty research (Duncan and Sweet 1992; RSS Task Force 1993) as well as the new research on welfare reform (Weber, Duncan and Whitener 2000) have focused on poor families in urban areas. When rural and urban comparisons are made, national level data are used, which obscure significant rural/urban differences in welfare use, poverty, and employment (Weber et al. 2000). As mentioned in the previous chapter, this book helps to fill that void in the academic literature.

West Virginia demonstrates the negative effects of rural location on every single economic indicator analyzed in this chapter. This is also true when comparing West Virginia to the rest of the Appalachian region. The University of Kentucky Center for Poverty Research reports that over a twenty year period West Virginia has a much lower employment-population ratio (ratio of employed people to the total population) and real per capita personal income than the rest of the South (as well as the rest of the United States). West Virginia also has consistently higher poverty rates, unemployment rates, AFDC/TANF recipients (with the exception of 1997-2000), Food Stamp participation, and Medicaid recipients than the remaining Southern region and the United States (www.ukcpr.org/EconomicData/statedata). As a result, if one of the most effective ways to test a program designed to provide income security to low-income families is to examine how effective it is in areas experiencing economic hardship, then studying welfare reform in West Virginia, a rural, Appalachian, Southern state with consistently high unemployment and poverty rates, should prove both useful and informative to the academic, practitioner, and policymaking communities alike.

References

America's Second Harvest. 2002. http://www.secondharvest.org.

Appalachian Regional Commission. 2003. Socioeconomic Data: Barbour County, West Virginia. http://www.arc.gov/search/LoadQueryData.do?queryId=1&fips=54001.

Bertaux, Nancy E. 1991. "The Roots of Today's 'Women's Jobs' and 'Men's Jobs': Using the Index of Dissimilarity to Measure Occupational Segregation by Gender." *Explorations in Economic History* 28: 433-459.

Billings, Dwight B. 1974. "Culture and Poverty in Appalachia: A Theoretical and Empirical Analysis." *Social Forces* 53(2): 325-23.

Billings, Dwight B. and Kathleen M. Blee. 2000. *The Road to Poverty: The Making of Wealth and Hardship in Appalachia*. New York: Cambridge University Press.

Billings, Dwight B. and Ann R. Tickamyer. 1993. "Uneven Development in Appalachia." *Forgotten Places: Uneven*

Development in Rural America. ed. Thomas A. Lyson and William W. Falk, 7-29. Lawrence, KS: University Press of Kansas.

Bischak, Greg. 1997. "Briefing Paper: Welfare Reform and its Potential Impact on Appalachia." Washington, D.C.: Appalachian Regional Commission.

Bokemeier, Janet and Ann R. Tickamyer. 1985. "Labor Force Experiences of Nonmetropolitan Women." *Rural Sociology* 50(1): 51-73.

Burkett, Gary L. 1994. "Status of Health in Appalachia." *Sowing Seeds in the Mountains: Community-Based Coalitions For Cancer Prevention and Control*. ed. Richard Couto, Nancy K. Simpson, and Gale Harris, 43-61. Washington D.C.: The National Cancer Institute.

Child Welfare League of America. 2001. http://www.cwla.org/advocacy/statefactsheets/2001/westvirginia.htm.

Cho, Woong and S. Ogunwole. 1989. "Black Workers in Southern Rural Labor Markets." *Research in Rural Sociology and Development*. ed. William Falk and Thomas Lyson, 189-206. London: JAI Press.

Colclough, Glenna and Charles Tolbert. 1993. "Divisions of Labor and Inequality in High-Tech Centers." *Inequalities in Labor Market Areas*. ed. Joachim Singelmann and Forrest A. Deseran, 143-64. Boulder CO: Westview Press.

Couto, Richard A. 1994. *An American Challenge*. Dubuque, IA: Kendall/Hunt.

Cushing, Brian. 1994. "West Virginia's Economy, 1940-2000." *West Virginia in the 1990s: Opportunities for Economic Progress*. ed. Robert Jay Dilger and Tom Stuart Witt, 17-46. Morgantown, WV: West Virginia University Press.

Deavers, Kenneth and Robert Hoppe. 1992. "Overview of the Rural Poor in the 1980s." *Rural Poverty in America*. ed. Cynthia M.

Duncan, 3-20. New York: Auburn House.

Dewees, Sarah. 1998. "The Drive to Work: Transportation Issues and Welfare Reform in Rural Areas." Information Brief No. 5. Southern Rural Development Center. October.

Dilger, Robert Jay and Tom Stuart Witt. 1994. "West Virginia's Economic Future." *West Virginia in the 1990s: Opportunities for Economic Progress.* ed. Robert Jay Dilger and Tom Stuart Witt, 3-15. Morgantown, WV: West Virginia University Press.

Duncan, Cynthia M. 1992. "Persistent Poverty in Appalachia: Scarce Work and Rigid Stratification." *Rural Poverty in America.* ed. Cynthia M. Duncan, 111-133. New York: Auburn House.

Duncan, Cynthia M. and Stephen Sweet. 1992. "Introduction: Poverty in Rural America." *Rural Poverty in America.* ed. Cynthia M. Duncan, xix-xxvii. New York: Auburn House.

Energy Statistics Sourcebook. August, 1999. 14th edition. PennWell. Oil and Gas Energy Database.

Ergood, Bruce and Bruce E. Kuhre, Editors. 1991. *Appalachia: Social Context Past and Present.* Dubuque, IA: Kendall/Hunt.

Falk, William W. and Thomas A. Lyson. 1988. *High Tech, Low Tech, No Tech: Recent Industrial and Occupational Change in the South.* Albany, NY: State University of New York Press.

Findeis, Jill L., Mark Henry, Thomas Hirschl, Willis Lewis, Ismael Ortega-Sanchez, Emelie Peine, and Julie Zimmerman. 2001. *Welfare Reform in Rural America: A Review of Current Research.* Rural Policy Research Institute. P2001-5, University of Missouri, Columbia, MO.

Gorham, Lucy. 1992. "The Growing Problem of Low Earnings in Rural Areas." *Rural Poverty in America.* ed. Cynthia M. Duncan, 21-39. New York: Auburn House.

Goudy, Willis, Rogelio Saenz, Sandra Burke, and David Rogers. 1986. "Occupational Segregation in Selected Iowa Communities: 1960-1980." Paper presented at the Annual Meeting of the Rural Sociological Society, Salt Lake City, Utah.

Gramling, Robert. 1996. *Oil on the Edge*. Albany, NY SUNY-Albany Press.

Hannah, Karen L. 1993. *West Virginia Women: In Perspective 1980-1995*. Charleston, WV: West Virginia Women's Commission.

Harris, Kathleen Mulan. 1998. "Presentation." *Welfare to Work: Opportunities and Pitfalls*. ed. Kathryn Edin, Kathleen Mullan Harris, and Gary D. Sandefur, 6-9. Washington, D.C.: American Sociological Association.

Hawley, Clifford B. 1994. "Demographic Change and Economic Opportunity." *West Virginia in the 1990s: Opportunities for Economic Progress*. ed. Robert Jay Dilger and Tom Stuart Witt, 47-72. Morgantown, WV: West Virginia University Press.

Isserman, Andrew M. 1996. "Appalachia Then and Now An Update of 'The Realities of Deprivation' Reported to the President in 1964." Online Resource Center, Appalachian Regional Commission. http://www.arc.gov/images/reports/thenandnow/then.pdf.

Isserman, Andrew M. and Terrance Rephann. 1993. "The Economic Effects of the Appalachian Regional Commission: An Empirical Assessment of 27 Years of Regional Development Policy." *Journal of the American Planning Association* 69: 345-365.

Jensen, Leif, Jill L. Findeis, Wan-Ling Hsu, and Jason P. Schachter. 1999. "Slipping Into and Out of Underemployment: Another Disadvantage for Nonmetropolitan Workers." *Rural Sociology* 64(3): 417-438.

Jensen, Leif and Marta Tienda. 1989. "Nonmetropolitan Minority Families in the United States: Trends in Racial and Ethnic Economic Stratification, 1959-1986." *Rural Sociology* 54(4): 509-532.

Johnson, Kenneth M., John P. Pelissero, David B. Holian, and Michael T. Maly. 1995. "Local Government Fiscal Burden in Nonmetropolitan America." *Rural Sociology* 60: 381-398.

Koon, Richard L. 1997. *Welfare Reform: Helping the Least Fortunate Become Less Dependent*. New York: Garland Publishing, Inc.

Latimer, Melissa and F. Carson Mencken. 2003. "Socioeconomic Trends in Mining Dependent Counties in Appalachia." *Communities of Work: Rural Restructuring in Local and Global Contexts*. ed. William Falk, Michael Schulman, and Ann R. Tickamyer, 79-103. Athens, OH: Ohio University Press.

Lichter, Daniel. 1987. "Measuring Underemployment in Rural Areas." *Rural Development Perspectives* 3: 11-14.

Lichter, Daniel T. 1989. "Race, Employment Hardship, and Inequality in the American Nonmetropolitan South." *American Sociological Review* 54: 436-446.

Lichter, Daniel T. and Janice A. Constanzo. 1987. "Nonmetropolitan Underemployment and Labor-Force Composition." *Rural Sociology* 52(3): 329-344.

Lichter, Daniel T. and Diane McLaughlin. 1995. "Changing Economic Opportunities, Family Structure, and Poverty in Rural Areas." *Rural Sociology* 60(4): 688-706.

Lobao, Linda. 1990. *Locality and Inequality*. Albany, NY: SUNY Press.

_____. 1993. "Renewed Significance of Space in Social Research: Implications for Labor Market Studies." *Inequalities in Labor Market Areas*. ed. Joachim Singelmann and Forrest A. Deseran, 11-32. Boulder CO: Westview Press.

Lorence, Jon. 1992. "Service Sector Growth and Metropolitan Occupational Sex Segregation." *Work and Occupations* 19(2): 128-156.

McLaughlin, Diane, Dan Lichter, and Stephan Matthews. 1999. "Demographic Diversity and Economic Change in Appalachia: Executive Summary." Online Resource Center, Appalachian Regional Commission. http://www.arc.gov/images/reports/demographics/demographics.pdf.

McLaughlin, Diane and Carolyn Sachs. 1988. "Poverty in Female-Headed Households: Residential Differences." *Rural Sociology* 53(3): 287-306.

Maggard, Sally W. 1994. "From Farm to Coal Camp to Back Office and McDonald's: Living in the Midst of Appalachia's Latest Transformation." *Journal of Appalachian Studies Association* 6: 14-38.

Martinelli, David and Ronald W. Eck. 1994. "West Virginia's Transportation Infrastructure: Conditions, Trends, and Implications for Economic Growth." *West Virginia in the 1990s: Opportunities for Economic Progress.* ed. Robert Jay Dilger and Tom Stuart Witt, 195-220. Morgantown, WV: West Virginia University Press.

Maynard, Rebecca A. 1995. "Preparing Welfare Recipients for Employment." *Focus* 17(1): 46-47. University of Wisconsin-Madison: The Institute for Research on Poverty.

Mencken, F. Carson. 1996. "Income and Employment Change in Appalachia During the 1983-1988 Business Cycle Recovery: Locating Differential Effects in North, Central, and Southern Appalachia." *Journal of Appalachian Studies* 2(1): 77-85.

_____. 1997. "Regional Differences in Socioeconomic Well-Being in Appalachia." *Sociological Focus* 30(1): 79-97.

Murdock, Steve H., Md. Nazrul Hoque, and Kenneth Backman. 1993. "Determinants of 1980 to 1990 Net Migration in Texas Counties: The Role of Sustenance Specialization and Dominance in International Ecosystems." *Rural Sociology* 58: 190-209.

National Association of Community Health Centers, Inc. 2001. "2000 Access to Community Health Care." August. http://www.nachc.com.

Nord, Mark and A. E. Luloff. 1993. "Socioeconomic Heterogeneity of Mining-Dependent Counties." *Rural Sociology* 58: 492-500.

Ollenburger, Jane C., Sheryl J. Grana, and Helen A. Moore. 1989. "Labor Force Participation of Rural Farm, Rural Nonfarm, and Urban Women: A Panel Update." *Rural Sociology* 54(4): 533-550.

People's Appalachian Research Collective. 1991. "Why Study Appalachia." *Appalachia: Social Context Past and Present.* ed. Bruce Ergood and Bruce E. Kuhre, 3-7. Dubuque, IA: Kendall/Hunt.

Pfeffer Max. 1993. "Black Migration and the Legacy of Plantation Agriculture." *Inequalities in Labor Market Areas.* ed. Joachim Singelmann and Forrest A. Deseran, 191-214. Boulder, CO: Westview Press.

Rank, Mark Robert. 1994. *Living on the Edge: The Realities of Welfare In America.* New York: Columbia University Press.

Rank, Mark R. and Thomas A. Hirschl. 1993. "The Link Between Population Density and Welfare Populations." *Demography* 30(4): 607-623.

_____. 1988. "A Rural-Urban Comparison of Welfare Exits: The Importance of Population Density." *Rural Sociology* 53(2): 190-206.

Reece, William S. 1994. "Local Government Finance and Its Implications for West Virginia's Economic Development." *West Virginia in the 1990s: Opportunities for Economic Progress.* ed. Robert Jay Dilger and Tom Stuart Witt, 285-317. Morgantown, WV: West Virginia University Press.

Ross, Peggy and Elizabeth Morrissey. 1986. "Persistent Poverty Among the Nonmetro Poor." Paper presented to the Southern Rural Sociological Association. Orlando, Florida.

Rural Sociological Society Task Force. 1993. *Persistent Poverty in Rural America.* Boulder, CO: Westview Press.

Stafford, M. Therese and Mark A. Fossett. 1989. "Occupational Sex Inequality in the Nonmetropolitan South, 1960-1980." *Rural Sociology* 54: 169-194.

Tickamyer, Ann R. and Janet Bokemeier. 1988. "Sex Differences in Labor Market Experiences." *Rural Sociology* 53(2): 166-189.

Tickamyer, Ann and Cynthia Duncan. 1990. "Poverty and Opportunity Structure in Rural America." *Annual Review of Sociology* 16(1): 67-86.

Tickamyer, Ann R. and Melissa Latimer. 1993. "A Multilevel Analysis of Income Sources of the Poor and Near Poor." *Inequalities in Labor Market Areas.* ed. Joachim Singelmann and Forrest A. Deseran, 49-68. Boulder CO: Westview Press.

Tickamyer, Ann R. and Cecil Tickamyer. 1988. "Gender and Poverty in Central Appalachia." *Social Science Quarterly* 69(4): 874-891.

Tomaskovic-Devey, Donald. 1987. "Labor Markets, Industrial Structure, and Poverty: A Theoretical Discussion and Empirical Example." *Rural Sociology* 52(1): 56-74.

University of Kentucky Center for Poverty Research. 2003. Economic and Program Data. http://www.ukcpr.org/EconomicData/statedata.asp?URLState=West%20Virginia.

U. S. Department of Commerce, Bureau of the Census. 2000. State and County Quick Facts. http://www.quickfacts.census.gov/qfd/states/54000.html.

_____. 2000. Census 2000 Summary File 3. http://www.factfinder.census.gov/servlet/.

_____. 1998. Table A98-54 Estimated Number and Percent People of All Ages in Poverty by County: West Virginia 1998. http://www.census.gov/hhes/www/saipe/stcty/a98_54.htm.

_____. 1990. Census 1990 Summary Tape File 3. http://www.census.gov/td/stf3/abst_s3.html.

Weber, Bruce, Greg Duncan, and Leslie Whitener. 2000. "Rural Dimensions of Welfare Reform." *Poverty Research News* 4(5): 3, 4.

West Virginia Bureau of Employment Programs. 2003. West Virginia Economic Summary. http://www.state.wv.us/bep/lmi/ECONSUMM/.

_____.2003. Employment Programs News Release. http://www.state.wv.us/bep/lmi/datare1/.

_____. 2002. The 100 Largest Employers in West Virginia. http://www.state.wv.us/scripts/bep/lmi/statetop100.cfm (link no longer maintained).

_____. 2000. West Virginia Occupational Projections 2000-2010. http://www.state.wv.us/bep/lmi/occproj/opmenu.htm.

Zimmerman, Julie, Sarah Dewees, Lynn Reinschmiedt, and Tom Hirschl. 1999. *Rural America and Welfare Reform: An Overview Assessment*. Rural Policy Research Institute. P99-3, Columbia, MO: University of Missouri.

Chapter 3

Cash Assistance and Social Welfare Policy in the United States: The Political and Institutional Context

ROBERT JAY DILGER

The nation's cash assistance program for the poor, what the general public commonly refers to as welfare, has, throughout its history, generated considerable debate and controversy. There have been fundamental disagreements over almost everything: how the program should be structured, who should receive assistance, what recipients should be required or encouraged to do in exchange for benefits, the extent to which work should be emphasized, whether existing programmatic features were a success or a failure, and even how to measure success or failure. These policy differences stem from fundamental disagreements concerning government's role in American society and the best means to help the poor to achieve economic self-sufficiency (Washington Research Council 1998). In recent years, this debate has focused on the efficacy of the human capital development strategy (i.e., focusing on education and job training programs) versus the workforce attachment strategy (i.e., emphasizing immediate job placement) as the best way to help recipients leave, and remain off, welfare.

In 1996, a host of political and cultural changes converged that resulted in the adoption of the six-year, $110 billion *Personal Responsibility and Work Opportunity Reconciliation Act of 1996*. This landmark legislation purposively "delinked" eligibility for welfare (cash assistance) from other government safety net programs, including Medicaid and Food Stamps. It did this, in large part, by doing away with the Aid to Families With Dependent Children (AFDC) program and replacing it with a new cash assistance program called Temporary Assistance for Needy Families (TANF). This new program was designed to end welfare dependency by imposing a host of new rules and regulations, including mandatory work requirements and lifetime benefit limits for recipients as well as mandatory work participation rates and maintenance-of-effort requirements for states. It was a dramatic change in policy, with a much greater emphasis on personal responsibility, self-help, and the workforce attachment strategy.

English Origins

To fully understand the welfare reform movement and the current status of welfare policy in the United States and in West Virginia, it is first necessary to understand the program's history. America's welfare policies originated in the English tradition. Although English welfare policy dates back to the Middle Ages, the *Elizabethan Poor Law of 1601* is generally regarded as the single most important welfare law in England's history. It represented the culmination of a two-century process of government's increased responsibility for aid to the poor, first through "repressive" measures (see Chapter 8 for details) and later through more charitable means, such as direct grants to unemployable people, work for able-bodied adults, and education, foster care, and apprenticeship for children (Reid 1995). Although churches retained their long-prominent role as the primary source of support for the poor, the *Elizabethan Poor Law* was a milestone in welfare's transition from being primarily a private sector concern to a public sector concern in England. It also established four basic welfare principles that later influenced the scope and structure of contemporary welfare programs in both England and the United States (Reid 1995; Trattner 1999). First, it created a limited, decentralized organizational structure to deal with the poor. Localities were responsible for both financing and administering public assistance programs. Second, localities took care of their own by establishing lengthy residency requirements. This minimized costs by discouraging vagabonds, drifters, and others from migrating to their communities in search of better benefits. Third, "deserving" poor were divided into three categories: children, able-bodied adults (typically widows and abandoned women), and the mentally or physically incapacitated. Each category was expected to contribute toward its upkeep and prepare themselves, as best they could, for work. For example, children were required to attend school to learn how to read and write and were then apprenticed to learn a trade. Able-bodied adults were provided employment or required to find employment as a condition of receiving assistance. Fourth, a distinction was made between deserving and non-deserving poor, with the latter denied assistance. Local officials determined who was deserving and who was not deserving (Dilger 1989; Trattner 1999).

The American Context

American political culture, molded by the Protestant work ethic and "liberal" values of individualism, personal responsibility, the importance of work, and a general distrust of collectivism and centralized government, exerted a strong influence on the development of American welfare policy during the nineteenth and twentieth centuries. These values resulted largely from the collapse of feudalism in Europe and the rise, both in the American colonies and elsewhere, of a middle class that was defined not by right of birth, but by its usefulness to others. A person's worth was no longer defined by their birth right or land holdings; it was defined by their usefulness to others and by their contribution to the welfare of others. In this context, work was viewed as both a moral act and as an economic one (Reid 1995). As a result, American political culture demanded that America's welfare programs require able-bodied recipients to work, or, at the very least, engage in schooling or job-training activities to enable them to work in the near future (Hofstadter 1948; Leiby 1978; Reid 1995).

Initially, the American colonial governments did not view the poor as a threat to civil society or social order. As a result, providing aid to the poor during the late 1700s and early 1800s was, for the most part, left to churches and private charities. Government became involved only as a last resort. When government did become involved, it generally followed the *Elizabethan Poor Law's* guiding principles of decentralization, cost containment, emphasis on work and preparation for work, and establishing distinctions between those considered deserving and undeserving. As a result, welfare was handled primarily by local governments which, to contain costs, established relatively long residency requirements to qualify for public assistance (Leman 1980). Newly arrived paupers were encouraged to move on. Some towns went so far as to whip newly arrived paupers before sending them on their way to discourage others from arriving (Abramovitz 1998). Typically, able-bodied adults provided assistance were required to work, and children were apprenticed. Also, only deserving poor were given assistance, primarily those considered unable to care for themselves, such as widows, orphans, and the mentally or physically handicapped. Black men and women were typically denied assistance, regardless of their personal circumstances, as were unmarried mothers of illegitimate children (Gordon 1994; Abramovitz 1998).

During the 1820s and 1830s, many social commentators questioned the assumption that the poor were not a threat to civil society and social order. In their view, the poor were an indication of a breakdown in civil society. They wanted government to address poverty in a more aggressive manner. They advocated the use of almshouses (often called poorhouses) where through ". . . order, cleanliness, discipline, and routine, the poor could be transformed into useful and productive members of society" (Reid 1995, 2210). At that time, almshouses were not nearly as widespread in the United States as they were in Great Britain. The idea of institutionalizing people considered a threat to civil society spread beyond the poor to include the mentally ill and prisoners. As a result, during the 1820s and 1830s a large number of almshouses, asylums, and penitentiaries were constructed throughout the United States. The almshouse movement was relatively short-lived. By the 1850s, many almshouses in the United States were closed in the wake of a growing tide of complaints concerning the abuse of residents and poor living conditions. Once again, what was referred to as outdoor relief (allowing welfare recipients to live in their own or neighbor's home while working outside of the house) became the norm.

By the mid-1800s, state government involvement in welfare was relatively limited and indirect, but growing. By mid-century, most states reimbursed localities for providing temporary care for drifters who failed to meet local residency requirements. Some states also provided public assistance for the deaf, blind, mentally ill, and abandoned or orphaned children. However, for the most part, church and private charities continued to play the leading role in providing assistance to the poor. This was the case in West Virginia, which attained statehood in 1863. At that time, West Virginia's state government played a very limited role in relief efforts. State law required each of the state's county courts to act as the "overseer of the poor" in their respective counties. The county court administered relief programs for county residents who were not cared for by relatives, churches, or private charities. Typically, employable men were required to work on the county road system in exchange for relief. The elderly and infirm were usually housed in the county poor house. Orphans were housed in the county children's home (Davis et al. 1963).

The federal government's role in welfare was also very limited during the early and mid-1800s. For example, in 1848 a bill was introduced in Congress that would have granted states federal land for auction. The bill directed that the proceeds from the auction be used to fund mental hospitals. The bill was introduced in response to a grassroots, nationwide effort led by Dorothea Dix to improve the care and housing of the mentally ill. The bill languished in Congress for several years until it was passed in 1854. However, President Franklin Pierce vetoed the bill, claiming that it violated states' rights. As he explained at the time, "If Congress has the power to make provisions for the indigent insane . . . it has the same power for the indigent who are not insane. . . . I cannot find any authority in the Constitution for making the Federal Government the great almoner of public charity throughout the United States" (Karger and Stoesz 1998, 54). Pierce's veto is noteworthy because it provided the rationale and legal precedent used to prevent the federal government from providing social welfare services for the next seventy-five years.

The Post-Civil War Era

The industrialization of the American economy following the Civil War led to the increasing urbanization of American society. Cities, in turn, gave rise to sweatshops, urban slums, and, in the absence of well-funded sanitation departments, the spread of infectious diseases. The industrialization of the economy also gave rise to the development of the organized labor movement to defend workers' rights. Labor-management conflict often turned violent. Between 1880 and 1900, there were more than 30,000 strikes and lockouts involving over 10 million American workers (Reid 1995). In addition, millions of European immigrants, many of them Catholic, arrived searching for work, which created increased demands on local charities and increased religious and ethnic tensions throughout urban America (Garfinkel and McLanahan 1986). The national economy also began to experience periods of boom and bust. The southern states imposed Jim Crow laws, systematically restricting African-Americans' political and economic opportunities. All these changes challenged the existing social order.

Private charities responded to these changes in two ways. First, the charity organization movement, expanding on the efforts of earlier organizations such as the New York Association for Improving the Condition of the Poor, began in earnest in 1877 with the formation of the American Charity Organization Society in Buffalo, New York. By 1900, 138 charity organization societies operated in twenty-five cities. Typically, these organizations did not provide grant relief. Instead, they served as a clearinghouse for other charities in their community, maintaining registries of relief applicants, keeping records of the assistance provided, and referring individuals to appropriate relief agencies. They also fostered the principles of "scientific charity." These principles included an obligation to assist the poor, but held that assistance should be provided in an efficient, business-like manner that reflected a well-conceived plan for addressing the underlying causes of poverty. Also, these organizations held that poverty was primarily due to personal defects and poor judgement. Therefore, it was a waste of resources to provide the poor with assistance unless there was also a mechanism in place to reform the individual. These reforms typically included discouraging the use of alcohol and having a professional caseworker or other person (often called friendly visitors) diagnose the individual's deficiencies and recommend avenues for personal improvement (Reid 1995; Trattner 1999; Tannenbaum and Reisch 2001).

The settlement house movement formed, in part, to counter the charity organization societies. In 1886, the Neighborhood Guild in New York City created the first settlement house. In 1889, Jane Adams and Ellen Gates Starr founded Hull House, the most famous settlement house, in Chicago. Instead of focusing on the need to reform individuals, the settlement house movement focused on the need for governmental action to address the environmental causes of poverty. They advocated legislation prohibiting child labor, improving public health facilities, and creating social insurance programs. By 1910, there were more than 400 settlement houses in the United States. They lobbied actively for legislation to address several social causes, including civil rights legislation, labor rights law, temperance, and women's suffrage (Reid 1995; Trattner 1999; Tannenbaum and Reisch 2001).

The Progressives, a middle-class movement, also formed in reaction to the many changes taking place during the post-Civil War era. They called upon government to fund parks and beautify the urban landscape, improve educational systems, assist immigrants to become "Americanized," enact social insurance policies to help the poor, and adopt regulatory measures to combat corruption in government and promote fair competition in the marketplace. They also advocated the professionalization of social workers to better manage, plan, and design programs to aid the poor.

The Progressives' efforts to create social insurance programs to aid the poor met with mixed success. Between 1910 and 1921, most states enacted worker's compensation legislation. However, organized medicine and industrial interests opposed the Progressives' efforts to enact health care and unemployment insurance legislation. As a result, most states rejected these proposals. The Progressives also advocated programs to help the elderly and provide cash assistance to impoverished mothers and their children.

In 1907, Wisconsin became the first state to provide cash assistance to poor individuals who were not assigned to a private citizen's home or a public almshouse (often referred to as outdoor aid). Wisconsin's program provided cash to the blind. In 1911, Illinois and Missouri offered outdoor aid to poor mothers. By 1919, thirty-nine states had adopted cash assistance programs for poor mothers who were not assigned to a private citizen's home or a public almshouse. In 1923, Montana and Nevada became the first states to offer outdoor aid to the aged. By 1934, one year prior to the year in which the federal government enacted its own outdoor aid program, twenty-four states offered outdoor aid to the blind; twenty-eight states offered outdoor aid to the aged; and forty-two states offered outdoor aid to mothers. Still, churches, charities, and local governments continued to play the leading role in public assistance because state programs, for the most part, were not well funded. For example, during the 1920s, less than half of the states with outdoor assistance programs appropriated any money for them. Also, local governments continued to (1) provide less assistance than churches and private charities, primarily because of their relatively long residency requirements, (2) require able-bodied adults and children to work, and (3) make distinctions between deserving and undeserving poor (U.S. ACIR 1980).

The Great Depression and The Social Security Act of 1935

The October 24, 1929 stock market crash and the ensuing Great Depression (1929-1941) changed public attitudes about the poor and government's role in caring for them. Prior to the stock market crash, most Americans divided the poor into two groups, a relatively small group that were poor due to reasons largely beyond their control, such as orphans, widows, and the mentally and/or physically handicapped, and a larger group who were poor because they were either lazy or lacked good moral judgement (e.g., unmarried mothers of illegitimate children, drug addicts, alcoholics, etc.). Most Americans believed that the first group deserved assistance, and local government welfare programs, churches, and private charities were well-equipped to handle their needs. The Great Depression changed their minds (U.S. ACIR 1980; Garfinkel and McLanahan 1986).

In 1933, fifteen million able-bodied men and women, nearly one-third of the American workforce, could not find employment. Suddenly, the stereotype of the poor being lazy "good-for-nothings" was shattered. The belief in the adequacy of local government welfare policies and church and private charity assistance was also shattered as soup and bread lines stretched for blocks on city streets, street corners featured men and women holding signs reading, "Will Work For Food," and the lyrics to Bing Crosby's 1932 number 1 hit recording "Brother, Can You Spare a Dime" brought a tear to every American's eye (Lewis 2002). Importantly, economic adversity during the Great Depression was both widespread and lasting. The official unemployment rate averaged 18 percent during the 1930s. Virtually everyone had either experienced unemployment or knew someone who had lost their job. Under such circumstances, it was difficult to blame the poor for being impoverished (Garfinkel and McLanahan 1986).

States were asked to increase funding for public assistance programs. For example, in 1934, West Virginia's state government appropriated $3 million in emergency assistance to help cities and counties meet their soaring relief needs (Davis et al. 1963). However, states had to deal with their own fiscal crises. As businesses closed and consumer spending declined, state business and sales tax revenue fell precipitously across the nation. Because most state constitutions required a balanced budget, states were not in a position to increase spending for relief efforts to the extent necessary to meet their state's growing relief needs. Also, borrowing money to pay for public assistance programs was not an option for most states because most states had accumulated relatively large debts during the 1920s to pay for road construction and other infrastructure projects. States at that time found it difficult to make payments on their existing debt and, given the very uncertain economic times, were very reluctant to incur more debt. Given the fiscal squeeze on state budgets, welfare advocates turned their attention to the federal government (U.S. ACIR 1980).

At first, the federal government did not act. President Herbert

Hoover (R, 1929-1933) was a staunch fiscal conservative who believed that assisting the poor was a state and local government responsibility. It wasn't until 1933, following the election of Franklin Delano Roosevelt (D, 1933-1945) and an overwhelmingly Democratic Congress, that the federal government acted. At that time, it created the Federal Emergency Relief Administration, which provided emergency public assistance to able-bodied, employable individuals. Those considered unemployable, such as widows, orphans, and the mentally or physically disabled, remained the responsibility of private charities, the churches, and state and local governments (Leman 1980).

After prolonged debate over states' rights and definitions of deserving and undeserving poor, the federal government enacted the *Social Security Act of 1935*, which was part of an overall effort to stimulate the economy by increasing the purchasing power of the working class along the lines suggested by the new, Keynesian economics and to mute social unrest (Abramovitz 1995, 1998). It contained five programs. Old-Age Insurance, funded by business and individual payroll taxes, provided the elderly with income following their forced retirement. Unemployment Insurance, funded through payroll taxes, provided those laid off due to poor economic conditions with temporary income to help them manage until they could find work. Aid to the Blind provided temporary income to the blind who were unemployed because of their handicap. The funds were to be used to help them until they could find work. Old Age Assistance did the same for those who were unable to find employment because of age discrimination against the elderly. Finally, Aid to Dependent Children (ADC), patterned after the states' "mother's outdoor aid programs," provided income for children whose fathers had died, were incapacitated, or left the home ($18 per month for the first child and $12 per month for each additional child in the family). Because of constitutional concerns involving states' rights, ADC was a voluntary, intergovernmental grants-in-aid program. The federal government provided one-third of program costs, and states retained primary control over program implementation, including the determination of eligibility criteria (U.S. ACIR 1980).

Cash Assistance and Social Welfare Policy

The *Social Security Act of 1935* marked a significant departure for welfare policy in the United States. The federal government's presence in providing public assistance funding had a centralizing effect on intergovernmental administrative structures and on state welfare policies in general. For example, the *Social Security Act* encouraged states to assume a more proactive role in public assistance by requiring them to establish a state department of public assistance as a condition for receiving federal ADC funds. West Virginia was one of the states that did not have a state public assistance department. The state legislature held a special session in 1936 to create a Department of Public Assistance to administer ADC. The Department of Public Assistance Director then appointed a director of public assistance in each of the state's counties. That director, in consultation with a five-member public assistance council, administered that county's public relief program. As time passed, primarily because each of the county's public assistance directors reported to the state director, local administrative practices and policies began to look similar. In addition, in 1939, amendments to the *Social Security Act* required state departments receiving federal funds, including state departments of public assistance, to employ personnel systems based on merit principles. West Virginia was one of the states that lacked a merit system. In 1940, West Virginia reluctantly established a merit system that created a personnel classification system and a salary scale for employees in the Department of Public Administration. New applicants for positions within the Department of Public Administration were also required to pass written qualifying examinations (Davis et al. 1963). Also, in 1943, the county departments of public assistance were reorganized into nine districts to reduce administrative expenses and to promote more effective and uniform program implementation practices (Davis et al. 1963). These nine districts were later reorganized into the four districts in place today. All of these changes had a centralizing effect on public assistance's intergovernmental administrative structures across the state. This, in turn, reduced differences in benefits and eligibility requirements within the state. This centralizing and equalizing pattern occurred in states across the nation. Efforts to reduce differences in benefits and eligibility requirements among states came later.

Aid to Dependent Children

Initially, ADC enjoyed widespread political support. The prevailing belief in states' rights and the need to balance the federal budget limited federal involvement in public assistance to a select category of the poor for more than a quarter of a century. For example, until 1950, ADC prohibited assistance for the mother, or female caretaker, of eligible children. Men were not eligible for assistance until 1961 when states were allowed to provide assistance to unemployed fathers in two-parent families through the Aid to Dependent Children - Unemployed Parent (AFDC-UP) program. But, as mentioned in Chapter 1, the decision in 1950 to extend program eligibility to adult women set the stage for a fundamental shift in the nature of the debate concerning the program's future. Unlike earlier eras when welfare mothers were expected to work, the new, "modern" societal view was that welfare mothers, like their middle-class counterparts, should focus on raising their children, at least until their children were in school. As a result, instead of requiring work, welfare mothers were expected to "earn" their benefits by providing their children "... the physical and affectionate guardianship necessary . . . [to] rear them into citizens capable of contributing to society" (Garfinkel and McLanahan 1986, 102). There was a general fear that if welfare mothers were required to work, their children would lack the guidance necessary to keep them out of mischief, from associating with the wrong crowd, from ending up in jail, or otherwise becoming a burden upon society. This child-saving orientation had become particularly prominent by the late nineteenth century, and this was manifested in efforts to increase funding for sheltering orphans and for intervening against parents who were considered neglectful or abusive toward their children (Gordon 1994). However, as structural changes in the American economy later led to increased numbers of women entering the workforce, many began to question why welfare mothers were not

Cash Assistance and Social Welfare Policy

required to earn their benefits through work (Blank and Blum 1997).

The Human Capital Development Argument

Following World War II, the United States emerged as the world's economic and military leader. The national economy's expansion fueled the continued movement of people from rural to urban locations, and, increasingly, from both urban and rural locations to suburbs. As job growth continued and standards of living increased, the poor and their needs were not a high priority item in Congress. It was as if the poor had become, at least in the eyes of the general public and most congressional members, invisible. By 1960, Aid to Dependent Children remained a relatively small, inexpensive program, serving 3 million recipients (2.3 million children) at a cost of approximately $1 billion (SSA 2001). However, events in West Virginia would play an important role in placing welfare policy onto the national political agenda as a high priority. During the 1960 Democratic presidential primaries, Senator John Kennedy (D-MA) selected West Virginia as the battleground state for proving that a Catholic could win the presidency. He campaigned hard, personally crisscrossing the state, and defeated Senator Hubert Humphrey (D-MN), the party's odds-on favorite to win the presidential nomination, in the state's primary. In the process, Kennedy convinced Democratic party leaders, who, at that time, played a key role in determining who would receive the party's presidential nomination, that he could overcome religious prejudice by winning an election in a mostly Protestant state. He also convinced them that he could attract support outside the nation's major cities. His campaign effort in West Virginia also raised public awareness to the plight of the poor living in rural Appalachia. Just as importantly, then-Senator Kennedy was deeply moved by the extent of poverty in West Virginia's rural areas and resolved to do something about it once elected (White 1961).

Media reports of widespread poverty in Appalachia, and in urban America, heightened public awareness of poverty and helped to define it as a problem requiring a governmental solution. At about the same time, scholars promoting the structuralist view of society rose to prominence. The publication of John Kenneth Galbraith's *The Affluent Society* in 1958 and Michael Harrington's *The Other America* in 1962 were instrumental in shifting prevailing views concerning welfare. The structuralists argued that human behavior was primarily a product of social structure and the roles that structure created, and only secondarily by personal choices (Reid 1995). Harrington, for example, argued that as many as 50 million Americans were living in poverty and that existing government support programs, such as ADC, did little to help the poor because the programs were based on the erroneous assumption that it was relatively easy for any able-bodied American adult to find work and escape poverty. He argued that many of the nation's poor were hard-working, moral men and women trapped in an economic system that prevented them from escaping poverty. Harrington asserted that poverty was not caused by individual laziness or poor moral judgement. Instead, it resulted from the way the American economic system distributed wealth in society. For Harrington and other structuralists, ADC recipients were victims of an economic system that contributed to their economic deprivation. To correct this, government had an obligation to provide cash assistance to the poor to enable them to meet their immediate economic needs. It also had an obligation to provide them access to educational and job training programs necessary to acquire the skills needed to escape poverty. Specifically, benefit payments needed to be increased substantially to provide the poor with at least a subsistence standard-of-living and, preferably, with enough money to encourage them to avoid taking easier, but socially harmful, routes to economic self-sufficiency, such as theft, prostitution, and drug dealing. In addition, government funding for support services, such as vocational education and job training programs, needed to be increased dramatically to provide the poor with the skills necessary to compete for jobs with a future - ones that led to relatively high incomes and benefits (Harrington 1962; Murray 1984). The poor also needed the protection of laws that made racial and gender discrimination illegal and punished drug dealers and other criminals who ravaged their neighborhoods and presented poor role models for their children.

Cash Assistance and Social Welfare Policy

The structuralist argument provided the intellectual underpinning for what became known as the human capital development strategy to help welfare recipients to make the transition to economic self-sufficiency. It focused on support services, especially education and job training, to enable recipients to acquire the skills necessary to become economically self-sufficient.

Other scholars argued that if government were to provide additional support services for the poor, then the federal government had to take the lead because many states lacked either the political will or the fiscal resources to finance them. They pointed out that the poor generally do not vote, while those with middle and upper incomes generally do vote. Because state and local government officials are elected, this makes it difficult for them to respond fully to the poor's needs. In addition, even those state and local governments that have the political will to help the poor are caught in a "Catch-22" situation. Because many businesses and taxpayers can locate wherever they wish, states and communities that provide the poor with relatively high cash payments and support services face the danger of losing their tax base to states and communities that focus their resources on providing services for businesses and middle and upper income taxpayers. Moreover, by spending less on the poor, these communities can attract businesses and middle and upper income taxpayers to their communities by offering them relatively low tax rates. These scholars worried that without a strong federal presence in welfare policy interstate and inter-community competition for business investment would result in a "race to the bottom" when it came to providing benefits and support services for the poor (Peterson 1981, 1995). They also argued that the federal government needed to be involved in welfare policy because its fiscal policies affected the national economy and, in turn, employment opportunities (Nathan, Carleson, and O'Neil 1980; U.S. ACIR 1980).

The 1960s and the War on Poverty

By 1962, three changes in the political environment presented the opportunity for making a fundamental change in American welfare policy. First, the general public perceived that poverty was a problem, current government policies had failed to solve the problem, and new government policies were needed. Second, the structuralists and numerous welfare advocacy groups were advocating change. Third, President Kennedy (D, 1961-1963) was convinced that change was necessary and made welfare reform a priority item for his presidency. What emerged from congressional deliberations on welfare legislation in 1962 was a fundamental shift in the basic strategy underlying ADC. Instead of focusing on saving children, the program's emphasis shifted to preventing adult welfare dependency. This was to be accomplished through a mix of programs, most of them emphasizing the human capital development strategy for decreasing welfare dependency and others emphasizing the workforce attachment strategy. Specifically, the 1962 Amendments to the *Social Security Act* provided additional funding for recipient support services, including modest funding ($5 million annually) for childcare. It also increased the federal government's cost-share for social services to 75 percent and funded half the administrative costs of community work and job training programs. In an attempt to prevent family breakups, the previously mentioned, optional Unemployed Parent program (AFDC-UP), which had been enacted the pervious year on an experimental basis, was renewed. It allowed states to provide assistance to a second parent (fathers) in a family with an incapacitated or unemployed parent. Although previous legislation concerning program eligibility was gender neutral (e.g., providing funds to a relative or caretaker of eligible children), states had historically limited program eligibility to women. To appease those who opposed extending program eligibility to men, states were required to deny benefits to AFDC-UP families if the unemployed parent refused to accept work without "good cause." Although AFDC-UP was not mandatory, providing cash assistance to men was a significant departure from past policy and set the stage for heightened debate concerning the need to require recipients to work. As part of the new emphasis on family development, Aid to Dependent Children was renamed Aid to Families with Dependent Children (AFDC). Also, because work expenses, such as transportation to and from work, work clothes, childcare, etc., often caused recipients to be worse off if they left welfare for a job, states

Cash Assistance and Social Welfare Policy

were required to deduct work-related expenses from earnings before reducing benefits. This provision's intent was to encourage recipients to seek and retain work. At that time, most states reduced welfare benefits one dollar for each dollar the recipient earned (Garfinkel and McLanahan 1986; Abramovitz 1998).

West Virginia was one of the states that opted to extend eligibility to men through the AFDC-UP program. At that time, West Virginia required its entire AFDC-UP caseload to participate in mandatory work and training activities (Ball et al. 1984). As a result, West Virginia became a pioneer in establishing structured work and training activities for welfare recipients (Plein 2001).

The changes enacted in 1962 did not have their intended effect. Instead of decreasing, recipient caseloads and program costs increased. Also, in most states, recipient work participation rates did not change (Garfinkel and McLanahan 1986). No one will know how President Kennedy would have responded to these developments because he was assassinated on November 22, 1963 in Dallas, Texas.

On January 8, 1964, with the growing civil rights movement serving as a catalyst for change, and before a mostly-Democratic Congress not ideologically adverse to government spending, President Lyndon Baines Johnson (D, 1963-1968) announced his "War on Poverty" in his State of the Union address. Over the next several years, the federal government adopted a number of programs that significantly expanded its role in social welfare policy. Among the more notable programs was the *Economic Opportunity Act of 1964* (EOA), which established the Office of Economic Opportunity. It provided funds directly to local, nonprofit organizations (purposively bypassing local government officials) to design and implement anti-poverty programs at the local government level. The EOA also created a number of education, employment, and training programs to help the poor, including VISTA, Head Start, Job Corps, Neighborhood Youth Corps, Summer Youth Programs, Work Study, Upward Bound, and Legal Services. These programs were designed to improve the poor's ability to escape poverty by providing them with the skills and experiences necessary to find and retain employment. In 1965, the Food Stamp program was expanded in an attempt to allow the poor to focus on acquiring the education and job skills necessary to escape poverty without worrying about feeding their families. Also, in 1965, Medicaid was created to provide the poor access to health care. In addition, states that participated in Medicaid could use its reimbursement funding formula for most AFDC expenses (administrative expenses have a separate reimbursement rate, currently set at 75% for all states). Medicaid's reimbursement funding formula was, and still is, inversely related to the state's per capita income, primarily to encourage poorer states, like West Virginia, to participate in the program. Medicaid guarantees all states at least a 50 percent reimbursement rate and has a statutorily imposed maximum reimbursement rate of 83 percent. West Virginia's reimbursement rate has historically ranged between 70 and 78 percent, among the highest in the nation.

Increasing AFDC's reimbursement rate to at least 50 percent was designed to encourage states to raise recipient benefit levels and income thresholds for determining program eligibility. At the time, most states provided benefits that were far below the amount necessary for recipient families to reach the federal poverty level. Most states also imposed income thresholds for determining program eligibility that excluded millions of American families officially designated as being poor from participating in the program.

As the number and cost of federal government support programs increased, fiscal conservatives in both major political parties began to express concern about the potential adverse economic effects government spending and deficits might have on the national economy. Moreover, as the cost of the Vietnam War escalated, fiscal conservatives began to complain that the nation could not afford to expand the social welfare state and conduct a war simultaneously.

At the same time fiscal conservatives questioned the economic wisdom of expanding the social welfare state, several economists, led by Milton Friedman, offered a completely different alternative for addressing poverty. Friedman proposed that the federal government replace its social welfare programs, and what he viewed as their wasteful, expensive, and intrusive bureaucracies, with a check sent directly to every individual who failed to earn enough income to pay federal income taxes. He suggested that the check equal 50 percent of the difference between the individual's actual earned income and the amount exempted from the federal government's income tax. This guaranteed all Americans a minimum income while maintaining an incentive to seek and retain employment. The work incentive would be derived from the opportunity for every individual to keep half of the government subsidy for every dollar earned up to the amount exempted from the federal income tax (Friedman 1962, Friedman and Friedman 1979).

The negative income tax idea attracted support within the academic community, especially among economists, but it also generated significant opposition, particularly from politically active organizations whose members benefitted directly from the welfare state (e.g., agriculture and grocery store chains benefitted from Food Stamps, and the medical community benefitted from Medicaid). Critics also pointed out that it lessened, but did not eliminate the disincentive to work for those already on welfare. Moreover, it discouraged work by low-income males (who, in most states, were not eligible for AFDC at the time) because their income remained near the poverty level whether they continued to work or not (Anderson 1978; Moffett 1982). Opponents also argued that it encouraged family breakups because some low-income families would receive a larger subsidy under the negative income tax format if they separated and collected benefits independently. In addition, a negative income tax did not take into account cost-of-living differentials between urban and rural areas and among the nation's various regions (Levitan 1985). Finally, the negative income tax's cash value was far less than the benefits Medicaid provided for those needing long-term care in either a hospital or nursing home (Kosterlitz 1986).

As the debate over the negative income tax continued, welfare advocacy groups and representatives of the nation's cities, particularly the U.S. Conference of Mayors, lobbied Congress to force states to ease AFDC's eligibility requirements (Dilger 1989). As mentioned previously, in 1965, state reimbursement rates were increased to at least 50 percent of program costs to encourage states to ease eligibility requirements. However, most states continued to impose an income threshold for determining program eligibility that was far below the poverty level. Congressional members intent on expanding the welfare state (mostly Democrats) and those advocating the human capital development strategy for decreasing welfare dependency argued that states' income thresholds excluded many "deserving" families who needed the program's funding and related-support programs (especially job training and vocational education programs) to escape poverty. City officials opposed imposing low income thresholds because many of those excluded from the program lived in urban areas. Moreover, denying benefits to these individuals and their families often led to increased city expenses. For example, at that time, AFDC recipients automatically qualified for Medicaid benefits. City hospital administrators relied on Medicaid reimbursements for a significant portion of their revenue (Dilger 1989).

Fiscal conservatives in Congress, and those advocating the workforce attachment strategy for decreasing welfare dependency, opposed the imposition of higher income thresholds on states. Fiscal conservatives argued that higher income thresholds would result in higher caseloads and increased program costs. Other conservatives opposed the imposition of higher income thresholds on the grounds that it violated states' rights and restricted states' ability to design programs to suit their specific needs. Those advocating the workforce attachment strategy worried that raising income thresholds would diminish the incentive for those not currently eligible for cash assistance to seek and/or retain work.

In 1967, after much debate, Congress did not, as some had hoped, impose a national income threshold. However, it prohibited states from counting the first $30 of earned income (to account for the costs of getting to and from work) and one-third of all other earned income (to account for the cost of meals) against the state's income eligibility requirement. It also created the Work Incentive Program (WIN), which provided welfare recipients a mix of support services, including job training, education, and structured job searches. Some WIN programs also provided recipients with work experiences by placing them in public service agencies (Blank and Blum 1997).

Initially, recipient participation in WIN was voluntary. In 1971, welfare recipients were required to participate unless they had a special responsibility at home or preschool-age children.

Cash Assistance and Social Welfare Policy

Although WIN's proponents hoped that it would result in increased recipient work participation rates, program funding limitations (WIN's peak funding of $395 million in 1981 provided, on average, just $250 to serve each potential registrant) meant that it was less expensive for states to issue a check to the recipient than work with them to find employment. Moreover, WIN's implementation was complicated by the sharing of administrative responsibilities for job training and placement programs by state Departments of Labor and welfare agencies. As a result, for most recipients, even when WIN participation was mandatory, the work participation requirement became little more than a registration requirement (Blank and Blum 1997).

The imposition of federally mandated income disregards in 1967, coupled with increased efforts by social workers, especially in urban areas, to encourage eligible populations to apply for assistance, led to a dramatic increase in AFDC enrollments, from about 4.4 million recipients in 1967 to 9.7 million by 1970 (see Chart). Enrollment continued to climb until it leveled off at 10 to 11 million

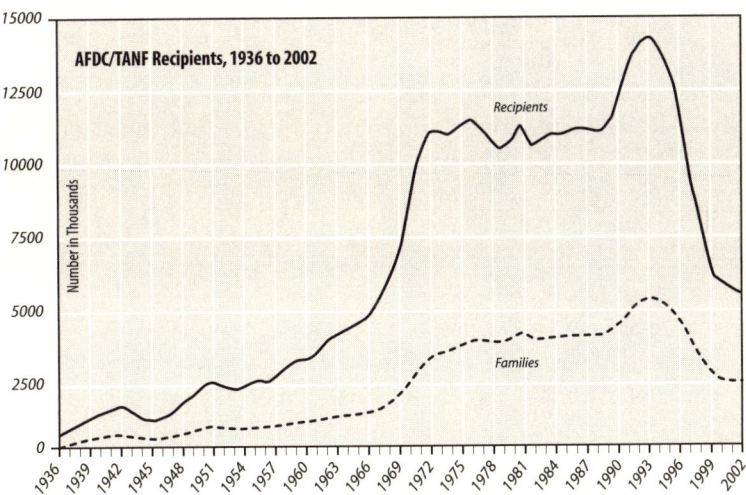

by the decade's end. As enrollment climbed, so did program costs, increasing from $1.3 billion in 1967, to $2.7 billion in 1970, and $5.2 billion in 1975 (DHHS 1998).

The 1970s and the Family Assistance Plan

President Richard Nixon (R, 1969-1974) was a fiscal conservative intent on reigning in what he considered "wasteful and profligate federal spending," especially on social welfare programs that, as he and other fiscal conservatives pointed out, had done little to reduce the national poverty rate, despite the expenditure of hundreds of billions of dollars over the previous decade. He was also, as one leading author described it, "anti-bureaucracy" (Nathan 1975). Most of the social welfare programs' bureaucracies at that time were staffed by careerists hired during previous Democratic administrations. Most of these bureaucrats were strong advocates of social welfare programs and participated actively in what academics called "iron triangles" (political alliances among bureaucrats, clientele interest groups, and congressional subcommittee chairmen) to continue the welfare state's expansion. Facing a heavily-Democratic Congress, ideologically committed to expanding social welfare programs, and the difficulty of effecting fundamental change in the face of congressional decentralization and entrenched iron triangles, President Nixon decided to endorse a variation of the negative income tax to replace AFDC. His 1969 Family Assistance Plan would have provided a guaranteed minimum income for families with children. A family of four without any income would have received $1,600 a year ($500 for each adult and $300 for each child). States could add to that amount if they wished. He argued that his plan would equalize benefit levels across the nation by creating a minimum income for everyone, regardless of their place of residency. Also, to encourage work, families could keep the first $60 of monthly earnings with no reduction in benefits, and their benefit would be reduced by only half for each dollar earned over that amount. Recipients also had to accept work or work-training if suitable jobs were available either locally or within commuting distance if transportation was provided. Those unable to work and mothers of preschool aged children were exempt from the work requirement, but the plan included additional funding for day care centers to make it possible for all mothers, including those with preschool age children, to work (Nixon 1969).

The Family Assistance Plan failed to win congressional approval, primarily because organizations benefitting directly from the social welfare state opposed it. There was also a lack of consensus concerning the size of the subsidy level to be provided, and no one was able to resolve the problem of how to deal with "income notches," where working more meant losing Medicaid or other program assistance that made the poor worse off under the Family Assistance Plan than under existing program arrangements (Nathan 1975; Anderson 1978; Salamon 1978; Leman 1980; Weaver 2000). A similar, but far less costly Earned Income Tax Credit (EITC) program was adopted in 1975. It was designed to supplement, not replace AFDC. EITC encourages work by allowing low-income wage earners with at least one child in their household to receive a refundable tax credit equal to the cost of Social Security and Medicare taxes and other work-related expenses, such as transportation costs. The EITC has since been expanded, with certain restrictions, to include working-age adults (25 - 64 years old) without children. Also, its cash value has increased over the years as the earnings threshold used to determine eligibility has increased (e.g., in 2004, the earnings threshold for a single adult with one qualifying child was $30,300).

In 1977, President Jimmy Carter's (D, 1977-1980) Program for Better Jobs and Income offered a revised version of the Family Assistance Plan. It would have replaced AFDC, Supplemental Security Income (SSI) (which provides cash to the low-income aged, blind, and disabled), and Food Stamps with two tiers of guaranteed income. Those expected to work (two-parent families and single-parent families with children over age fourteen) would receive less than those not expected to work (single parents with children under age fourteen). A family of four that was expected to work would receive $2,300 annually, with a 50 percent reduction of earnings over $3,800. A family of four not expected to work would have received $4,200 annually, with a 50 percent reduction of all earnings. President Carter's proposal also included a work requirement: single mothers with preschool aged children (under seven years old) were not required to work, those whose youngest child was seven to fourteen years old were required to work part-time, and those whose youngest child was fourteen years old or older were required to work full-time. The program also included public sector jobs and job training for up to 1.4 million welfare recipients and the working poor. The Carter Administration estimated that their proposal would cost $30 billion annually, or 10 percent more than maintaining the status quo. The Congressional Budget Office later indicated that the Administration's cost-estimate for the program was too conservative, leading many fiscal conservatives to oppose the program (Weaver 2000). The proposal died in Congress for many of the same reasons the Family Assistance Plan failed to win adoption earlier (e.g., opposition by organizations benefitting directly from the programs slated for elimination, the inability to resolve income notches, conservative opposition to additional spending, and opposition to extending government benefits to those without children).

The 1980s and the Reagan Presidency

By the end of the 1970s, some commentators, worried about the increasing percentage of adult recipients who were never married, divorced, or separated, argued that AFDC and other, related social welfare programs were creating a "culture of poverty" that promoted a life of casual social relationships, irresponsibility, immediate gratification, and sexual license among the poor. In their view, some of the poor exhibited such different and hostile behavioral patterns that programs designed to help them achieve economic self-sufficiency were doomed to fail (Auletta 1983; Cochran 1982). Other AFDC critics continued to question whether AFDC was helping the poor. They noted that AFDC spending increased dramatically during the 1970s, but poverty rates did not decline. In fact, the national poverty rate increased from the 10 to 12 percent level during the early 1970s to the 13 to 15 percent level during the early 1980s. They were convinced that poverty rates did not improve because welfare recipients correctly reasoned that their standard of living would fall if they went to work. Although AFDC's monetary value was relatively small, most recipients also received Medicaid,

Cash Assistance and Social Welfare Policy

Food Stamps, and housing assistance. The combined value of these programs often exceeded the monetary value associated with the types of jobs available to recipients. These jobs typically offered wages at or near the national minimum wage and, importantly, usually did not provide health benefits (Anderson 1978; Murray 1984). AFDC's critics also argued that states had little incentive to innovate or encourage welfare recipients to leave the rolls because AFDC was an open-ended, reimbursement program. If the state did a poor job of helping AFDC recipients leave the welfare rolls, AFDC enrollment increased and the state received more money, not less. Finally, they noted that state and federal bureaucrats had little reason to encourage program innovation because their jobs were linked to the number of clients served. If enrollment dropped, the need for government caseworkers, and mangers to supervise the caseworkers, also dropped.

In 1981, when President Ronald Reagan (R, 1981-1989), a fiscal conservative strongly opposed to the expansion of social welfare programs, entered the White House, AFDC had 11 million recipients and cost the federal government $7.8 billion (DHHS 1998). Initially, the Reagan Administration did not advocate fundamental welfare reform. The Reagan Administration opposed the negative income tax on the grounds that it encouraged dependency on government funding. Although he often spoke of his support for state's rights, President Reagan advocated changes to specific AFDC rules that infringed on state autonomy because he wanted to reduce program costs. For example, the *Omnibus Budget Reconciliation Act of 1981* imposed more stringent asset limits on states when determining program eligibility (lowering maximum allowable assets to $1,000, excluding home equity and the value of one car), limited the $30 plus one-third income disregard when determining program eligibility to the first four months of employment, reduced deductions for work-related and childcare expenses when determining eligibility, excluded those engaged in labor strikes from the program, and limited eligibility to those with incomes below 150 percent of the state's standard of need, regardless of the recipient's income disregards and other deductions (Weaver 2000). These changes reduced AFDC's caseload that year by more than 700,000 recipients, most of them working mothers, and further strengthened the federal government's role in determining the general outlines of state welfare policies across the nation.

The *Omnibus Budget Reconciliation Act of 1981* also revamped the federal government's job training programs. First, it reduced federal funding for job training 50 percent between 1981 and 1986. Funding for the *Comprehensive Employment and Training Act* (CETA), which provided job training for welfare recipients and others, was eliminated entirely, primarily because it was criticized for placing most of its participants in temporary public-service jobs instead of moving them into permanent positions in the private sector. Funding for the Work Incentive Program was cut sharply, from $365 million in 1981 to $110 million in 1987. Nationwide, WIN moved only about 130,000 people off welfare in 1985, approximately 1 percent of AFDC adult recipients. Second, the *Job Training Partnership Act* (JTPA) was adopted to replace CETA and supplement WIN. It emphasized the workforce attachment strategy, with the goal of placing recipients in private sector jobs as quickly as possible. Instead of focusing on education programs and job training activities that may take participants months or even years to complete, participants were provided job-search techniques and offered short-term training to move them into the workforce as expeditiously as possible. Although JTPA was available to many disadvantaged groups, its focus was on reducing welfare dependency. It subsequently placed 61 percent of its participants in jobs, much higher than previous job training programs. However, some analysts argued that JTPA's success was overstated because its administrators routinely engaged in "creaming," where participants with previous job experience or a high school degree were placed into employment situations that, arguably, they could have gotten themselves. Those deemed not job ready were discouraged from participating in the program, artificially inflating JTPA's placement rates (Whitman 1987). Third, states were allowed to operate Community Work Experience (CWEP) programs, also called workfare. These experimental programs tested the efficacy of the workforce attachment strategy as a tool to decrease welfare dependency by providing AFDC recipients work experience in public or nonprofit organizations. Instead of receiving wages, recipients continued to receive benefits from AFDC, Medicaid, Food Stamps, and other related government support programs.

West Virginia was one of the states that implemented CWEP, and one of only three states that elected to implement it statewide. In 1983, it extended CWEP's work obligation to all West Virginia AFDC recipients who were required to participate in the WIN program (all adult AFDC-UP recipients and all adult AFDC recipients without a child under the age of six). As mentioned previously, West Virginia has a history of emphasizing the work attachment strategy, having been one of the few states to establish large-scale work programs for adult AFDC-UP recipients during the 1960s. At that time, West Virginia engaged nearly half of its adult AFDC-UP population in work-related activities in both public and private sector settings (Ball et al. 1984).

West Virginia's implementation of its CWEP program was relatively aggressive compared to efforts undertaken in other states. In 1984, 40 percent of its adult AFDC-UP recipients (men) and approximately 10 percent of its WIN-eligible adult AFDC recipients (women) participated in the program. At that time, there were about 5,000 AFDC-UP cases in the state and 21,000 AFDC cases (7,000 eligible for CWEP). West Virginia experienced its highest CWEP participation rates in its more urban areas, where job placement opportunities were more plentiful. The state experienced its lowest participation rates in more rural areas, where job placement opportunities were more difficult to locate (Ball et al. 1984). A mid-term analysis of West Virginia's CWEP program conducted in 1984 indicated that women proved to be more difficult to place because they tended to have less work experience, a greater hesitation to leave their children, and more health-related problems than men. Staff also had a more difficult time placing women because they were required to ensure that women who participated in the program had access to adequate childcare. Staff also had a history of placing adult AFDC-UP recipients (men) into work and work-related activities, but little or no experience placing other AFDC recipients (women) into work and work-related activities (Ball et al. 1984). Overall, West Virginia's implementation of CWEP during the 1980s, especially for adult AFDC-UP recipients, was viewed as a model for other states. Although program expenses were higher, participants reported little increase in skill development, and participation had little effect on earnings, participants believed that their work made a valuable contribution to the sponsoring agency, a view their agency supervisors shared. As one report noted, although West Virginia's CWEP program had little positive effect on earnings, it made a large pool of unemployed labor available for community service, provided participants an opportunity to contribute in a productive way to the life of their community, and enhanced participants' self-esteem (Friedlander et al. 1986). Most of the participants (almost 80%) also reported that requiring work in exchange for their welfare check was either a satisfactory or very satisfactory arrangement (Ball et al. 1984). As will be discussed in later chapters, CWEP continued to play a relatively large role in West Virginia's implementation of AFDC throughout the 1980s and 1990s (Plein 2001).

In 1982, President Reagan decided not to wait to see the results of the various experimental, state workfare demonstration programs that were being conducted to determine the feasibility of emphasizing the workforce attachment strategy to reduce welfare dependency. He proposed that AFDC and Food Stamps be turned over to states in exchange for nationalizing Medicaid (Conlan and Walker 1983). President Reagan's 1982 swap proposal was never formally introduced in the Congress, primarily because welfare advocacy groups and state and local government interest groups opposed it. The National Governors Association, for example, worried that the Reagan Administration would cut funding for Medicaid after its takeover, forcing states to pick up the slack. Also, many welfare advocacy groups and the cities' two leading lobbying organizations, the National League of Cities and the U.S. Conference of Mayors, worried that poor states would engage in a "race to the bottom" in the absence of federal minimum standards if given sole authority over AFDC and Food Stamps (Weaver 2000).

Although the Reagan Administration's swap proposal failed, economic, social, and political factors were aligning that increased support for making fundamental changes to AFDC. By the mid-1980s, structural changes in the increasingly global economy had led millions of women, many of them with children, into the workforce. Also, the feminist movement, coupled with the increased number of women in the workforce, caused changes in public expectations concerning women's role in society. As a result of the increased presence of women in the workforce, many women, and men, began to wonder why working and middle class women were able to find and retain work, even if they had young children at home, while welfare mothers could not. Increasingly, gender and being a single parent were no longer viewed as legitimate excuses for not working (Garfinkel and McLanahan 1986; Blank and Blum 1997; Weaver 2000). Also, national opinion polls conducted throughout the 1980s indicated that most Americans believed the country was spending too much on AFDC (Weaver 2000). As a result, members of Congress from both political parties who had previously emphasized the human capital development strategy for reducing welfare dependency began to look more favorably on the workforce attachment strategy as a viable option. Moreover, in 1986, the private, non-profit Manpower Demonstration Research Corporation released a study of eight state welfare-to-work programs which indicated that although the gains were not dramatic, work-focused programs for welfare recipients could increase employment and be cost-effective. Their study encouraged those historically opposed to the work attachment strategy to consider it as a viable policy option (Gueron 1986; Blank and Blum 1997).

The growing political support for the workforce attachment strategy was reflected in the passage of the *Family Support Act of 1988*, which required states to participate in the AFDC-UP program starting in 1990 (at that time, only twenty-seven states had elected to participate in the program). States that had not offered AFDC-UP in the past were allowed to limit payments to the first six months of the year. Also, indicative of the movement toward the workforce attachment strategy, at least one of the parents in the AFDC-UP family had to engage in a community work experience or another work-related activity for at least sixteen hours a week (Weaver 2000). The *Family Support Act* also strengthened the emphasis on work and work readiness preparation for other AFDC recipients by requiring states to establish a Job Opportunities and Basic Skills

(JOBS) program. With few exceptions, AFDC recipients from sixteen to fifty-nine years old who were not disabled or already working thirty or more hours a week were required to participate in JOBS. Although federal funding for the work program (approximately $1 billion over five years) fell short of the amount needed to put all AFDC recipients to work, states were required to meet federal work participation rates, starting at 7 percent in FY 1990 and rising to 20 percent in FY 1995. States that did not meet the requirement would lose a portion of their AFDC funds.

Federal law required the state's JOBS program to include the following: high school education or equivalency education, basic literacy education, English as a second language, job-skills training, job-readiness activities, and job-development and job-placement activities. In addition, each state had to have at least two of the following: job search requirements (clients were required to bring in weekly proof of a specified number of job search contacts with businesses), on-the-job training, work supplementation (subsidized jobs where the state pays all or part of the wages), and community work experience (work relief where clients are required to work off their grants - the number of required hours was determined by dividing their grant amount by the minimum wage). States were also allowed to offer vocational, technical school, or college education programs. States could not require recipients to participate in JOBS if necessary childcare or transportation services were not available. However, states were required to guarantee childcare and transportation for all JOBS participants once they entered the program, provided they continued to make "satisfactory progress" while in the program.

The *Family Support Act of 1988* also reflected changing attitudes on Capitol Hill by toughening federal laws concerning child support payments. The Federal Office of Child Support Enforcement was established in 1975. It administered an open-ended, reimbursement grant program that provided states 75 percent (later reduced to 66%) of costs for programs that collected past-due child support payments from non-custodial parents. Initially, states designed their own programs. The federal government later mandated enforcement practices that proved to be effective in collecting unpaid child support. For example, in 1984, states were required to create state income tax refund interception programs for delinquent custodial parents after several states had implemented similar programs and found them to be an effective means of collecting past-due child support payments. To encourage welfare recipients to cooperate with child enforcement officers, states were required to pass through to the recipient the first $50 of child support payments received each month from the delinquent parent, and to disregard that income when determining welfare benefits and eligibility. The *Family Support Act of 1988* went further by requiring states to impose immediate wage withholding on non-custodial parents by January 1994 for all new child support orders. The mandate was modeled on the experiences of several states that had imposed wage withholding on non-custodial parents who were delinquent in their child support payments and of a few states that had imposed immediate wage withholding programs, even before the non-custodial parent had fallen behind on his or her payments. To ensure consistency across families, states were required to establish statewide child support guidelines that judges were required to use when issuing child support orders (RAND 1988; Sorensen and Halpern 1999).

From AFDC to TANF: The Turbulent 1990s

When President Bill Clinton (D, 1993-2001) began his first term of office in the White House, AFDC's enrollment had reached a record high of 14.2 million recipients (9.5 million children). The federal government's costs had risen to $14.9 billion, and many members of Congress from both political parties were demanding that the program be changed to reduce costs, target resources to the "truly deserving," and emphasize work. Also, most Americans at that time expressed deep dissatisfaction with AFDC and the "welfare system." In one national survey, 79 percent of respondents said the welfare system was not working well (Garin, Molyneux and DiVall 1994). People from different ethnic and racial groups as well as different political viewpoints shared this view. The most common complaint was that welfare discouraged work. Another national survey asked the American public what bothered them most about the welfare system. Nearly half (49%) said welfare discouraged work, 14 percent cited its cost, and 13 percent said it caused families to break up (Kaiser/Harvard Program 1995). Moreover, the Republican Party gained majority status in both the U.S. House of Representatives and in the U.S. Senate following the November 1994 congressional elections, clearing the path for congressional action on welfare reform legislation.

Initially, the Clinton Administration responded to these changes in the political and cultural landscape by granting states an unprecedented number of federal welfare rule and requirement waivers. In March 1996, President Clinton announced proudly before the National Governors Association that he had granted waivers for fifty-three different welfare reform projects in thirty-seven states, covering nearly 75 percent of all welfare recipients. Many of these waivers encouraged or required recipients to work. The Clinton Administration also sponsored or endorsed welfare reform legislation, but opposed radical change. For example, on June 14, 1994, President Clinton endorsed legislation to increase welfare spending by $9.3 billion over five years. The additional funds were to be used to finance work-first programs for recipients who had received assistance for more than two years, had not been able to find employment, and were born after 1971. Congress held hearings on the proposal, but decided to wait to see how the 1994 congressional elections turned out before taking final action. When the Republican Party captured both the House and Senate, the President's proposal was shelved in favor of more stringent, and less expensive, Republican proposals.

After much debate, and despite the threat of a presidential veto, Congress passed H.R. 4, *The Welfare Reform Act*, in late December 1995. It imposed mandatory work requirements, a sixty-month time limit on the receipt of benefits, and it capped future program spending. The U.S. General Accounting Office estimated that it would reduce federal expenditures by $58 billion over seven years. Also, the U.S. Office of Management and Budget estimated that an earlier version of the bill would push another one million children into poverty. Importantly, it removed the entitlement status from AFDC, SSI, and a number of nutrition programs. President

Cash Assistance and Social Welfare Policy

Clinton vetoed the bill on January 9, 1996. He argued that it did not include sufficient funding for childcare and health coverage for low-income families, needed additional requirements to ensure that states supported the program in the future, and lacked a contingency fund to deal with an increase in recipients resulting from economic downturns and population growth.

In an attempt to ameliorate political damage from Republican charges that he was totally opposed to reforming welfare, on May 18, 1996, President Clinton granted Wisconsin's request for a waiver to implement Wisconsin Works. It contained several provisions that were included in the welfare reform bill he vetoed. For example, it required welfare recipients to work and ended the program's entitlement status. In the meantime, the Republican House and Senate held hearings and subsequently passed the six-year, $110 billion *Personal Responsibility and Work Opportunity Reconciliation Act of 1996* by wide margins (328 to 101 in the House and 78 to 21 in the Senate). It contained many of the provisions that led President Clinton to veto the previous welfare reform bill. It also reduced federal expenditures by $24 billion over six years by denying benefits to both illegal and legal immigrants (most of the savings resulted from eliminating legal immigrant eligibility for SSI - approximately 500,000 legal immigrants were affected) and saved another $23 billion by reducing Food Stamp funding 13 percent. President Clinton objected to both denying benefits to legal immigrants and the Food Stamp cuts. However, he convinced the Senate to remove provisions pertaining to Medicaid that he opposed. He also convinced congressional leaders to include additional funding for childcare services, state maintenance-of-effort provisions to ensure that states continue to support the program in the future, and a contingency fund to deal with population growth and unexpected economic downturns. They also agreed to later consider funding a new children's health insurance program to expand health insurance coverage to uninsured children from low-income families (the ten-year, $40 billion State Children's Health Insurance Program (CHIP) was subsequently adopted as part of the *Balanced Budget Act of 1997*). Facing intense political pressure to do something about welfare, and convinced that he had bartered the best deal possible, President Clinton reluctantly signed the bill into law on August 22, 1996.

The Act's Four Primary Goals and Key Provisions

The new law had four primary goals: (1) provide assistance to needy families so that children may be cared for in their own homes or in the homes of relatives, (2) prevent and reduce the incidence of out-of-wedlock births, (3) reduce single-parent child-rearing, and (4) reduce welfare dependency (*Federal Register* 1999).

The first goal was to be met by increasing funding for childcare assistance to $14 billion over the program's six years, an increase of $3.5 billion. Also, a new $1 billion annual Child Care and Development Block Grant was created. Recipients were also guaranteed at least one year of transitional Medicaid when leaving welfare for work. The second goal was to be achieved by providing states "bonus" money for devising programs that reduced the number of out-of-wedlock births that occurred in that state. The third goal was to be accomplished by requiring recipients to cooperate with state child support enforcement agencies. In the past, recipients were encouraged to cooperate. Also, states had to require employers to report all new hires within twenty days to child support enforcement authorities. They, in turn, placed the name in a new National Directory of New Hires. The directory then matched social security numbers and other identifying materials to determine if the new employee was under a child support order. The goal was to reduce delays in implementing immediate wage withholding and to prevent non-custodial parents from evading their child support responsibilities by changing jobs frequently. The fourth goal was to be accomplished by replacing the AFDC and JOBS with the state-centered Temporary Assistance for Needy Families Block Grant (TANF).

TANF was to end welfare dependency by eliminating its entitlement status and imposing mandatory work requirements and lifetime benefit limits on recipients and mandatory work participation rates and maintenance-of-effort requirements on states. For the first time, federal funding was no longer linked to the number of recipients served. Instead, each state received a set amount each year based on its funding levels prior to the new law's enactment. West Virginia's share of federal funds was set at $92 million annually, with the state contributing another $39 million. By providing each state a set amount of funding, states were encouraged to experiment with innovative programs to remove recipients from the rolls. In the past, states had little incentive to move people from the rolls because fewer recipients meant less federal funding. Also, most recipients were required to work after they had received cash assistance for twenty-four months. In addition, states were required to demonstrate that ever-increasing proportions of their adult TANF recipients were engaged in a work activity. In FY 2002, the overall minimum participation rate reached 50 percent (90% for two-parent households). States that failed to meet the mandatory work participation rates were subject to forfeiture of 5 percent of their federal TANF funds during the first year of noncompliance, and an additional 2 percent of funding for each consecutive year they continued in noncompliance, up to a maximum of 21 percent of their federal TANF funding (NCSL 1997).

The Congressional Budget Office predicted that none of the states would meet the work participation rate requirements. However, federal rules allowed states with caseload reductions of 25 percent or more to count that reduction as a credit against the work participation rate requirements. Also, later administrative rulings expanded the definition of work to include some educational and training activities. Thanks in large part to these rulings and the dramatic reduction in caseloads across the nation, West Virginia, and most other states, were able to meet the overall work participation rate requirements. However, some states, including West Virginia, failed to meet the 90 percent threshold for two-parent families.

Under the work requirements, single parents were required to be engaged in a work activity for at least thirty hours per week. Depending on family circumstances, married couples had to work a combined thirty-five to fifty-five hours per week. Single parents with children under age one and single parents with a child under age six who were unable to find childcare were exempt from the work requirement. If non-exempt recipients refused to participate in work activities, they could be sanctioned by having their benefits reduced and, eventually, terminated. The work requirement could be met through either unsubsidized or subsidized employment, on-the-job training, work experience, community service, up to twelve months of vocational training, providing childcare services to individuals participating in community service, and up to six weeks of job search (DHHS 2000b).

TANF also limited cash assistance to a maximum of five cumulative years. States could impose shorter time limits (nine states elected to do so) and exempt up to 20 percent of their caseload from the time limit for "good cause." States were allowed to define good cause. Most states elected to consider severe physical and mental handicaps and domestic violence situations as good causes for exemption purposes.

States were also required to demonstrate a maintenance-of-effort by spending at least 80 percent of what they spent on AFDC and related programs in FY 1994 in order to receive their full allotment of TANF funds. That threshold was reduced to 75 percent if they met their work participation rate requirements. States also had to maintain spending at 100 percent of FY 1994 levels to access a $2 billion contingency fund designed to assist states affected by high population growth or economic downturn. In addition, they had to maintain 100 percent of FY 1994 or FY 1995 spending on childcare (whichever was greater) to access additional childcare funds beyond their initial TANF allotment (DHHS 2000b).

States were also granted additional flexibility concerning other programmatic features, such as income disregards, asset limitations, benefit payments, etc. Some congressional members, welfare advocacy groups, and academics opposed these changes, fearing that the additional flexibility would result in states racing to the bottom by imposing more stringent eligibility requirements, less generous benefit levels, and fewer support services.

Additional Federal Action

A large number of technical issues confronted states as they began implementing the new law (see Chapters 4-6). The federal government addressed many of these issues in the *Welfare Reform Technical Corrections Act of 1997*. For example, it specified that two-parent families with one disabled parent were to be treated as a single-parent family in determining compliance with the work participation rate requirement, the thirty-five hour per week work requirement was spread between both parents in a two-parent family, and technical language concerning childcare funds was corrected to assure that unspent funds were redistributed to states and not returned to the U.S. treasury. Also, the *Budget Reconciliation Act of 1997* created the previously mentioned ten-year, $40 billion CHIP program, restored legal immigrant eligibility for SSI, and created a $3 billion Welfare-to-Work Program (administered initially by private industry councils and later by local workforce investment boards).

The Welfare-to-Work Program was designed to help adult recipients who had received cash assistance for long periods of time (thirty months or more) or were within twelve months of losing their eligibility under the sixty-month time limitation and faced at least two of three specific employment barriers: (1) no high school diploma or General Educational Development credential (GED) and low reading or math skills, (2) a substance abuse problem, or (3) a poor work history. It also provided employment services to non-custodial parents of welfare children (mainly poor fathers), to improve their economic outcomes and thereby increase their ability to support their children (Nightingale et al. 1999; Trutko et al. 1999).

The *Taxpayer Relief Act of 1997* expanded the Work Opportunity Tax Credit and created the Welfare-to-Work Tax Credit. It is available to employers who hire welfare recipients. Finally, the five-year, $68 billion *Workforce Investment Act of 1998*, administered by local workforce investment boards in partnership with local elected officials, provided educational and job training services to youth, adults, and dislocated workers. It provided the unemployed (including TANF recipients) a single point of contact (through one-stop career centers) to a number of employment-related services. Included among these services were a preliminary assessment of their skill levels, aptitudes, abilities, and support service needs; information about local education and training service providers; help filing claims for unemployment insurance and evaluating eligibility for job training and education programs or student financial aid; job search and placement assistance; career counseling; and access to up-to-date labor market information, which identifies job vacancies, skills necessary for in-demand jobs, and information about local, regional and national employment trends (DOL 1998).

West Virginia's Initial Response to Welfare Reform

When the *Personal Responsibility and Work Opportunity Reconciliation Act of 1996* was passed, West Virginia already had a welfare reform plan under development. Called WV WORKS, West Virginia's program was implemented on a county-by-county basis through the latter part of 1997. By early 1998, WV WORKS was operating across the state. A thorough analysis of WV WORKS features and implementation is provided in Chapters 4-6. Importantly, the program's initial emphasis was to provide recipients with the means to leave welfare. This was accomplished by promoting work, pursuing child support payments, and providing education and training to those needing additional job skills. Like the welfare reform programs implemented in many other states, WV WORKS was essentially a "work-first" program.

Caseloads Plummet Unexpectedly

TANF's work requirements and other sanctions had an immediate and dramatic effect on welfare caseloads across the nation. Between January 1997 and June 1999, more than 4.5 million people (39.7%) left the program, reducing total enrollment from 11.4 million to 6.9 million people. The reductions were even more dramatic in West Virginia. Over that same time period, more than two out of every three TANF/WV WORKS recipients (67,658 out of 98,690) left the rolls (68.5%) (DHHS 2000a).

Initially, most state policymakers viewed TANF's dramatic enrollment declines as an indication that welfare reform was working. The reductions, it seemed, indicated that the new law was meeting its goal of stemming the rising tide of welfare dependency. At first, most commentators assumed that TANF enrollments were declining because the law's provisions were encouraging welfare recipients to find work at a time when the national economy was booming and jobs, especially entry-level jobs, were relatively plentiful. However, state welfare agency data revealed that, nationwide, fewer than half of the recipients who left the welfare rolls were finding jobs. In West Virginia, fewer than one-third of those who left TANF/WV WORKS following the new law's enactment entered the workforce (Fischer 1998; WV WORKS 1998). Policymakers across the nation, and in West Virginia, began to ask the same questions:

- "What is happening to these people?"

- "Are they on the road to economic self-sufficiency, or are they likely to return to welfare if the economic expansion weakens?"

- "If they do return in large numbers, will states have the fiscal capacity and the political will to finance programs to assist them?"

Leavers

Scholars and practitioners in the field speculated that the unexpectedly high number of leavers was due to a combination of factors. First, the relatively robust national economy and favorable job market for entry-level positions obviously played a key role for those leavers who found work. Second, some leavers were already working at "under-the-table" jobs on a cash only or barter basis. Many left the system because the new work requirements would have required them to work at two places at the same time. When forced to chose which job to take, many chose the under-the-table job. Third, some recipients received relatively small amounts of cash assistance and determined that they would rather "go it alone" than deal with the welfare bureaucracy and the new rules and regulations.

As mentioned in Chapter 1, states are not required to provide detailed reports on the status of former welfare recipients. As a result, the only systematic data available on families who left welfare shortly after the implementation of the *Personal Responsibility and Work Opportunity Reconciliation Act of 1996* was from state-sponsored research efforts designed to meet their information needs (GAO

1999). Fortunately, the National Conference of State Legislatures (NCSL) has tracked these efforts and serves as a central repository of information concerning those who have left welfare since the *Personal Responsibility and Work Opportunity Reconciliation Act of 1996* went into effect. To date, NCSL has obtained information from thirty states, plus the District of Columbia, concerning leavers (NCSL 2003).

Collectively, these studies suggest that leavers are having a difficult time making ends meet. Nationally, only about half of adult leavers are working, and most of those who are working are employed in the service and retail trade industries earning between $6 and $7 an hour. Nearly all leavers remain in poverty. Most leavers receive some form of government assistance, such as Medicaid and Food Stamps, but the incidence of government assistance declines after leaving TANF. Most also report that life is generally better than when they were on welfare, but they continue to struggle financially. In most states, between 10 and 20 percent of leavers report that they have been forced to go without food or have experienced times when they did not have enough money to purchase food. Approximately one-quarter of families who leave TANF return within several months (Tweedie 2000).

West Virginia's leavers are also experiencing financial difficulty. When surveyed in 1999, fewer than half of West Virginia's leavers (43%) reported that they were working and, like their national counterparts, most were employed in the service and retail trade industries. The median wage for West Virginia's leavers in 1999 was $5.90 per hour. Nearly all of West Virginia's leavers live in poverty. Although a majority of West Virginia's leavers had a relatively positive view of their own personal well-being, their future, and their children's future, many reported that after leaving WV WORKS they experienced times when they did not have enough money to buy food (42.9%), medicine (40.2%), or glasses (59.3%); and they did not have enough money to go to the dentist (48.9%) or to the doctor (39.6%). Also, participation in other public assistance programs, such as Medicaid and Food Stamps, declined after leaving the rolls, even though respondents' answers to other questions suggested that they were eligible for continued assistance. Medicaid enrollment, for example, dropped from 76.8 percent while on TANF to 58.4 percent after leaving the program. Food Stamp enrollment dropped from 72.6 percent to 51.8 percent. Similar declines were reported for other government assistance programs, including free or reduced price school meals, school clothing vouchers, the low-income energy assistance program, women, infant and children (WIC) nutrition programs, and housing assistance. Support from private sources, such as food pantries and church assistance, increased marginally, but not nearly to the extent that government assistance declined (Dilger et. al. 1999).

Surprise: States Did Not Race to the Bottom

When the *Personal Responsibility and Work Opportunity Reconciliation Act of 1996* was adopted, many scholars, state officials, and welfare advocacy groups worried that the shift from being an open-ended reimbursement program to having set funding levels might force states to choose between increasing state welfare expenditures or reducing benefits and support services if caseloads increased. However, the dramatic reduction in caseloads nationwide provided states a relative abundance of fiscal resources. With fewer recipients to serve, states were able to reduce their own contribution to the program and still spend more per case than previously. Nationally, spending per case increased 49 percent between FY 1994 and FY 1999. Instead of a race to the bottom, most states made only marginal changes to benefit levels and, initially, banked much of the program's unspent funds in rainy day funds to hedge against enrollment increases during a recession (Tweedie 2000).

The dramatic caseload declines across the nation not only provided states a relative abundance of fiscal resources, it also increased programmatic flexibility in other ways. Because states wanted to avoid federal sanctions, most states, including West Virginia, initially adopted work-first approaches, emphasizing job searches and immediate job placements, often at the expense of vocational education and job training programs. But, the rapid decline in caseloads eased the pressure to meet the federal work participation requirements because, as mentioned earlier, federal rules allowed states with caseload reductions of 25 percent or more to count that reduction as a credit against the federal work participation requirement. For example, West Virginia received a caseload reduction credit of 38.9 percent in FY 2000. As a result, the federally mandated 35 percent work participation rate in force at that time was reduced to 0 percent. As this case demonstrates, because caseloads fell throughout the nation, states had little difficulty meeting the federally mandated work participation rates (although a few states, including West Virginia, were unable to meet the work participation rate requirement for two-parent families). Once states realized that they were not going to be sanctioned for failing to meet the work participation requirement, states broadened their focus from immediate job placement and job search activities to other issues, such as how to improve leavers' job retention and earnings progression and move families out of poverty permanently. As this shift in focus occurred, and the national economy remained fairly strong, states increased spending on support services, such as childcare and transportation assistance programs, and on educational and job training programs (Tweedie 2000). State spending on support services accelerated in 2000 and 2001 as Congress debated several proposals that would have rescinded unspent TANF funds to help balance the national budget. State government officials worried that if they did not spend their funds quickly, they might lose them.

Like many other states, when West Virginia realized that it was not going to be subject to large federal sanctions (the state was penalized small amounts in 1997, 1998, and 2000 for failing to meet work participation requirements for two-parent families), it began to shift from its earlier reliance on work-first strategies. For example, the state created the "In Service to West Virginia" program, which provides recipients who have used up most of their TANF eligibility with work experience in public service and other work projects. It also increased the average monthly cash assistance check by $200 to make it easier for recipients to make ends meet while on WV WORKS. The state also increased the monthly income disregard used to determine program eligibility from 40 to 60 percent (DHHR 2000a, 2000b).

West Virginia also increased spending for supportive services designed to help individuals transition off welfare. For example, it

Cash Assistance and Social Welfare Policy

increased funding or created new programs to supply recipients with clothing, car repairs, relocation, tools and equipment, transportation, and other needs. Administration of many of these programs was contracted out to nonprofit organizations, creating new and expanding existing partnerships with West Virginia's nonprofit sector. For those in financial crisis, the state offered applicants more generous diversion payments that did not count against the individual's sixty-month time limit. The state also committed additional resources to help recipients pursue post-secondary education. New state legislation redefined what were considered acceptable work activities, making it easier to substitute education for work activities.

West Virginia also increased funding for services that benefit children. The state redirected a large percentage of its $120 million TANF budget to childcare and social services. For example, in FY 2000 the state obligated $22 million to its Child Development Block Grant and more than $28 million to its Child Welfare and Social Service programs (DHHR 2000a). In addition, the state increased funding for various prevention programs that were contracted out to other government and non-government organizations. These funds were used for truancy diversion, adolescent education programs that focus on preventing risky behaviors, parenting classes, and other initiatives aimed at addressing children's needs and preventing welfare dependancy.

Best of Both Worlds

The United States' relatively robust economic times from 1997 through 2000 created an unexpected financial windfall for state welfare administrators across the nation. This windfall ultimately led to a relatively generous allotment of resources for recipient support services, vocational and non-vocational educational programs, job training services, and transition benefits. In addition, the nation's economic expansion created an ideal opportunity for work-first programs to succeed. Proponents of the workforce attachment strategy pointed out that the percentage of TANF recipients working increased from a self-reported 7 percent in 1992 to 11 percent in 1996 and to 34 percent in 2000 (28% in paid employment situations) (DHHS 2000c, 2002). However, West

Virginia's work participation rate (17.1% in 2000) remained far below the national average. Proponents of the workforce attachment strategy also pointed to research in several states, which suggested that parental work reduced children's behavior problems, improved school performance, and reduced domestic violence (DHHS 2000c). Moreover, although poverty reduction was not one of the new law's stated goals, proponents of the workforce attachment strategy noted that poverty rates declined during the program's implementation, suggesting that work-first strategies may have contributed to the decline. Others countered that the decline in poverty was due to the nation's economic expansion and had nothing to do with welfare reform. They argued that the workforce attachment strategy's real test would come when the nation entered into a recession.

The Economic Slowdown

The national economy began to weaken during the first quarter of 2001. To avoid a recession, the Federal Reserve Board eased monetary policy, systematically reducing its prime interest lending rate. Nevertheless, the economy continued to slow, and, during the summer of 2001, the national economy recorded its first negative quarterly economic growth rate in nearly a decade, marking the beginning of a recession. Then, on September 11, 2001, America was changed forever as hijackers crashed two airliners into the World Trade Center in New York City and another into the Pentagon. A fourth hijacked plane, apparently targeting Camp David in the mountains of western Maryland, crashed in Shanksville Township, Pennsylvania, east of Pittsburgh. Thousands of lives, and America's sense of security, were lost forever. As the horrific events of that fateful morning unfolded, the U.S. stock market was closed and remained closed for the remainder of the week. When it reopened, stocks plummeted. In an attempt to avert an economic panic and restore consumer confidence in the economy, the federal government adopted a $40 billion emergency relief package to rebuild New York City and a $15 billion relief package for the airline industry (air passenger levels fell more than 20 percent in the months following the attacks, forcing airlines to lay off more than 100,000 employees). The Federal Reserve Board also aggressively reduced the prime

Cash Assistance and Social Welfare Policy

interest lending rate until it reached 4.75 percent on December 12, 2001, the lowest prime interest lending rate since the 1960s.

Although consumer spending later rebounded, the national economy's 4 to 5 percent annual economic growth rates, commonplace during the late 1990s, were now only fond memories. For the first time since welfare reform legislation was adopted in 1996, welfare recipients nationwide were required to do what West Virginia's welfare recipients had been doing for years, find and retain work in a tight job market. Thus, the terrorist attacks of September 11, 2001 not only harmed the national economy and permanently scarred our collective sense of security, but they also made the already difficult task of moving welfare recipients from government dependency to economic independence even more difficult. Fortunately, the recession was relatively short-lived and, by mid-2002, the national economy was growing again, although at half the pace experienced during the late 1990s. As a result, the 1996 welfare reform law's emphasis on the workforce attachment strategy has not been tested under prolonged adverse economic conditions. However, this is not entirely uncharted water. West Virginia's economy has experienced difficulties for more than a generation. Thus, examining West Virginia's experiences with welfare reform should prove useful to policymakers and practitioners in other states as they implement their own versions of welfare reform, especially during recessionary times. Examining West Virginia's experiences with welfare reform should also prove useful to national policymakers as they deliberate on future versions of federal welfare reform legislation. As will be shown, implementing welfare reform in West Virginia proved to be a particularly difficult task, suggesting that "one size fits all" welfare policies may not be appropriate for states, like West Virginia, whose recipients face multiple employment barriers and whose bureaucracies lack the administrative capacity and resources necessary to fully reinvent themselves into employment centers.

References

Abramovitz, Mimi. 1998. *Regulating the Lives of Women: Social Welfare Policy from Colonial Times to the Present*. Boston: South End Press.

_____. 1995. "Aid to Families With Dependent Children." *Encyclopedia of Social Work.* 19th Edition. ed. Richard Edwards. New York: National Association of Social Workers Press.

Anderson, Martin. 1978. *Welfare: The Political Economy of Welfare Reform in the United States.* Stanford, CA: Hoover Institution.

Auletta, Ken. 1983. "Dependency and Dignity." *New Republic* (February 7): 33, 34.

Ball, Joseph, Gayle Hamilton, Gregory Hoerz, Barbara Goldman, and Judith Gueron. 1984. *Interim Findings on the West Virginia Community Work Experience Demonstrations.* New York: Manpower Demonstration Research Corporation.

Blank, Susan W. and Barbara B. Blum. 1997. "A Brief History of Work Expectations for Welfare Mothers." *Welfare to Work* 7:1 (Spring): 1-11. http://www.futureofchildren.org/usr_doc/vol7no1ART3.pdf.

Cochran, Clarke E., T.R. Carr, Lawrence C. Mayer, and N. Joseph Cayer. 1982. *American Public Policy: An Introduction.* New York: St. Martin's Press.

Conlan, Timothy J. and David B. Walker. 1983. "Reagan's New Federalism: Design, Debate, and Discord." *Intergovernmental Perspective* 8:4 (Winter): 6-22.

Davis, Claude J., Eugene R. Elkins, Carl M. Frasure, Mavis Mann Reeves, William R. Ross, and Albert L. Sturm. 1963. *West Virginia State and Local Government.* Morgantown, WV: West Virginia University Bureau for Government Research.

Dilger, Robert Jay. 1989. *National Intergovernmental Programs.* Englewood Cliffs, N.J.: Prentice-Hall, Inc.

Dilger, Robert Jay, Eleanor Blakely, Karen V.H. Dorton, Melissa Latimer, Barry Locke, Carson Mencken, L. Christopher Plein, Lucinda A. Potter, David Williams, and Dong Pil Yoon. 1999. *West Virginia Works Case Closure Study.* Morgantown, WV: West Virginia University Institute for Public Affairs. Reprinted in *The West Virginia Public Affairs*

Reporter 17:1 (Winter 2000): 2-15.

Federal Register. 1999. "Part II: Department of Health and Human Services. 45 CFR Part 260, et al. Temporary Assistance for Needy Families Program (TANF), Final Rule." (April 12): 17720-17931.

Fischer, Karin. 1998. "Officials say state welfare program has been reduced by two-thirds." *Charleston Daily Mail*, September 14, 1A.

Friedlander, Daniel, Marjorie Erickson, Gayle Hamilton, and Virginia Knox. 1986. *West Virginia: Final Report on the Community Work Experience Demonstrations.* New York: Manpower Demonstration Research Corporation.

Friedman, Milton. 1962. *Capitalism and Freedom.* Chicago: University of Chicago Press.

_____ and Rose Friedman. 1979. *Free to Choose.* New York: Avon Books.

Garfinkel, Irwin and Sara McLanahan. 1986. *Single Mothers and Their Children: A New American Dilemma.* Washington, D.C.: Urban Institute Press.

Garin, Geoffrey, Guy Molyneux, and Linda DiVall. 1994. *Public Attitudes Toward Welfare Reform: A Summary of Key Research Findings.* Washington, D.C.: Peter D. Hart Research Associates and American Viewpoint.

Gordon, Linda. 1994. *Pitied But Not Entitled: Single Mothers and the History of Welfare 1890-1935.* Cambridge, MA: Harvard University Press.

Gueron, Judith M. 1986. *Work initiatives for welfare recipients.* New York: Manpower Demonstration Research Corporation.

Harrington, Michael. 1962. *The Other America: Poverty in the United States.* New York: Macmillan Press.

Hofstadter, Richard. 1948. *The American Political Tradition.* New York: Vintage Books.

Kaiser/Harvard Program on the Public and Health/Social Policy.

1995. *Survey on Welfare Reform: Basic Values and Beliefs; Support for Policy Approaches; Knowledge About Key Programs*. Menlo Park, CA: Henry J. Kaiser Family Foundation; cited in Dan Bloom. 1997. *After AFDC: Welfare-to-Work Choices and Challenges for States*. New York: Manpower Development Research Corporation.

Karger, Howard Jacob and David Stoesz. 1998. *American Social Welfare Policy*. Third Edition. New York: Longman.

Hofstadter, Richard. 1948. *The American Political Tradition*. New York: Vintage Books.

Kosterlitz, Julie. 1986. "Income Security Focus." *National Journal* (August 30): 2092.

Leiby, James. 1978. *A History of Social Welfare and Social Work in the United States*. New York: Columbia University Press.

Leman, Christopher. 1980. *The Collapse of Welfare Reform: Political Institutions, Policy, and the Poor in Canada and the United States*. Cambridge, MA: MIT Press.

Levitan, Sar A. 1985. *Programs in Aid of the Poor*. 5th Edition. Baltimore: The Johns Hopkins University Press.

Lewis, Steven. 2002. Bing Crosby Internet Museum. http://www.kcmetro.cc.mo.us/pennvalley/biology/lewis/crosby/bing.htm.

Moffett, Robert A. 1982. "The Effect of a Negative Income Tax on Work Effort: A Summary of the Experimental Results." *Welfare Reform in America: Perspectives and Prospects*. ed. Paul M. Sommers. Boston: Kluwer-Nijhoff Publishing.

Murray, Charles. 1984. *Losing Ground*. New York: Basic Books.

Nathan, Richard. 1975. *The Plot That Failed: Nixon and the Administrative Presidency*. New York: John Wiley & Sons.

Nathan, Richard, Robert Carleson and Paul H. O'Neil. 1980. "Welfare Reform: Federalism or Federalization." *Common Sense* (Winter): 1-30.

National Conference of State Legislatures (NCSL). 2003. *Description of State Leaver Studies*. Denver, CO: National Conference of State Legislatures. http://www.ncsl.org/statefed/welfare/leavers02.htm.

_____. 1997. *Analysis of the Personal Responsibility and Work Opportunity Reconciliation Act of 1996*. Denver, CO: National Conference of State Legislatures. http://www.ncsl.org/statefed/wel913.htm#tanf.

Nightingale, Demetra Smith, John Trutko and Burt S. Barnow. 1999. *Status of the Welfare-to-Work (WtW) Grants Program After One Year*. Washington, D.C.: The Urban Institute. http://www.urban.org/welfare/wtw_labor.html.

Nixon, Richard M. 1969. "Television Address on the New Federalism." cited in Richard Nathan. 1975. *The Plot That Failed: Nixon and the Administrative Presidency*, 101-112. New York: John Wiley & Sons.

Peterson, Paul E. 1981. *City Limits*. Chicago: The University of Chicago Press.

_____. 1995. *The Price of Federalism*. Washington, D.C.: The Brookings Institution.

Plein, Christopher L. 2001. *Welfare Reform in a Hard Place: The West Virginia Experience*. Rockefeller Report No. 13. Albany, NY: The Nelson Rockefeller Institute of Government.

Rand Corporation. 1988. "The Family Support Act of 1988: Appendix and Implementation and Effects." June 29. Internet articles. http://www.rand.org/publications/R/R4170.pdf/a.R4170.app.pdf and http://www.rand.org/publications/R/R4170.pdf/a.R4170.ch5.pdf.

Reid, P. Nelson. 1995. "Social Welfare History." *Encyclopedia of Social Work*. 19th Edition. Ed. Richard Edwards. New York: National Association of Social Workers Press.

Salamon, Lester M. 1978. *Welfare: The Elusive Consensus*. New York: Praeger Publishers, Inc. Social Security Administration (SSA). 2001. *Social Security Bulletin, Annual Statistical Supplement, 2001*. Washington, D.C.: Social Security Administration.

Sorensen, Elaine and Ariel Halpern. 1999. *Child Support Enforcement Is Working Better Than We Think.* Washington, D.C.: The Urban Institute. http://newfederalism.urban.org/html/anf_31.html.

Tannenbaum, Nili and Michael Reisch. 2001. "From Charitable Volunteers to Architects of Social Welfare: A Brief History of Social Work." *Ongoing* (Fall): n.p. http://www.ssw.umich.edu/ongoing/fall2001/briefhistory.html.

Trattner, Walter I. 1999. *From Poor Law to Welfare State.* 6th Edition. New York: The Free Press.

Trutko, John, Nancy Pindus, Burt S. Barnow and Demetra Smith Nightingale. 1999. *Early Implementation of the Welfare-to-Work (WtW) Grants Program.* Washington, D.C.: The Urban Institute. http://www.urban.org/url.cfm?ID=410336

Tweedie, Jack. 2000. "From D.C. to Little Rock: Welfare Reform at Mid-term." *Publius: The Journal of Federalism* 30:1-2 (Winter/Spring): 69-97.

U.S. Advisory Commission on Intergovernmental Relations (U.S. ACIR). 1980. *Public Assistance: The Growth of a Federal Function.* Washington, D.C.: U.S. Advisory Commission on Intergovernmental Relations.

U.S. Department of Health and Human Services (DHHS). 2002. *Temporary Assistance to Needy Families, Fourth Annual Report to Congress.* Washington, D.C.: U.S. Department of Health and Human Services. http://www.acf.dhhs.gov/programs/opre/ar2001/indexar.htm.

_____. 2000a. "Temporary Assistance for Needy Families: Fact Sheet." Washington, D.C.: U.S. Department of Health and Human Services, September 5, 2000. http://www.acf.dhhs.gov/programs/opa/facts/tanf.htm.

_____. 2000b. "State by State Welfare Caseloads since 1993 (Recipients)." Washington, D.C.: U.S. Department of Health and Human Services, August 8, 2000. http://www.acf.dhhs.gov/news/stats/caseload.htm.

_____. 2000c. "Temporary Assistance for Needy Families: Annual Report to Congress, August 2000." Washington, D.C.: U.S.

Department of Health and Human Services. http://www.acf.dhhs.gov/programs/opre/director.htm.

———. 1998. *Aid to Families with Dependent Children, Baseline Report.* Washington, D.C.: U.S. Department of Health and Human Services, Office of the Assistant Secretary for Planning & Evaluation. http://aspe.hhs.gov/hsp/AFDC/afdcbase98.htm.

U.S. Department of Labor Employment and Training Administration (DOL). 1998. "Summary of Workforce Development Provisions of *The Workforce Investment Act of 1998* (P.l. 105-220)." Washington, D.C.: U.S. Department of Labor. http://usworkforce.org/summarywia.htm.

U.S. General Accounting Office (GAO). 1999. *Welfare Reform: Information on Former Recipients' Status.* Washington, D.C.: U.S. Government Printing Office. GAO/HEHS-99-48. April.

Washington Research Council. 1998. *Catching Up on Welfare Reform.* Washington, D.C.: Washington Research Council.

Weaver, R. Kent. 2000. *Ending Welfare as We Know It.* Washington, D.C.: The Brookings Institution.

West Virginia Department of Health and Human Resources (DHHR). 2000a. *WV WORKS, West Virginia's Welfare Reform Program, 2000 Annual Report.* Charleston, WV: West Virginia Department of Health and Human Resources. http://www.wvdhhr.org/ofs/2000AnnualReport.htm.

———. 2000b. *State Plan for Temporary Assistance for Needy Families: Submitted to the U.S. Department of Health and Human Services.* Charleston, WV: West Virginia Department of Health and Human Resources.

White, Theodore H. 1961. *The Making of the President, 1960.* New York: Atheneum House.

Whitman, David. 1987. "The Key to Welfare Reform." *The Atlantic Monthly online*. June. http://www.theatlantic.com/politics/poverty/whitmaf.htm.

WV WORKS. 1998. "Caseload By County." Charleston, WV: West Virginia Department of Health and Human Resources. http://www.wvwelfarereform.org/Statistical%20Information.html (link no onger maintained).

Chapter 4

Managing Welfare Reform in West Virginia: Lessons Learned

L. CHRISTOPHER PLEIN AND DAVID WILLIAMS

This chapter examines West Virginia's Department of Health and Human Resources' (DHHR) administrative capacity to implement welfare reform, focusing on its activities following the enactment of the *Personal Responsibility and Work Opportunity Reconciliation Act of 1996*. Administrative capacity has been evaluated by taking into account hard assets, such as fiscal resources, management information systems, and organizational staffing and expertise. Administrative capacity has also been evaluated by taking into account more qualitative assets, such as organizational culture, institutional memory and experience, the leadership skills of senior administrators and officials, the attention senior administrators and officials dedicate to the policy, and the extent of the agency's political capital and autonomy. The best studies address both dimensions (Nathan and Gais 1999; Gais et al. 2001; Liebschutz 2000).

In many ways, this chapter is a story of DHHR's limited control over unfolding events and how political pressures forced it to shift priorities and practices over time. In a nutshell, DHHR was granted substantial discretion to design a welfare-to-work program just months prior to the enactment of the *Personal Responsibility and Work Opportunity Reconciliation Act of 1996*. The new law forced DHHR to shape its implementation strategy to fit priorities set in

Washington, D.C. However, some of the technical language in the new law was vague. For example, it was unclear which activities could be counted toward the new work requirements. Worried that their decisions might result in federal sanctions, DHHR proceeded cautiously. DHHR's cautious response upset many stakeholders, especially welfare advocacy groups. Ultimately, DHHR's actions led to greater legislative scrutiny and oversight of the Department's administrative actions. As the implementation process progressed, it became increasingly clear that DHHR lacked the administrative capacity necessary to manage the changes needed to meet the 1996 welfare reform law's goals.

Seizing and Losing the Initiative: Federal Reform Trumps State Initiatives

The *Personal Responsibility and Work Opportunity Reconciliation Act of 1996* created new opportunities and challenges for states. Existing state policy and institutional arrangements, as well as underlying social, political, and economic conditions, shaped the law's implementation. The different mix of contextual, institutional, and programmatic factors contributed to a variety of state responses to welfare reform in the late 1990s. Some states, including Michigan and Wisconsin, responded to the new law by fundamentally reinventing their welfare systems (Weissert 1999; Barnow et al. 2000). Responding to the law's goal of moving recipients into employment, some states reassigned work placement and job training responsibilities from welfare bureaucracies to existing labor departments or to new agencies. Others, such as New Jersey, Florida, and Mississippi, contracted out welfare case management at the local level (Roper 1998; Crew and Davis 2000; Breaux et al. 2002). This general trend in reinventing welfare systems became the subject of considerable attention in the academic literature and welfare policy community (Nathan and Gais 1999; Blank and Haskins 2001).

West Virginia responded to the new law in an incremental fashion. When the law was passed, West Virginia had in place a relatively centralized institutional structure for administering health and human services. DHHR managed program operations in the state capital (Charleston) and implemented programs at the local level through state-run field offices. This centralized administrative structure evolved from various reorganization efforts spanning the 1970s, 1980s, and 1990s. The Department's Bureau for Children and Families administered Aid to Families with Dependent Children (AFDC), Food Stamp, and Medicaid eligibility determination and case management, along with a host of social service programs for "at-risk" individuals. Community Services Managers oversaw the many programs administered and delivered at the local level. In addition, DHHR's thirty-eight district offices were grouped into four administrative regions, each headed by a regional director accountable to the Commissioner of the Bureau for Children and Families (Plein and Williams 1997).

Initially, DHHR's senior administrators were optimistic about the prospects of implementing successful reform. They were convinced that a reorganized organizational structure, coupled with a long history of involvement in welfare-to-work initiatives dating back to the 1960s, provided them the institutional capacity to successfully implement reforms. Perhaps most importantly, they had already developed a welfare-to-work plan that was designed to accomplish the goals the new federal law outlined. The program, titled WV WORKS, had been designed in anticipation of being granted a waiver from the U.S. Department of Health and Human Resources. Numerous states had utilized AFDC waivers to develop welfare-to-work demonstration programs. DHHR's plan was a combination of home-grown ideas, program components inspired by other state experiences, and input and validation by out-of-state consultants versed in welfare-to-work program design.

Governor Gaston Caperton (D, 1989-1997) was the catalyst behind West Virginia's decision to seek a waiver. In 1995, he directed DHHR to devise a welfare-to-work program that would qualify for a federal waiver under the AFDC program. According to senior DHHR administrators, Caperton became interested in creating a welfare-to-work program in West Virginia through his interaction with other governors in his capacity as an executive officer for the National Governors Association. He was particularly impressed by welfare-to-work programs in Wisconsin and Vermont. He created two working groups to examine the issue and form the broad outlines of a plan to implement a welfare-to-work program in West Virginia. The "governor's working group" was asked to explore ways in which various departments and agencies could cooperate in implementing a welfare-to-work initiative. A DHHR working group was created to design the program (Plein and Williams 1997). The governor gave DHHR significant leeway in developing the program. After creating the plan's basic outline, DHHR formed fourteen implementation teams across the state to provide feedback from field office staff and other stakeholders. These teams included more than 200 representatives from local government and the private sector (DHHR1996a, 1997).

The WV WORKS program that emerged bore many similarities to welfare-to-work programs in other states, especially Wisconsin WORKS. For example, like Wisconsin WORKS, participants were required to sign a personal responsibility contract (PRC), which established a set of conditions that they negotiated with their caseworker. These conditions included a wide range of activities and commitments. The most common PRC components dealt with job search and educational and training activities, as well as agreements requiring parents to ensure that their children received vaccinations, attend parenting classes, and seek training for "soft" skills, such as business etiquette and family budgeting. Another element common to other state welfare-to-work programs was WV WORKS' diversion payment option. Instead of enrolling in WV WORKS, participants could receive a lump sum payment to pay for essentials. Another similarity was the proposed use of transition loans to help individuals purchase items necessary for work, such as uniforms and clothing.

In early 1996, briefings were held with state legislative leaders to review WV WORKS' goals and structure. At this time, DHHR officials were highly cognizant of the winds of change swirling around AFDC. They warned state legislators that significant federal reforms might be on the way (DHHR 1996b). In March 1996, the state legislature adopted legislation granting DHHR authority to seek federal permission to operate a demonstration welfare-to-work program. However, because DHHR knew that federal welfare reform was certain to pass, it opted to withdraw its waiver and wait to see what the federal government was going to do.

The *Personal Responsibility and Work Opportunity Reconciliation Act of 1996* embodied many of the reforms pioneered in the states (Heclo 2001). On the surface, the new law appeared to give states greater autonomy and flexibility in designing and managing their welfare programs by replacing AFDC with the Temporary Assistance for Needy Families (TANF) block grant. Initially, many commentators believed that TANF was going to end AFDC's rule-bound regime with numerous regulations and policies emanating from Washington D.C. Many believed that TANF was going to usher in a new era in program administration that embraced popular philosophies of devolution and reinvention (Heclo 2001; Breaux et al. 2002). West Virginia and other states quickly learned otherwise. The new law contained many conditions, some starkly clear and others more ambiguous, that hampered innovation and did much to reinforce AFDC's legacy of rule-bound behaviors at the state and local level.

Welfare reform took place within an intergovernmental context. Although the political rhetoric emanating from Washington D.C. promised states additional programmatic flexibility, the new law included many rules and regulations that states had to meet or they would lose all or portions of their federal funding. As a result, federal standards and expectations often displaced state priorities. However, states were used to federal directives. Their biggest complaint was that Washington sent ambiguous signals concerning federal performance measures in the areas of workforce participation and budgetary controls (Heclo 2001; Nathan and Gais 1999; Gais et al. 2001). In this uncertain environment, with the threat of sanctions hanging over their heads, many states, including West Virginia, decided to proceed cautiously. Although welfare reform advocates hoped that the 1996 welfare reform law would encourage re-invention and innovation, the ambiguities concerning how to meet the new rules and regulations discouraged it.

Lesson One: When Faced With Ambiguity the Past Holds Sway

> The Department of Human Resources will be entering a period of enormous change with the implementation of WV WORKS. Not only will the program change for clients, staff will also be dealing with that change. WV WORKS moves away from a system that is focused on rules and process to a system that emphasizes results - employment. Staff will be adjusting to this shift. All staff will be attending culture change training, which will focus on the 'new way' of doing business. Basically, the welfare office will become an employment office.
>
> – West Virginia Department of Health and Human Resources (1996c, 2-3)

During 1996 and 1997, DHHR promoted WV WORKS with great fanfare. It touted the promise of reform and guaranteed that it would free itself from the rule-bound shackles that had made it an unresponsive welfare bureaucracy in the past. The promise of organizational change was common in the rhetoric of welfare reform across the nation, but like many agencies in other states, West Virginia's DHHR found it difficult to keep that promise. Substantive reform takes time and requires clear signals backed by law, consistent and timely release of guiding regulations that give direction to new law, and new management policies to effect change. Reform is only symbolic when it lacks legal guidance to implement the new paradigm. Habitually risk-adverse, worried about the possibility of failing to meet federal work participation rates, and uncertain about what was allowed under the new law, the Department's safest course was the most familiar: rely on past practices. Ironically, the *Personal Responsibility and Work Opportunity Reconciliation Act* encouraged such behavior by allowing states to count closed cases toward the federal work participation requirements (Tweedie 2000; Heclo 2001). Proficient in the arts of eligibility determination and application procedures, DHHR found it relatively easy to create substantial barriers to enrollment.

The rhetoric of reform stipulated, as then-Presidential candidate Bill Clinton announced in 1992, that success was "ending welfare as we know it" by moving individuals into economic self-sufficiency. This was to be accomplished by reinventing welfare bureaucracies into employment and job training centers. These reinvented bureaucracies were also to help families overcome preexisting employment barriers by enforcing child support payments, providing funds for childcare, and providing training in business etiquette, family budgeting, parenting skills, and other "soft skills." As detailed in Chapter 5, this heightened sense of responsiveness to recipient needs informed much of the intent and generated much of the enthusiasm that surrounded WV WORKS during its demonstration phase in 1997. However, by 1998, DHHR discovered that it lacked the fiscal resources and administrative capacity to retain that heightened sense of responsiveness to client needs when it implemented WV WORKS statewide.

By setting state-by-state funding levels and imposing mandatory work participation rates, the 1996 welfare reform law forced states to look for ways to meet the work participation rates in an economically efficient manner. States knew that caseload reductions counted toward the work participation rate, which, in FY 2002, was 50 percent of the total adult caseload and 90 percent of two-parent families. They then compared the cost and, in light of local economic conditions, the efficacy of retooling administrative and case management arrangements to become employment centers to the cost of implementing onerous eligibility procedures and other case clearing tactics. Case clearing won (Plein 2001a).

DHHR determined that the most cost-effective means of avoiding federal sanctions and staying within budget was to establish a redetermination process that effectively cleared the welfare rolls. When WV WORKS came online in 1997 and 1998, West Virginians receiving AFDC cash assistance had to reapply. Confronted with new, unfamiliar, and complex application procedures, many decided to forego WV WORKS (see Chapter 5 and Plein 2001a). Several other states also adopted this strategy as a means of complying with federal work participation rules and keeping costs low (Nathan and Gais 1999).

In short, the 1996 welfare reform law's caseload reduction credit encouraged states, especially those with difficult labor markets, to follow old, rather than new administrative behaviors. Instead of reinventing themselves into flexible employment centers, most local offices in West Virginia continued to act like the rigid, unfriendly income maintenance bureaucracy of the past. West Virginia was not the only state to take this route. Many state welfare agencies continued to be rule-bound, oriented more toward complying with state and federal regulations than serving client needs (Meyers 2000; Tweedie 2000; Riccucci and Lurie 2001). This rule-bound mentality spilled over into the administration of other human services programs, including Medicaid and Food Stamps. Indeed, reinventing welfare bureaucracies was a tall order. For many years these bureaucracies had been subjected to, and had become accustomed to, tight legal and political controls (Weir et al. 1988; Roberston and Judd 1989).

As Riccucci and Lurie (2001) noted, entrenched behaviors designed to minimize errors when determining Medicaid, AFDC, and Food Stamp eligibility work against the implementation of new programs and services designed to provide recipients with jobs. In West Virginia, DHHR's "bunker mentality" was reinforced by the actions of others. For example, in the late 1990s, the U.S. Department of Agriculture (USDA) cited DHHR for its poor performance in minimizing Food Stamp eligibility determination errors. Also, in 1997, the West Virginia State Legislature's Office of Legislative Auditor audited DHHR's Medicaid eligibility determination process and concluded that "inefficient training, a complex reference manual, and insufficient supervisory case review" had contributed to errors in Medicaid eligibility determination (Legislative Auditor 1997, 7). These findings caused DHHR to become preoccupied with avoiding errors. This preoccupation, in turn, made it difficult for DHHR to accomplish the administrative "cultural changes" needed to achieve more proactive and flexible approaches to welfare case management.

The first lesson learned from West Virginia's experience with implementing welfare reform is that program change is as much a "cultural change" as an "organizational and regulatory change." Past practices, mind-sets, philosophies, and regulations tend to seep over into program change, even when entrenched behaviors and norms are inimical to achieving the new policy's goals. The influence of prior mind-sets, philosophies, and regulations is particularly potent when there is uncertainty and ambiguity in the new program's directives.

Lesson Two: When it Rains it Pours - The Converging Paths of Reform

> Through accountability, DHHR can accomplish short-term goals. Short-term accomplishment enables DHHR to engage in long-term goals and build a rock-solid record of achievement. As you are well aware, we have emphasized extensive accountability from fiscal responsibility to customer service to responsiveness to the Legislature for requests for information. Our goal has been, and continues to be, to have the right answer at the right time. I hope you will agree that the DHHR today is very different from that of three years ago.
> – Joan Ohl, Secretary,
> West Virginia DHHR (Ohl 2000)

Joan Ohl made these comments at a budget presentation to the state legislature in February 2000. She announced that DHHR had committed itself fully to reforming and reorganizing its operations, had become more responsive and sensitive to public needs, and was now more attentive and accountable to those principals involved in agency oversight. What was also telling from her budget presentation was how vast DHHR's responsibilities were, and continue to be. In addition to welfare, Secretary Ohl's office was responsible for Medicaid, childcare regulation and subsidization, child support enforcement, foster care and adoption, public health, rehabilitative services, Food Stamps, and a wide variety of social services. In short, the budget presentation made it clear that welfare reform was just one of many health and human service programs undergoing significant administrative change.

The *Personal Responsibility and Work Opportunity Reconciliation Act of 1996* set into motion a number of changes by replacing AFDC with TANF. It also made substantial administrative and programmatic changes to both Food Stamps and Supplemental Security Income (SSI). Moreover, in 1997, the *Balanced Budget Act* fundamentally reordered Medicaid's funding mechanisms, encouraged states to use managed care approaches to reduce expenses, and prohibited spending Medicaid funds for various social service, public health, and rehabilitative programs (Plein 1999). These changes, coupled with the introduction of the new Children's Health Insurance Program (CHIP) for low-income families (see Chapter 3), presented DHHR with a full plate of programmatic changes that severely tested its administrative capacity.

If contending with Medicaid changes and welfare reform were not enough, the *Workforce Investment Act of 1998* (WIA) encouraged states to focus additional attention and resources on job training and development for the unemployed and underemployed. Although DHHR was not directly involved in crafting West Virginia's WIA plan, it had to cope with a rapidly changing job training and job placement system. These changes further complicated DHHR's efforts to reinvent itself into an employment center. In addition, DHHR did not have administrative control over job search and job training services. The Bureau for Employment Programs handled those responsibilities. As a result, DHHR was forced to develop a working partnership with the Bureau for Employment Programs as part of its effort to reinvent itself into an employment centered agency (Plein and Williams 1997). Unfortunately, WIA work training activities did not necessarily match those the *Personal Responsibility and Work Opportunity Reconciliation Act of 1996* identified. As a result, WV WORKS recipients engaged in a WIA-sponsored program did not necessarily satisfy TANF's work requirements. Furthermore, the Bureau for Employment Programs had its own administrative and financial problems, making DHHR's efforts to reinvent itself into an employment center even more difficult (Plein and Williams 2000).

DHHR's struggles with Food Stamp management provide a sobering illustration of the difficulties of managing reform amidst a complex network of social and human services programs. In the early 1990s, the USDA cited the state for failing to address problems in Food Stamp eligibility determination. In 1993, the state averted a $5.3 million federal sanction by agreeing to develop a correction and compliance strategy that improved training and coordination in Food Stamp management (*West Virginia Executive Budget* 1998).

However, DHHR continued to fail to meet federal performance requirements. DHHR's failure led to the threat of additional federal sanctions and additional efforts to improve program management. By the late 1990s, DHHR's Food Stamp eligibility determination error rate improved, but not without significant attention and effort by state, regional, and local administrators (Ohl 2000). DHHR's Food Stamp experiences during the 1990s made avoiding federal sanctions during the implementation of WV WORKS, and the embarrassment of being labeled, once again, a "failure" by the federal government, a very high priority among DHHR's senior administrators.

The convergence of multiple reform paths placed an unusual burden on DHHR's administrative capacity. Instead of following a carefully drawn, systematic plan that focused on achieving long-term goals, DHHR typically reacted to issues as they arose, focusing on immediate problems and concerns rather than long-term goals. Given all of the other issues demanding attention, DHHR's senior administrators did the best they could, but they lacked the time necessary to give welfare reform the attention it required.

Lesson Three: Under Devolution States Still Listen to Washington

> For a variety of reasons states were slow to spend their TANF block grant in the first few years, namely because of the delay in the issuance of final regulations.
> – National Governors Association (2001)

Bureaucratic power is largely a function of autonomy and resources. Autonomy is measured by the agency's independence and authority to make and carry out policy. Resources are measured, at least in part, by the relative wealth and protection accorded to the agency's funding streams (Meier 1993). In a federal system, autonomy is relative and measured in context of the horizontal relationships between institutional actors at various government levels. Thus, a state agency's autonomy can be, and often is, constrained by federal conditions and requirements. But, relative to other state actors, such as governors and state legislators, state agencies can be quite autonomous. Terry Sanford (1967) described the autonomy of state agencies as a byproduct of "picket fence" federalism. State elected officials were often left out of the policymaking loop as federal law and regulations preempted state legislative action, but allowed state and local bureaucracies to exercise discretion while implementing the law. Although "picket fence" federalism advanced national policy priorities in a fragmented federal system (Robertson and Judd 1989), state elected officials worried that voters would hold them accountable for programs over which they had little or no control. In addition, federal regulations and requirements prevented state legislators and governors from directing the actions of their state agencies, which were often seen as "hiding behind the rules." Scholars and practitioners often cited the complex tangle of federally funded and directed health and human services programs as epitomizing the excesses of "picket fence" federalism. Such perceptions and practices helped to fuel the ongoing political debate over the need for program devolution (Reagan 1972; Nathan and Doolittle 1987; Dilger 1989; Heclo 2001). The 1996 welfare reform law was supposed to represent a breakthrough for the programmatic devolution movement. However, as the new welfare law was implemented, it became increasingly clear that state welfare bureaucracies remained closely tied to their federal counterparts in Washington, D.C..

Proponents of the new law promised that states would be freed of the federal government's bureaucratic shackles. However, many states, including West Virginia, continued to look to Washington for guidance and direction. The new law directed the U.S. Department of Health and Human Services (DHHS) to issue rules and regulations defining what constituted a TANF case and which activities, other than job placement, counted toward the mandatory work participation rate. It took DHHS more than two years to issue these rules. Lacking guidance from Washington, and worried that they might later be subjected to sanctions for failing to comply with federal rules, DHHR officials proceeded with extreme caution, focusing on providing basic services to those on WV WORKS and a work-first strategy. DHHR's actions seemed justified when DHHS issued preliminary rules in 1997 that included short-term assistance in its definition of what constituted a TANF case and a narrow definition of what constituted a work activity. The National Governors Association, other prominent public interest groups, and welfare advocacy groups argued that DHHS' definitions would stifle state innovation. DHHS subsequently issued rules during fall 1999 that clarified what constituted a TANF case (short-term assistance did not count) and issued a broader definition of a work activity that included job training and educational activities (Plein 2001b).

Once the rules were clarified, DHHR embarked on new program initiatives to assist those who had left the rolls and were at risk of returning. Like many other states (Tweedie 2000; Gais et al. 2001), West Virginia provided more generous supportive services and aid to those on welfare and to those who had left the program (Plein 2001a; Dilger et al. 2001). By early 2000, DHHR had reoriented WV WORKS' priorities to provide greater attention to the needs of those on, leaving, and off the welfare rolls (Plein 2001a). A new adjective, rarely applied to DHHR's welfare bureaucracy in the past, was now appropriate. DHHR was, on the whole, becoming *responsive* to the varied needs of those who came in contact with the welfare system. The most notable steps included:

- Reversing, though only after state legislative action and a probable court reversal, the counting of SSI in eligibility determinations. This policy, which forced thousands off the rolls, was eliminated in June 1999.

- Increasing the average monthly cash benefit by $200 between 1999 and late 2000. This action vaulted West Virginia from among the lowest cash benefit states to 15th in the nation.

- Increasing the monthly income disregard for determining WV WORKS eligibility from 40 to 60 percent of earnings. This change allowed hundreds of families to retain their eligibility for WV WORKS benefits after they entered the workforce.

- Allowing new applicants to receive cash diversion payments of up to the equivalent of four months of cash assistance. Under this diversion option, the lump sum payment did not count against the individual's sixty-month lifetime benefit limit. Previously, any diversion payment resulted in a three-month deduction in the applicant's sixty-month lifetime benefit limit.

- New supportive services were offered to assist those on and off welfare obtain and retain employment. Among the services offered were: clothing vouchers, personal grooming expenses, test fees, and other employment related services, payments to purchase commercial driver, regular driver, and chauffeur driver licences, relocation costs, tools and equipment, vehicle insurance payments, and transportation reimbursement.

- New supportive services were offered to help families and individuals at the community level, such as truancy diversion, pregnancy prevention, and parenting and teen mentoring classes.

- A number of initiatives were implemented to improve front line service delivery and to reconnect those who had left welfare, but were still eligible for Medicaid, Food Stamps, and CHIP.

DHHR undertook these actions because politics created the mandate for action; practical experience drove home the wisdom of being more responsive to recipient and potential recipient needs; and new federal rules pointed the way for action. But, none of these actions would have been possible if DHHR had not proceeded cautiously and accumulated tens of millions of dollars in unspent federal TANF dollars.

Lesson Four: The Consequences of Inertia in the Devolution Era - The Surplus Blues

We are aggressively looking for ways to spend this money. ... We are keenly aware that if we don't spend the money in a timely manner, it will be extremely tempting for Congress to take some of it back.
– Sharon Phares, DHHR spokesperson, quoted in the *New York Times* (Pear 1999)

During the first two years of welfare reform, states across the nation built up considerable TANF surpluses, which resulted from the unintended, unexpected, and dramatic caseload reduction that occurred across the nation. With federal funding fixed by statute, and enrollment a third to a half of previous levels, states found themselves in the enviable position of having to figure out how to spend the money. Many states announced that they were setting aside money as "rainy-day" funds in the event of an economic downturn; however, the situation was actually more complex. For example, DHHR announced that it was setting aside monies to prepare for potential hard times ahead, but, in actuality, that was only part of the reason. It also set aside the funds because, in the absence of clear federal guidelines, it was worried that it might have to repay the money with state dollars if the federal government later determined that DHHR had spent the funds inappropriately. By June 2000, West Virginia, in proportional terms, had one of the largest unspent federal TANF balances in the United States. With more than $160 million on hand, West Virginia had carried over approximately half of its first two years of federal TANF funds, compared to 6 percent nationally (Miller 2000a). The result was an embarrassment of riches that led to considerable political controversy. DHHR came under intense political pressure to spend the money.

The surplus controversy generally followed events at the national level. By early 1999, welfare advocacy groups throughout the nation were asking why states were accumulating such large surpluses (Pear 1999). They wanted states to "invest" that money in programs to help both those on and off the rolls. Some in Congress raised the possibility of taking back unspent TANF funds to reduce the national deficit. State groups, such as the National Governors Association, were angered that Congress considered reneging on its pledge to allow states to benefit from program efficiencies. Moreover, they argued that states should not be punished because they would have spent more money if federal guidelines clarifying TANF's rules and regulations had been issued earlier (National Governors Association 1999a, 1999b).

By spring 2000, unspent TANF funds became an issue of intense interest in West Virginia, drawing both legislative and media attention. Matters came to a head in June 2000 when, before a state legislative oversight committee, a senior DHHS administrator admonished the state to spend more of its unspent funds on childcare, health care, transportation support, and education (Miller 2000a, 2000b; Miller 2000).

In response to these demands, DHHR initiated spending in three areas. First, and most significantly, in FY 2001 DHHR transferred $43 million of the unspent funds to the state's Bureau of Social Services to fund various programs, including the state's controversial and expensive juvenile foster care program. It also obligated $22 million for childcare services. These funds were used to increase childcare subsidy rates for the poor and build child and day care facilities across the state. DHHR obligated similar amounts, $41.5 and $22.5 million, respectively, in FY 2002 (DHHR 2001). Because the funds came from the surplus, the DHHR's Secretary did not have to request supplemental appropriations from the state legislature. Making such requests in the middle of the state fiscal year had become common practice, providing an opportunity for state legislators to scrutinize and criticize DHHR's executive management decisions.

Second, with legislative and gubernatorial encouragement, DHHR increased cash assistance benefits for those on WV WORKS and expanded support services and other benefits for both those on the rolls and those who had recently left welfare. As detailed in this chapter's previous section, these steps included raising the average cash assistance payment by approximately $200 a month, providing more diversionary support for families considering applying for WV WORKS, and adding various supportive services to help those both on and off the rolls find and retain employment.

Third, DHHR provided funding for a wide array of community-based programs that benefitted those on WV WORKS as well as those in the general population with certain "at-risk" characteristics, such as a job displacement, behaviors that might lead to adolescent pregnancy, and juvenile delinquency. Also, some of the accumulated federal funds were used to substitute for state funding of existing programs and to expand other programs already in place. This was done in such areas as family planning and truancy diversion. The truancy diversion program, for example, was expanded from relatively few counties to a statewide initiative. These programs served a diverse clientele that included current WV WORKS recipients, former WV WORKS recipients, and other "at-risk" populations. The new federal guidelines allowed states to fund such activities under the 1996 welfare reform legislation's family formation goals.

By October 2000, West Virginia had committed $69.5 million of its $160 million in carry over funds (DHHR 2000a, 2000b). Welfare advocacy groups and the media praised DHHR for becoming a more responsive and supportive agency. Some singled out new efforts to help low-income families find housing and make home improvements, provide after-school training and mentoring services to children considered at risk of dropping out of high school, and supplementing family planning programming (Miller 2000b). However, as the fall 2000 gubernatorial election approached, welfare reform and health and human services administration became embroiled in campaign politics. In fall 2000, the incumbent governor, Republican Cecil Underwood, raised cash assistance payments by $100 a month. Some claimed that he was trying to win votes by doing so. At the same time, he came under heavy fire from his Democratic challenger, Robert Wise, concerning CHIP's administration. Wise argued that the Underwood Administration had failed to administer the program effectively, implying that Governor Underwood was insensitive to the needs of the poor and working families. The debate over the course of health and human services administration continued throughout the campaign and spilled into the new year as well.

Lesson Five: It's All About Politics – the Limits of Administrative Autonomy

> 'Everything is open,'[Secretary of Health and Human Resources] Nusbaum said. 'It's going to be a heck of a deficit, and we're going to have to look at what programs we are by law required to provide.'
> – Paul Nusbaum, Secretary, DHHR
> ("State Welfare Grant Program
> May Face Deficit in 2003" 2001)

When Robert Wise became West Virginia's Governor in January 2001, the state entered a new phase of welfare reform. By June, the tenor of change was apparent when DHHR's new Secretary, Paul Nusbaum, announced that the state was facing a welfare funding crisis. The problems of spending accumulated federal TANF funds had changed, seemingly overnight, to the problems of running a deficit. Nusbaum announced that unless current policies were changed, the state's welfare budget would face a $90 million deficit by October 2003. He blamed the funding crisis on his predecessors, arguing that they were guilty of profligate spending. Before state legislative committees and the press, he promised DHHR would engage in a careful strategic planning process to account for how the state's welfare dollars would be spent and to maximize program effectiveness. He also called for the appointment of a blue-ribbon council to assist him in identifying program priorities and recommending spending cuts.

In December 2001, the special TANF advisory council released its recommendations for cost savings and program reductions. It noted that more than half of the projected $90 million deficit could be prevented by eliminating DHHR's transfer of federal TANF dollars to the Office of Social Services. The council, and later Governor Wise, recommended that the Office of Social Services find other sources of federal and state funds (TANF Advisory Council 2001). The state legislature later accepted a gubernatorial request to provide an additional $20 million in state funds for the Office of Social Services (Kabler 2002a).

The advisory council suggested that the other half of the deficit could be resolved by cutting or reducing funding for programs that directly assist those on and off TANF, such as support services and diversion payments. Approximately $20 million in cuts were recommended, including funding for some of the changes that had won DHHR the most praise from welfare advocacy groups and various media outlets. For example, the council proposed that the earned income disregard be reduced from 60 percent back to 40 percent (TANF Advisory Council 2001). The council also recommended that the remainder of the deficit could be met by scaling back and/or eliminating contracts and grants provided to community-level service providers.

Welfare advocacy groups and nonprofit organizations complained bitterly about the proposed reductions and appealed to both DHHR and the state legislature to preserve their programs and minimize cuts (Miller 2002a, 2002b). By the end of the 2002, state legislative session attention, once again, turned to DHHR and its decisions. A "revamp committee," comprised of DHHR staff and welfare advocacy group representatives, developed a set of recommendations to trim administrative costs and improve case management (Miller 2002c). Most significant were proposals to reduce various support services and to tighten eligibility guidelines for receiving these services. DHHR also began the difficult task of determining which contracts to various social service providers would be reduced or eliminated. In May 2002, DHHR presented a plan to the state legislature to eliminate 107 contracts for a savings of $27 million (Kabler 2002b). Among the programs cut were a statewide truancy diversion initiative for elementary and middle-school youth.

West Virginia was not the only state that found itself in the unenviable position of having to cut back on welfare services funded by federal TANF dollars. Many other states also faced deficits in their welfare budgets (Haynes 2002). Moreover, like West Virginia, states across the nation were having a very difficult time finding state revenues to replace federal dollars. The national economic slowdown that began in 2001 and was accelerated by the tragic events of September 11, 2001, caused state budget difficulties across the nation, and many states were able to fund only part of the projected shortfall (Rosenbaum 2002).

As it attempted to address the projected deficit, DHHR discovered that changing its course of action was more difficult than anticipated. For example, DHHR allocated $11.03 million for supportive services during calendar year 2000. Of this, 39 percent was spent on services for non-WV WORKS recipients. During the first five months of 2001, DHHR spent $7.02 million on supportive services, with 31 percent allocated to non-WV WORKS recipients. In the five months following Secretary Nusbaum's announcement about the looming funding crisis in June 2001, DHHR spent $6.88 million on support services, approximately the same amount it spent during the first five months of the year. The allotment of support services payments to non-WV WORKS recipients, 27 percent, also remained about the same.

As West Virginia's TANF funding "crisis" reveals, politics can strongly influence program delivery and evolution. Change, especially when it involves funding reductions, is often more difficult than anticipated.

Lesson Six: If it Works There, Shouldn't it Work Here? The Limits of Fungibility

> "It's Working in Wisconsin: What West Virginia Can Learn from Governor Tommy G. Thompson About Welfare Reform."
> – Conference Sponsored by West Virginia Roundtable and others (1997)

Governor Tommy Thompson (R, Wisconsin) and one of his senior aides traveled to West Virginia in June, 1997 to meet with then-Governor Cecil Underwood. He gave a presentation about Wisconsin's welfare reform experiences to state policymakers and others from West Virginia's welfare community. The visit's purpose was to enable West Virginia to learn from Wisconsin's experiences with welfare reform. Wisconsin WORKS was viewed as a model for other states to emulate (Mead 2002). Such policy learning and sharing is a hallmark of American federalism. States look to others who have achieved success to pattern their programs. Indeed, the federal waiver program that allowed states to pilot welfare-to-work programs under AFDC was designed to encourage experimentation and learning among the states.

Rose (1993) has written convincingly about how states learn about and borrow programs from each other. However, he notes that the transferability, or fungibility, of any program or policy is conditional. Differences in context and issues require states to adapt and revise successful approaches borrowed from others. In short, one size does not fit all. What appears to be a best practice in one state may, in the long run, not be so successful in another. The advantage of learning from others is that when results and outcomes are not as expected, policymakers can change existing arrangements. However, when lessons learned from states are codified into law and imposed upon states, as was the case with the *Personal Responsibility and Work Opportunity Reconciliation Act*, such discretion is denied.

Although Wisconsin WORKS has been lauded as the model for welfare reform, it has also been criticized as an artificial success - the product of a good economy, selective program application, and atypical fiscal and political support from policymakers (Barnow et al. 2000). Whatever the assessment of its performance, two components of Wisconsin's program, work requirements and time-limited eligibility, became the keystones of the 1996 federal welfare reform law, and they have shaped state responses to welfare reform across the nation. Arguably, this had a dampening effect on progressive reform in states. The feasibility of meeting work participation rates became a fixation in state priorities. Instead of reinventing the welfare system into job training and employment centers, states focused on caseload reduction to meet work participation requirements (Tweedie 2000). The irony is that federal welfare reform promised greater state flexibility while actually curtailing state innovation.

In March 2002, the Bush administration announced its welfare reform reauthorization plan. Although it touted state flexibility, the proposal actually included even stricter controls on state discretion than those in the *Personal Responsibility and Work Opportunity Reconciliation Act of 1996*. For example, under the proposal, states will no longer have the option of using caseload reduction credits to meet the work participation rate. States will also have to meet higher work participation rates (70% of adults by 2007). The proposal also requires states to be more specific in establishing state goals for moving clients into work, facilitating economic self-sufficiency, and promoting family formation. As under existing law, the U.S. Secretary of Health and Human Services must approve state plans. In addition, states must establish measurable objectives and develop evaluation procedures to assess progress toward these goals (Bush 2002).

In May 2002, the Republican-controlled U.S. House of Representatives adopted a slightly modified version of the administration's plan (Goldstein and Eilperin 2002). The Democratic-controlled Senate, advocating somewhat higher funding levels and increased state flexibility concerning recipient work participation requirements, held up final action on the bill until after the November 2002 congressional elections. The Republican Party maintained its control of the U.S. House of Representatives and, by a single seat, narrowly won control of the U.S. Senate. In February 2003, the Republican-controlled U.S. House of Representatives adopted, once again, a slightly modified version of the administration's plan. The Senate is likely to force the House to accept somewhat higher funding levels and grant states somewhat greater discretion in the use of TANF funds. However, the overall tenor of welfare reform remains the same. The emphasis continues to be on work.

In summary, West Virginia's response to welfare reform was shaped and reshaped by external events and demands. The *Personal Responsibility and Work Opportunity Reconciliation Act of 1996*, with its fixed funding formula, work participation requirements, and caseload reduction credits, caused DHHR to reorder its priorities. DHHR's preoccupation with budgetary issues, coupled with its lingering concern over the possible imposition of federal sanctions, led it to abandon its initial attempt to reinvent itself into a job training and employment center. Then, when political pressure was applied to encourage DHHR to spend accumulated federal TANF funds, DHHR did not reinvent itself. Instead, it contracted with numerous nonprofit organizations to provide additional support services for recipients and non-recipients considered at-risk of joining the welfare rolls. Although welfare advocacy groups and others applauded this action, the benefits of these programs were relatively short-lived; and DHHR's organizational structure, and its tendencies to be reactive instead of proactive and to proceed with caution, remained unchanged. As a result, West Virginia's experiences with welfare reform suggest that, at least in this state, instead of creating a new environment of opportunity and change, the *Personal Responsibility and Work Opportunity Reconciliation Act of 1996* reinforced entrenched bureaucratic behaviors.

Conclusion: The Past as Guide to Future

> Over the past three and a half years I have done everything in my power as President to promote work and responsibility, working with forty-one states to give them sixty-nine welfare reform experiments.
> – President Bill Clinton (Clinton 1996)

> The administration proposes to discontinue the few remaining state welfare reform waivers granted prior to the 1996 welfare reform legislation. Flexibility under current law allows states to accomplish all the purposes of TANF without waivers. *Furthermore, the requirements of TANF no longer represent an experiment.*
> – Bush Administration's Reauthorization Plan (Bush 2002, emphasis added)

Welfare reform was presented to the American public as a new partnership between states and the federal government to develop new approaches, best practices, and tools to reinvent welfare systems and help families move off the welfare rolls. Ideally, it was seen as an opportunity to build on past state practices. As the National Governors Association observed on the one-year anniversary of the *Personal Responsibility and Work Opportunity Reconciliation Act of 1996*: "the signing of the federal law one year ago merely accelerated changes that were already underway" (NGA 1997). However, the 1996 federal welfare reform law did not result in a fundamental restructuring of welfare systems across the nation, primarily because the new law did not provide states enough margin for trial and error. TANF's work participation requirements, time limits on eligibility, and fixed funding mechanism caused DHHR and many other state welfare bureaucracies across the nation to proceed cautiously in a risk-averse climate. In West Virginia, the initial optimism about welfare reform under a federal waiver gave way to an overriding concern about meeting federal work participation requirements. Although a fair portion of the blame for not reinventing itself into job training and employment centers must fall upon DHHR's shoulders, it had no control over the one-size-fits-all rules and regulations emanating from Washington D.C. It also lacked the authority to force DHHS to issue clarifying rules and regulations in a more expeditious manner, and it was not responsible for the weak labor markets that have plagued most of West Virginia for decades, making the task of meeting federal work participation rates so difficult to achieve. The clearest lesson that can be learned from West Virginia's welfare reform experience is that implementing change in an environment marked by lack of time, resources, and clarity is not conducive to forming a coherent and broad-based strategy of change. Instead, the institutional response is likely to be reactive, cautious, crisis-driven, and piecemeal and the programmatic outcomes are likely to be less than hoped for, and they are often at the expense of those among us who can least afford to be ill-served.

References

Barnow, Burt, Thomas Kaplan, and Robert Moffit, Editors. 2000. *Evaluating Comprehensive State Welfare Reform: The Wisconsin Works Program*. Albany, NY: Rockefeller Institute Press.

Blank, Rebecca and Ron Haskins, Editors. 2001. *The New World of Welfare*. Washington, D.C.: The Brookings Institution.

Breaux, David A., Christopher Duncan, C. Denise Keller, and John C. Morris. 2002. "Welfare Reform Mississippi Style: Temporary Assistance for Needy Families and the Search for Accountability." *Public Administration Review*. 62(1): 92-103.

Bush, President George W. 2002. *Working Toward Independence (Personal Responsibility and Work Opportunity Reconciliation Act Reauthorization Proposal)*. Washington, D.C. March.

Clinton, President Bill. 1996. "Remarks on Welfare Reform and an Exchange with Reporter, July 31, 1996," *Public Papers of the President of the United States: William J. Clinton, Book II*, 1233-1233. http://www.gpoaccess.gov/pubpapers/browse.html.

Crew, Robert E. and Belinda Creel Davis. 2000. "Florida Welfare

Reform: Cash Assistance as the Least Desirable Resource for Poor Families." *Managing Welfare Reform in Five States: The Challenge of Devolution.* ed. Sarah Liebschutz. Albany, NY: Rockefeller Institute Press.

Dilger, Robert Jay. 1989. *National Intergovernmental Programs.* Englewood Cliffs, NJ: Prentice Hall.

_____, Eleanor Blakely, Melissa Latimer, Barry Locke, Carson Mencken, L. Christopher Plein, Lucinda M. Potter, and David Williams. 2001. "WV WORKS: The Recipients Perspective." *The West Virginia Public Affairs Reporter* 18(3): 2-19.

Gais, Thomas, Richard Nathan, Irene Lurie, and Thomas Kaplan. 2001. "Implementation of the Personal Responsibility Act of 1996." *The New World of Welfare.* ed. Rebecca Blank and Ron Haskins, 35-69. Washington, D.C.: The Brookings Institution.

Goldstein, Amy and Juliet Eilperin. 2002. "House Clears GOP-Backed Welfare Bill." *Washington Post.* May 17, A01.

Haynes, V. Dion. 2002. "Welfare in Jeopardy as States Consider Cuts." *Charleston Gazette.* April 17, 5A.

Heclo, Hugh. 2001. "The Politics of Welfare Reform." *The New World of Welfare.* ed. Rebecca Blank and Ron Haskins, 169-200. Washington, D.C.: The Brookings Institution.

Kabler, Phil. 2002a. "'Best Evaluation Budget Ever,' Senator Boasts." *Charleston Gazette.* March 18, 1A, 7A.

_____. 2002b. "Deficit Forces Cuts in Welfare," *Charleston Gazette.* May 21, 1A, 11A.

Liebschutz, Sarah F., Editor. 2000. *Managing Welfare Reform in Five States: The Challenge of Devolution.* Albany, NY: Rockefeller Institute Press.

Mead, Lawrence. 2002. "Welfare Reform: The Institutional Dimension." *Focus* 22(1): 39-45.

Meier, Kenneth H. 1993. *Politics and the Bureaucracy.* 3rd Edition.

Belmont, CA: Wadsworth Press.

Meyers, Ken. 2000. "How Welfare Offices Undermine Welfare Reform." *American Prospect* (June 19-July 3): 40-45.

Miller, Dawn. 2002a. "Child-care Cuts Delayed, Cutoff Threshold Raised." *Charleston Gazette*. January 23, 1C.

_____. 2002b. "Nonprofits That Serve Poor Kids, Families Ask for Public Support." *Charleston Gazette*. March 8, 1C, 2C.

_____. 2002c. "Welfare Needs New Focus, Report Says." *Charleston Gazette*. May 3, 10A.

_____. 2000a. "State Urged to Use Extra Welfare Cash." *Charleston Gazette*. June 13, 1A, 9A.

_____. 2000b. "State Devises Job Projects for Low-Income Families." *Charleston Gazette*. June 14, 1C.

Miller, Tom. 2000. "Welfare Funds could be Forfeited." *Charleston Gazette*. June 20.

Nathan, Richard and Thomas Gais. 1999. *Implementing the Personal Responsibility Act of 1996: A First Look*. Albany, NY: Nelson A. Rockefeller Institute of Government.

Nathan, Richard and Fred C. Doolittle. 1987. *Reagan and the States*. Princeton, NJ: Princeton University Press.

National Governors Association. 2001. "HR-36 (HHS-21) Welfare Reform Policy." Policy Position. April 10. http://www.nga.org/nga/legislativeUpdate/1,1169,C_POLICY_POSITION^D_554,00.html.

_____. 1999a. "Letter to House Leadership and House Appropriations Committee Opposing TANF cuts included in the fiscal 2000 Labor–HHS Appropriations Bill." September 28. http:// www.nga.org/nga/legislativeUpdate/1,1169,C_LETTER%5ED_1575,00.html.

_____. 1999b. "Letters to House and Senate Chairmen and Ranking Members Opposing Cuts in TANF Block Grants." March 3. http://www.nga.org/nga/legislativeUpdate/1,1169,C_LETTER%5ED_1580,00.html

———. 1997. "Welfare Reform: Governors Mark Law's First Anniversary." *Governors' Bulletin*, Online Web Edition August 18, Vol. 31, No. 17. http://www.nga.org/welfare/WelfareDocs/bul-970818.htm (accessed on September 20, 1997; link no longer maintained). http://www.nga.org.

Ohl, Joan. 2000. "Department of Health and Human Resources FY 2001 Budget Presentation." Testimony before the Senate Finance Committee, February 1, 2000, and the House Finance Committee, February 10, 2000. Charleston, WV: West Virginia Department of Health and Human Resources.

Pear, Robert. 1999. "States Declining to Draw Billions in Welfare Money." *New York Times*. February 8, A1, A9.

Plein, L. Christopher. 2001a. "Welfare Reform in a Hard Place: The West Virginia Experience." *Rockefeller Report* No. 13. July. Albany, NY: Nelson A. Rockefeller Institute of Government.

———. 2001b. "The Use of Federal Rulemaking Process to Shape the Implementation of New Welfare Law." Paper presented at the 43rd Annual Meeting of the Western Social Science Association. Sparks, Nevada. April 19.

———. 1999. "The Administrative Burdens of Change: The Convergence of Multiple Paths of Reform." Paper presented at the Annual Meeting of the Association of Public Policy Analysis and Management. Washington, D.C. November.

Plein, L. Christopher and David G. Williams. 2000. "State Capacity Study: Second Round Study on TANF and Social Service Programs in West Virginia." Albany, NY: The Nelson A. Rockefeller Institute of Government.

———. 1997. *West Virginia's Welfare Reform Experience: First Report*. State Capacity Study. Albany, NY: The Nelson A. Rockefeller Institute of Government.

Reagan, Michael D. 1972. *The New Federalism*. New York: Oxford University Press.

Riccucci, Norma A. and Irene Lurie. 2001. "Employee Performance

Evaluation in Social Welfare Offices." *Review of Public Personnel Administration* 21(1): 27-37.

Robertson, David B. and Dennis R. Judd. 1989. *The Development of American Public Policy: The Structure of Policy Restraint.* Glenview Il: Scott, Foresman, and Company.

Roper, Richard. 1998. "A Shifting Landscape: Contracting for Welfare Services in New Jersey." *Rockefeller Reports.* December.

Rose, Richard. 1993. *Lesson Drawing in Public Policy.* Chatham, NJ: Chatham House Publishers.

Rosenbaum, David E. 2002. "States Make Cuts and Increase Fees as Revenues Drop." *New York Times.* May 16, A1, A20.

Sanford, Terry. 1967. *Storm Over the States.* New York: McGraw Hill.

"State Welfare Grant Program May Face Deficit in 2003." 2001. *Bluefield Daily Telegraph.* June 13. http://www.bdtonline.com/archives/

TANF Advisory Council. 2001. *Report and Recommendations.* Charleston, WV. December 7.

Tweedie, Jack. 2000. "From D.C. to Little Rock: Welfare Reform at Mid-term." *Publius: The Journal of Federalism* 30(1-2): 69-97.

Weir, Margaret, Ann Shola Orloff, and Theda Skocpol. 1988. "Introduction: Understanding American Social Politics." *The Politics of Social Policy in the United States.* ed. Margaret Weir, Ann Shola Orloff, and Tend Skocpol, 3-35. Princeton, NJ: Princeton University Press.

Weissert, Carol, Editor. 1999. *Learning from Leaders: Welfare Reform in Five Midwestern States.* Albany, NY: Rockefeller Institute Press.

West Virginia Department of Health and Human Resources (DHHR). 2001. *Annual TANF Report.* Presented to the Legislative Oversight Commission on Health and Human Resources Accountability. Charleston, West Virginia. June 10.

_____. 2000a. *WV WORKS, West Virginia's Welfare Reform Program,*

Annual Report. Charleston, WV: West Virginia Department of Health and Human Resources. October.

———. 2000b. "Welfare Reform Report, August 2000." Briefing materials provided to the Legislative Oversight Commission on Health and Human Resources Accountability. Charleston, WV: West Virginia Department of Health and Human Resources. August 21.

———. 1997. Information Packet on West Virginia Works. Charleston, WV: West Virginia Department of Health and Human Resources

———. 1996a. *State of West Virginia State Plan for Temporary Assistance for Needy Families, November 1996, Submitted to the U.S. Department of Health and Human Services.* Charleston, WV: West Virginia Department of Health and Human Resources.

———. 1996b. "WV Works Brief." Briefing Handout. Office of Family Support. Charleston, WV: West Virginia Department of Health and Human Resources.

———. 1996c. "West Virginia WORKS/Personal Responsibility and Work Opportunity Reconciliation Act Briefing Paper." Charleston, WV: Bureau for Children and Families. October 8.

WV Executive Budget for Fiscal Year 1999. 1998. Charleston, WV: Office of the Governor.

West Virginia State Legislature, Office of Legislative Auditor. 1997. *State of West Virginia Full Performance Evaluation of the Department of Health and Human Resources: Medicaid Eligibility, Eligibility Determination Error Rate.* Charleston, WV: Office of the Legislative Auditor. December.

West Virginia Roundtable, West Virginia Human Resources Association, West Virginia Rural Development Council. 1997. "It's Working in Wisconsin: What West Virginia Can Learn from Governor Tommy G. Thompson About Welfare Reform." Charleston, WV: West Virginia Rural

Chapter 5

Implementing Reform in West Virginia: The Evolution of Field Level Administration

L. CHRISTOPHER PLEIN

The *Personal Responsibility and Work Opportunity Reconciliation Act of 1996* was designed to modify the behavior of welfare recipients and administrators (Nathan and Gais 1999). One of the law's primary goals was to "reinvent" state and local welfare bureaucracies, reorienting them from a focus on determining eligibility and case management to moving recipients from the rolls and into employment. Indeed, the 1996 welfare reform law and subsequent amendments were part of an ongoing movement to make organizations more responsive to public desires by making them more entrepreneurial, more decentralized, and less rule bound. The reinvention movement was also seen in efforts to devolve federal program responsibilities to states (Portz et al. 1999; Breaux et al. 2002).

Welfare reform advocates recognized the importance of local implementation. They purposely sought to reform and reorganize welfare systems across the states. They knew that it would take a significant "culture change" in local welfare offices to create the local administrative systems necessary to place recipients into jobs. Indeed, the rule bound organizational cultures and income assistance-oriented organizational missions in place at that time were viewed as part of the problem rather than the solution to welfare reform. As a result, welfare reform was more than simply an effort to change recipient behavior; it was also a rallying cry for reinventing welfare systems across the nation.

Many observers have argued that the success or failure of welfare reform rests largely in the hands of those responsible for program implementation at the local/community level. Indeed, some observers, such as Nathan and Gais (1999) have stressed that "second order" devolution involving local administrative systems is just as important to understanding welfare reform as "first order" devolution involving the transfer of responsibilities from the federal to state governments. A number of researchers have examined the dynamics of welfare reform at the local level. Some have examined how state policy preferences are communicated and transferred to the local level. Others have examined the diversity of local system operations in the post-Aid to Families With Dependent Children (AFDC) era now that case management and job placement activities have been contracted out or privatized in many localities (Liebschutz 2000a). Others have studied the role front line workers and their embedded behaviors have on program implementation, noting how these behaviors can complicate program implementation by failing to accept, internalize, and practice new behaviors mandated by policy change (Lurie 2001; Tickamyer et al. 2000). Recent research has focused on whether local personnel evaluation systems match TANF's new program management goals. For example, Riccucci and Lurie (2001) argue that performance standards continue to be rooted in the more rule bound imperatives of the past, which emphasized minimizing error rates when reviewing applications and making eligibility determinations. More broadly, several scholars have emphasized the need to evaluate not only the outcomes but the administrative processes involved in welfare reform implementation (Nathan and Gais 1999; Boehnen and Corbett 2000).

This chapter examines how local welfare system practices in West Virginia evolved over time, focusing on the implementation of welfare reform from 1996 to 2002. It is argued that West Virginia's effort to reorganize and reform front line practices was less of a sustained effort to put into place a clear, well-conceived plan than it was a series of improvisations and adjustments driven by changing issues, events, and priorities. The analysis relies on research the author conducted as part of the Nelson A. Rockefeller Institute of Government's state capacity study, as well as personal interviews and interactions with the West Virginia Department of Health and Human Resources (DHHR). The research was augmented by data from the 1999 WV WORKS' leaver and 2000 WV WORKS' current recipient surveys conducted by West Virginia University's Interdisciplinary Research Task Force on Welfare Reform (Dilger et al. 2000; and Dilger et al. 2001).

Background:
Reorganization, Reform, and the West Virginia Context

State welfare systems have always varied. They vary even more now that the *Personal Responsibility and Work Opportunity Reconciliation Act of 1996* has been implemented. In general, welfare systems are either state-centered or shared systems. In state-centered systems, program direction emanates from the state capital, and program delivery is carried out by state agency field offices. In shared systems, the state makes policy and provides program direction and local governments are responsible for service delivery. In recent years, both state and local governments have relied increasingly on other organizations to carry out case management and job training activities through contracted arrangements. West Virginia is a state-centered system that has retained its core case management functions within its field offices.

Thirty-five states relied on state-centered systems immediately prior to the enactment of the 1996 welfare reform law (Liebschutz 2000b). The law led to substantial variation among these states. Some states viewed the new law and prior demonstration welfare-to-work programs as opportunities to overhaul and reorganize state level bureaucracies and field operations to emphasize job training and employment placement. For example, Wisconsin, New York, and Florida substantially reorganized or created new state agencies to manage their TANF programs. Wisconsin, which created a Department of Workforce Development from its Department of Health and Social Services and Department of Industry, Labor, and Human Relations, received considerable media and scholarly attention (Liebschutz 2000a). Other states, such as Mississippi, experimented with new forms of privatization and contracting, only to experience less than stellar results, primarily due to poor program design and weak accountability systems (Breaux et al. 2002). West Virginia was not quite as ambitious in its response to welfare reform. It decided to reform, but not radically, the fundamental structure of DHHR's bureaus and agencies.

West Virginia's current DHHR organizational structure reflects an ongoing series of reorganizations that have been underway since the 1970s. These changes culminated in 1995 when the system was redesigned in favor of a more coordinated approach to state, regional, and district management. At the state level, the Office of Income Maintenance and the Office of Work and Training were merged into a new Office of Family Support. The state was also organized into four regions, with a director assigned to each region. They were asked to improve communication and control between Charleston (the state capital) and DHHR's thirty-eight district level field offices. The position of Community Services Manager was established at the district level. They were asked to manage all of the services DHHR offered in that office. These included AFDC (later TANF/ WV WORKS), Medicaid, Food Stamps, and a vast array of social service programs, including child support enforcement, foster care placement, behavioral health referral, and various emergency and short-term public assistance programs.

WV WORKS (West Virginia's response to the new TANF program established by the *Personal Responsibility and Work Opportunity Reconciliation Act of 1996*) also combined income maintenance and work and training-staff functions into an integrated case manager position called the Family Support Specialist. At the district level, Family Support Supervisors oversaw TANF implementation. Those not receiving TANF benefits but eligible for Food Stamps, Medicaid, and other public assistance programs encountered a more fragmented income maintenance system staffed by economic support specialists and their supervisors. Figure 5.1 outlines the new positions organized under WV WORKS.

Implementing Reform in West Virginia

Office of Family Support Positions

Community Support Managers: Coordinate and supervise local district office activities, including TANF/WV WORKS, Medicaid, Food Stamps, and other social services.

Family Support Supervisor: Manages TANF/WV WORKS program at the local district level.

Family Support Specialist: TANF/WV WORKS case manager, responsible for eligibility determination, benefits administration, job and training counseling, etc.

Economic Support Supervisor: Manages inflow and application process in local offices for public assistance inquiries and supervises case management of Medicaid and Food Stamps for non-TANF recipients.

Economic Support Specialist: Under AFDC, managed eligibility and income maintenance functions. Under TANF/WV WORKS, provides case management for Food Stamps, Medicaid, and other benefits and services for non-TANF eligibles.

Source: L. Christopher Plein and David G. Williams. 1997. WEST VIRGINIA'S WELFARE REFORM EXPERIENCE: FIRST REPORT. Albany, NY: Nelson A. Rockefeller Institute of Government, State University of New York.

Figure 5.1: Key West Virginia Office of Family Support Positions

In devising its welfare-to-work program, West Virginia's reorganization was limited to redesigning welfare case management at the local level through its DHHR field offices. WV WORKS' designers felt that it was critical that organizational change be accompanied by a "cultural change" among front-line workers and managers. The idea was to reinvent local offices as employment centers. DHHR was inspired by efforts undertaken in other states to focus case management activities on job placement. West Virginia subsequently discovered that achieving this goal was not easy.

Local field offices were transformed, but they were not reinvented as employment centers. What is essential to understanding West Virginia's implementation story is that change did not come about through proactive design and planning. Instead, the transformation of front line offices in West Virginia was more a product of adaptation and adjustment to changing circumstances and policy priorities. In an administrative environment of shifting program needs and objectives, it is difficult, and perhaps not desirable, to sustain a long-term plan of organizational change. West Virginia's experience is a multifaceted story of program evolution marked by four distinct periods of development.

The Promise of Reform: 1996-1997

Prior to the *Personal Responsibility and Work Opportunity Reconciliation Act of 1996*, the U.S. Department of Health and Human Services' Administration on Children and Families devised and implemented procedures allowing states to experiment with welfare-to-work programs. With federal permission, states could diverge substantially from AFDC guidelines. These "waiver" programs allowed states to implement reform in a piecemeal fashion and to focus energies in those areas where conditions were most amenable to experimentation. This flexibility was critical to developing what was generally considered the model of welfare reform - Wisconsin's WORKS and WORKS2 programs (Barnow et al. 2000; Liebshutz 2000a).

West Virginia developed its WV WORKS program in anticipation of securing a federal waiver. However, passage of the 1996 welfare reform law derailed these plans. The state withdrew its waiver application and, instead, used WV WORKS as the template for TANF implementation. The new welfare law created many challenges for program implementation, but it did have two unintended benefits. First, it allowed the state to implement WV WORKS on a piecemeal basis until January 1998. Second, while negotiating for its waiver, federal officials pressured the state to engage in the "random assignment" of control and to target groups as a means of evaluating the demonstration program's efficacy. The new law absolved the state from this latter requirement.

West Virginia was very selective in choosing demonstration sites. Rather than dictating which district offices would be the first to experiment, DHHR invited district offices to apply for the honor of being selected as a demonstration site. Eighteen districts submitted applications, and six were chosen. Their selection created a sense of *elan* for those six districts (covering nine counties) during the first months of implementation. They were seen as pathfinders and leaders in the new welfare reform experiment. From their experiences, they were expected to share insights, best practices, and cautionary lessons for the other counties that would follow. Interviews with both state and local administrators conducted during the first months of WV WORKS' implementation revealed that they were both enthusiastic and excited about their pioneering roles (Plein and Williams 1997).

State administrators were convinced that "cultural change" in district offices was the key to creating an employment focus in local administration. Their strategy included: personnel reclassification, training programs aimed at reorienting front line staff attitudes toward employment placement, and allowing greater flexibility and discretion at the local level. Position reclassification resulted in the creation of a new cadre of Family Support Specialists to work exclusively with WV WORKS' recipients on a one-to-one basis. The new rhetoric of reinvention considered WV WORKS recipients "customers" whose personal Family Support Specialist would manage all their benefits and services. Instead of treating recipients as ongoing beneficiaries, Family Support Specialists were to encourage their "customers" to obtain employment. They were also encouraged to abandon the rule-bound mindset associated with AFDC eligibility and review requirements. The promise of flexibility meant that field office management could arrange office responsibilities as they saw fit and devise new approaches to case management and service provision. By helping individuals move off the rolls, Family Support Specialists were supposed to devote more time and attention to those remaining on the rolls who faced more difficult barriers and obstacles to self-sufficiency (Plein and Williams 1997).

In the months that followed, central and field level administrators pointed to a number of successes achieved in the demonstration counties. One district reinstituted the long-abandoned practice of home visits to welfare clients. This practice allowed the caseworker to better understand the conditions and circumstances families faced and to keep in touch with their clients. Another district, in order to bring the skills of different front line staff to bear on case management, created response teams of specialists to assist Family Support Supervisors in their work with TANF families. One district worked with local community service nonprofit organizations to establish a clothing pantry for WV WORKS recipients preparing for job interviews and employment. In late 1997, all districts were mandated to initiate the conversion to WV WORKS by January 1998. Staff from demonstration districts shared best practices and approaches to the new program at regional conferences and in visits to other districts (Plein and Williams 1997).

The demonstration program was not without controversy. Its emphasis on work activities and implementing new eligibility guidelines caused enrollments to drop dramatically. Between January and June 1997, welfare cases in West Virginia declined by 7,500. Approximately 50 percent of the decline occurred in the nine demonstration counties. More than 44 percent of the families on welfare in these counties left the rolls during this period, compared to 17 percent in the remaining forty-six counties (Miller 1997; Plein and Williams 1997). In some districts this rate was even higher. For example, in the DHHR district for Greenbrier, Monroe, and Pocahontas counties caseloads fell 55 percent in the first six months of 1997, and the Mercer County district caseload fell 51 percent (Plein and Williams 1997). Local field office managers believed that much of the decline was due AFDC recipients' reluctance to engage in structured work activities. As one local manager put it, when word came down that there would be a work requirement, "people were flinging themselves into employment" (Plein and Williams 1997).

However, much of the demonstration counties' caseload reductions resulted from families being forced off the rolls due to excessive income. Unlike AFDC, WV WORKS counted Supplemental Security Income (SSI) when determining eligibility. For example, in the first six months of 1997, caseloads in the Mercer district fell 51 percent. More than half (64%) of that reduction was due to the new SSI policy. In the Greenbrier-Monroe-Pocahontas district, the effect was not as great but still notable, with more than a third of the caseload decline attributed to the counting of SSI income in eligibility determination (Plein and Williams 1997). Throughout 1997, the practice of counting SSI income was carried out only in those districts that had converted to WV WORKS. Other districts continued to exempt SSI benefits when determining eligibility. This apparent "inequity" led to a class action lawsuit, claiming that those in demonstration counties were being treated unfairly. The lawsuit, however, did not proceed to trial and was dismissed on the grounds that all counties would soon convert to the new system (Plein and Williams 1997). In 1999, the state legislature ordered DHHR to repeal its SSI policy after judicial actions made it clear that the provision would not likely withstand a court challenge.

DHHR's enthusiasm for its new welfare program was not universally shared by other government actors. In late 1997, the West Virginia Office of the Legislative Auditor criticized WV WORKS. Among other things, the Legislative Auditor's Office found that instead of placing recipients in private sector jobs, WV WORKS relied heavily on subsidized and publicly-funded work activity programs, such as the Community Work Experience Program (CWEP), for placing welfare recipients in job activities (Office of Legislative Auditor 1997). DHHR had used CWEP for more limited forays into welfare-to-work efforts since the early 1980s. The Legislative Auditor's Office suggested that the DHHR was too dependent on these arrangements. A crucial question that emerged was whether they relied on these placements out of necessity or convenience. Some argued that the state's anemic economy and weak job market forced DHHR to focus on CWEP and other publicly-funded work activities. Others suggested that DHHR took the more familiar and easier route to job placement and failed to make a concerted effort to forge new partnerships with the private sector and other organizations because that route was more difficult and time consuming. These concerns returned in full force when WV WORKS was implemented statewide in 1998.

L. Christopher Plein

The Harsh Realities of Statewide Implementation: 1998-1999

The welfare reform demonstration "honeymoon period" came to an abrupt halt in early 1998. As the state implemented WV WORKS statewide it faced the daunting task of complying with federally-mandated work participation rates and keeping WV WORKS within budget. Financial constraints meant that the flexibility the six demonstration districts enjoyed could not be extended statewide. Fearing federal sanctions, DHHR abandoned the emphasis on job placement and the idea of making local district offices "employment centers" (see Chapter 4). Instead, it concentrated on caseload reduction. DHRR officials recognized that federal rules allowed states with caseload reductions of 25 percent or more to count that reduction as a credit against the federal work participation requirement. DHHR officials quickly realized that it would be easier to meet the federal work participation rate requirements by clearing individuals off the rolls and claiming the federal caseload reduction credit than to find individuals training and/or employment activities that counted toward the work participation rates. In the short run, the case-clearing strategy was cheaper, easier, and faster. For a state uncertain about its capabilities in employment placement, certain about the limited job prospects of a poor economy, and fearful of federal sanctions, case clearing became the foundation of program implementation in 1998 and much of 1999. West Virginia was not alone. Many other states also adopted this strategy (Nathan and Gais 1999; Tweedie 2000).

WV WORKS became a "work-first" program. Applicants were expected to work as soon as they were enrolled in the program. Lifetime eligibility was limited to sixty months, and very few exemptions to the sixty-month limit were granted. To keep enrollments as low as possible, front line administrators were encouraged to provide new applicants with short-term diversion payments, Food Stamps, and Medicaid instead of enrolling them in WV WORKS. If success was measured by organizational preferences, WV WORKS' first year of implementation was an unqualified success. WV WORKS caseloads fell swiftly and deeply. Caseloads dropped from 23,821 to 10,205 between January 1998 and January 1999 and continued to fall during the first quarter of 1999 (DHHR 2000).

Central to DHHR's case closure strategy was the requirement that all AFDC recipients be subject to redetermination. Because WV WORKS' eligibility requirements differed from AFDC's, all recipients had to be recertified before being enrolled in WV WORKS (see Chapter 4). DHHR effectively created a gate through which recipients had to pass to enroll in WV WORKS. The redetermination process provided front line workers in district level offices an opportunity to screen applicants and deliver the "hard line" on welfare. For example, one of the original demonstration districts required WV WORKS applicants to demonstrate that they had made ten job inquiries or contacts before they were allowed to enroll in the program (Plein and Williams 1997). This practice, and others like it, aided DHHR's overall effort to clear the rolls during the initial months of TANF's implementation.

As part of its reorganization process, DHHR created a two-tiered system for delivering health and human services. It spent considerable time and effort creating a new case management system for WV WORKS. It left intact the existing, more fragmented case management system for those not enrolled in WV WORKS but still receiving other benefits, such as Medicaid and Food Stamps. Separating WV WORKS case management from other public assistance programs enabled DHHR to steer individuals seeking public assistance from WV WORKS. When West Virginians entered a DHHR field office, they were often referred to several workers, making the enrollment process impersonal and daunting. In short, field level reorganization, aimed at putting a more "human face" on WV WORKS case management and client services improved WV WORKS case management, but also served to limit program enrollment and did little to improve the case management process for thousands of West Virginians seeking other types of public assistance, such as Medicaid and Food Stamps.

The creation of the two-tiered case management system also had the unintended consequence of creating a "disconnect" between government assistance programs and welfare leavers. Once they became separated from their Family Support Specialist, who typically alerted recipients to the existence of available support programs and helped them wade through the application process, many WV WORK leavers opted not to pursue other forms of government assistance, such as Medicaid and Food Stamps, even though they were eligible for assistance. This disconnect was reflected in the reduction in the number of West Virginians participating in Medicaid and other governmental assistance programs between 1997 and 1998. West Virginia's Medicaid enrollment, for example, fell 13 percent (Plein 2001b). Moreover, survey data from the 1999 WV WORKS' leavers study revealed that many leavers stopped participating in a number of governmental support programs, such as Food Stamps, even though they remained eligible for assistance (Dilger et al. 2000). For example, when they were on WV WORKS nearly all of the survey's respondents reported that they were enrolled in Medicaid and received Food Stamps. After they left, only 58 percent reported receiving Medicaid, and only 52 percent reported receiving Food Stamps (Dilger et al. 2000).

As mentioned earlier, WV WORKS was a "work-first" program. Recipients were informed that they were expected to work. But, as in many other states, "work-first" in West Virginia was a political term that did not always reflect reality. In 1998, only one-third (33%) of WV WORKS recipients were engaged in work activities, broadly defined to include both paid and unpaid employment. In 1999, only one in four (26%) WV WORKS recipients, one of the lowest work participation rates in the nation, were engaged in work activities (DHHS 1999, 2000).

West Virginia, and many other states, failed to meet the federal government's mandated work force participation rates. West Virginia escaped federal sanctions, as did all other states, by using the federal caseload reduction credit to meet the participation rate threshold. West Virginia's relatively poor job placement performance was, at least partially, due to its anemic economy. Most of the state, with notable exceptions, including the Eastern Panhandle, the Kanawha Valley, and the Morgantown area, suffered from high unemployment and weak job growth. As a result, front line administrators relied heavily on CWEP and Community Services Programs (CSP) to place recipients in work activities. Nearly half (49%) of all WV

WORKS' job placements in 1999 took place in these types of work activities, compared to 13 percent nationally (DHHS 2000; Plein 2001a). DHHR relied on CWEP and CSP because it was easier to utilize existing arrangements to meet the work requirements than to engage in the more labor-intensive process of prospecting for and cultivating new and existing relationships with the private sector.

Many scholars have noted that program implementation at the district level is critical to a program's success. For example, Lurie (2001) found that even when federal, state and local front line administrators were in full agreement with a policy's goals, there were often misunderstandings concerning programmatic details, rules, and regulations as well as gaps in administrative capacity that ultimately led to unintended consequences and/or failure to meet programmatic objectives. In West Virginia, misunderstandings and uncertainties concerning the precise meaning of federal rules and regulations (see Chapter 3) and the resulting concerns about being sanctioned for spending money inappropriately, led DHHR officials to proceed cautiously when spending money. This, coupled with a lack of administrative capacity at the local district level, led front line administrators to focus on clearing the rolls to meet the federal work requirements.

The West Virginia Legislative Auditor's Office noted the lack of administrative capacity in DHHR's field offices during its evaluation of DHHR's performance implementing WV WORKS. It noted that DHHR provided front line staff just a week, and sometimes less than a week, of specialized training to prepare them for their new responsibilities as job counselors. The Legislative Auditor's Office cited a Community Service Manager's contention that front line staff required at least two months of intense training to do their jobs well (Office of Legislative Auditor 1997). This lack of training, coupled with a weak job market in most districts, helps to explain why West Virginia's front line workers relied so heavily on CWEP and CSP for job placement.

Another part of the explanation for DHHR's decision to focus on case clearing and on CWEP and CSP for job placements was its difficulty with its new management information system, called RAPIDS. This computer program, designed to assist case managers in determining program eligibility and managing case information, was installed early in 1996. In most respects, RAPIDS was an excellent system for meeting AFDC's programmatic goals, which focused on determining program eligibility. Unfortunately, RAPIDS was not designed to accommodate the goals of the *Personal Responsibility and Work Opportunity Reconciliation Act of 1996*. RAPIDS could tell the front line worker if the person sitting in front of them was eligible for assistance, but it could not help them find the applicant a job or suggest the best course of action for that applicant to become job ready. As the system's limitations came to light, DHHR tried repeatedly to upgrade and update it. At one point, DHHR used three management information systems simultaneously (Plein and Williams 1997). The term "work around" became part of the everyday parlance of front line workers as new ways were developed to circumvent software barriers.

DHHR's implementation difficulties were not lost on welfare client groups and advocates. They were very critical of the Department, especially for focusing on case clearing which, they were convinced, was behind the Department's decision to count SSI income when determining program eligibility. Welfare advocates also pointed to anecdotal evidence suggesting that DHHR font-line workers were unduly harsh and insensitive to applicant needs. The authors' 1999 WV WORKS leaver study provided some support for this contention. The most frequent response to the open-ended question, "If there was one thing that you could change about WW WORKS, what would it be?" was the need to improve the sensitivity of DHHR employees (17% of the respondents). Another14 percent wanted DHHR to provide additional help finding employment (Dilger et al. 1999).

Correcting the Disconnects in Front Line Management and Administration: 1999-2001

After experiencing dramatic caseload reductions in 1998 and early 1999, WV WORKS' enrollment stabilized in 2000 and then began to increase. It was about this time, when enrollments had stopped declining, that DHHR officials realized there were now three welfare populations in West Virginia: those on WV WORKS, those in the process of leaving WV WORKS, and those at risk of being on WV WORKS. Politics, practical experience, and new regulatory arrangements converged to make DHHR more responsive to those leaving and off WV WORKS. In political terms, the legislature's reversal of DHHR's SSI policy, coupled with continued and mounting pressure from the state legislature and welfare advocacy groups to spend down the state's unspent "rainy day" TANF funds, spurred DHHR to become more responsive to client needs. Moreover, practical experience gained from the first year of implementation indicated that the benefits of focusing on case closure (avoiding federal sanctions) had come at a high price. Political support in the legislature was lacking. Various media outlets, led by the influential *Charleston Gazette*, provided additional coverage, much of it sympathetic, to the complaints welfare advocacy groups voiced, and it was becoming increasingly clear that DHHR's strategy was doing little to help, and perhaps was harming, the well-being of those who had left the rolls.

In 1999, the U.S. Department of Health and Human Services released regulations clarifying the meaning of various rules and regulations contained within the 1996 welfare reform law. These clarifications provided states additional flexibility in responding to the needs of both those still on and off TANF (see Chapter 4). This flexibility, combined with the political pressure the state legislature and welfare advocacy groups exerted and the fact that it was a gubernatorial election year, all worked to encourage DHHR to shift strategies and alter front line practices. Instead of focusing almost exclusively on WV WORKS recipients, DHHR provided greater attention to leavers and those currently off the rolls but at risk of returning. For example, in 2000, DHHR officials in Charleston asked district offices to increase efforts to enroll eligible children in Medicaid and the Children's Health Insurance Program (CHIP), facilitate the provision of supportive services to current recipients (ranging from vouchers and reimbursement for clothing, transportation, and professional and business license fees to referrals to job training and skills development programs), and provide transitional assistance to families leaving WV WORKS (Plein 2001b). While keeping families off WV WORKS was still a high priority, keeping those in need within the larger health and human services system was also emphasized.

DHHR also instituted a broad array of supportive services for those on WV WORKS and for former recipients whose family incomes were equal to or below 185 percent of the federal poverty level. Interviews with state level and field level personnel revealed that administrators were ahead of front line staff in promoting efforts to assist families. As one senior administrator explained, it was difficult for DHHR, as an organization, to adapt to the new flexibility allowed under federal TANF regulations. The organizational culture was traditionally rule bound and tended to conceptualize things as either "black or white" (Plein and Williams 2000). A district level manager noted that one of DHHR's continuing major challenges is to encourage front line workers to be more flexible and helpful when helping families apply for WV WORKS and other services and benefits (Plein 2001b).

The new emphasis on providing assistance to non-WV WORKS recipients was a critical development in implementing welfare reform in West Virginia. By 2001, DHHR had put into place an integrated application process for all public assistance programs, and RAPIDS had finally reached a point in its development that it was considered a help, as opposed to a hindrance, in assisting front line workers as they processed applications for Medicaid, Food Stamps, and other services. DHHR also provided front line workers additional training (Plein 2001b). Another important development was posting the Income Maintenance Manual, the bible of case management, on-line, and introducing e-mail communications between district management staff and policy specialists in Charleston. With information more readily available, local field office staff reported that they now felt more comfortable with case management (Plein 2001b).

To address the disconnect that often occurs when families leave WV WORKS, DHHR authorized front line workers to work with WV WORKS leavers for ninety days after they had officially left the rolls (Plein and Williams 2000). At least one district office practiced transitional case management for up to twelve months after a family left WV WORKS (Plein 2001b). By mid-2000, DHHR was making good progress in providing transitional Medicaid and Food Stamp benefits to those employed while on WV WORKS. The authors' 2000 WV WORKS' recipient survey revealed that 92 percent of recipients engaged in a work activity reported receiving Food Stamps, and 87 percent were enrolled in Medicaid (Dilger et al. 2001).

Some local offices also forged partnerships with community-based service providers and organizations to coordinate outreach and enrollment efforts for programs other than WV WORKS. These initiatives were funded from a variety of sources, including earmarked federal dollars, state TANF funds, and philanthropic gifts. Several of these initiatives were designed to increase enrollment in CHIP and Medicaid and were carried out in schools, hospitals, health clinics, and other community level venues. Other initiatives targeted at-risk populations. These initiatives included, additional job training and skill development programs, parenting classes, truancy diversion, after school programs, adolescent mentoring, and teen pregnancy prevention.

New priorities emanating from Charleston created new challenges for front line workers still becoming accustomed to their roles as employment counselors. However, despite the changes taking place, the authors' 2000 survey of WV WORKS recipients revealed that most WV WORKS recipients were satisfied with front line services. Approximately two-thirds (65%) reported that they were either satisfied or very satisfied with their overall experiences with their caseworker. And, more than half (56%) reported that they were satisfied or very satisfied with their overall experiences with their district office (Dilger et al. 2001). However, as Dilger notes in Chapter 9, those facing multiple employment barriers reported significantly less satisfaction with field operations and caseworker service. In a detailed analysis of the survey data, Dilger argues that the statistically significant differences discovered between the survey responses provided by recipients most at risk of not achieving economic self-sufficiency and other recipients suggest that DHHR's front line workers may have engaged in "creaming," where preference and attention was focused on recipients viewed as relatively easy to place in a work-related activity rather than on more "high-maintenance" recipients viewed as relatively difficult to place in a work-related activity and who require more case management.

DHHR's implementation of welfare reform was complicated by relatively high turnover rates among front line staff. Nearly one out of every five Family Support Specialists left DHHR during FY 1999. This high turnover rate, in the midst of significant programmatic change, resulted in a loss of institutional memory, a need for closer supervision, and the need for more training and orientation resources. DHHR subsequently provided front line staff relatively significant salary raises, which helped to reduce turnover. In January, 2000, DHHR reported a turnover rate of slightly more than 3 percent during the last five months of 1999 (DHHR 2000). Nevertheless, entry-level salaries remain quite low. For example, in 2001, an entry-level Economic Services Specialist earned $1,539 a month, or $18,468 annually, and the starting salary for a Family Support Specialist was $1,647 a month, or $19,764 annually. It is not beyond the realm of possibility that the clients applying for supportive services earn as much or more than the person processing their application. Recent interviews with field and state level staff revealed that the morale of front line workers is not high. The most commonly voiced concern is that state employees are ineligible for CHIP even though they would be eligible if employed outside of government (Plein 2001c).

DHHR's implementation of welfare reform was also complicated by varied workloads across the state. Although welfare reform caused the number of recipients to fall dramatically across the state, it also dramatically increased front line workers' responsibilities. Fewer recipients did not mean less work. Some district offices, particularly in the southern part of the state, which has a relatively weak economy, were nearly overwhelmed by their new responsibilities. By May 2000, the caseload differential across districts had grown substantially. At that time, the average caseload for Family Support Specialists ranged from a low of twenty-one WV WORKS cases to a high of 1,035 cases. The state did not anticipate this imbalance.

Table 5.1 illustrates the state's regional caseloads and caseload ratios per Family Support Specialist. When WV WORKS was developed, each district was allotted one Family Support Specialist for every 100 AFDC cases. Three years later, variations in caseloads

Implementing Reform in West Virginia

meant that some Family Support Specialists carried larger caseloads than others. As Table 5.1 indicates, by 2000 the caseload ratio varied considerably across districts. Such variation can have significant effects for individual district offices. For example, there is a stark difference between the two counties that traditionally have the highest caseloads - Kanawha County, a relatively prosperous county where the state capital is located, and McDowell County, which is located in the heart of the economically distressed southern coalfields. Kanawha County's ratio fell to 1:28 while McDowell County's ratio fell, but to only 1:65.

	Regional Caseloads (May 2000)		
	CASES	POPULATION	FSS/CASE RATIO
REGION I	2878	511,667	1:37
REGION II	4992	592,397	1:40
REGION III	1973	341,599	1:44
REGION IV	4151	362,648	1:50

Sources: Figures calculated by authors from county case load data prepared by the West Virginia Department of Health and Human Resources for legislative briefings and from county population statistics published in the **West Virginia Kids Count Data Book** (2000) derived from 1997 Census Bureau data. Each case represents about 2.5 individuals. Population refers to total regional population. Ratio data is determined by comparing family support specialist allocations to May 2000 data. We determined allocations by looking at 1997 AFDC/TANF average monthly case load data prepared by the West Virginia Department of Health and Human Resources. This table originally appeared in Christopher Plein and David G. Williams. 2000. **State Capacity Study: Second Round Study on TANF and Social Service Programs in West Virginia.** Albany, NY: Nelson A. Rockefeller Institute of Government, State University of New York.

Table 5.1: Regional Caseloads

L. Christopher Plein

Conclusion: The Remaining Challenges

West Virginia entered a new phase of welfare reform in January 2001 when Governor Robert Wise (D, 2001-2005) replaced Governor Cecil Underwood (R, 1997-2001). By June 2001, the tenor of this change was apparent when Paul Nusbaum, the new Secretary of Health and Human Resources, announced to the state legislature and public that West Virginia faced a TANF funding crisis. He blamed the crisis on the poor planning and practices of his predecessors. The Secretary predicted that if the state continued current policies and spending patterns it would face a $90 million deficit in its TANF program by FY 2003. The governor subsequently appointed a task force to address the projected shortfall and, in December 2001, it delivered its recommendations on cost cutting and program priorities. As detailed in Chapter 4, the task force recommended eliminating and/or reducing many programs and supportive services provided under TANF.

The latest phase of welfare reform in West Virginia is focused on the need for belt-tightening and service cutbacks at local offices. Approximately $20 million of the suggested reductions were aimed at support services developed for those leaving the welfare rolls or those who have left but are at risk of re-entering the rolls. More than $6.1 million in savings was to be achieved by reducing supportive service payments to WV WORKS leavers (TANF Advisory Council 2001).

Ironically, these funding reductions were announced as the national and state economy continued to weaken, and the demand for support services was increasing. WV WORKS' monthly caseload, which bottomed out at around 10,000 cases in late 1999, had slowly increased, ranging from 13,000 to 15,000 cases. Given the implementation difficulties encountered with 10,000 cases, welfare advocacy groups and others wondered what would happen to service levels now that WV WORKS' caseload was increasing. Ironically, given the reductions in support services and the continued uncertainties concerning West Virginia's economy, it is likely that the rolls may continue to experience increases, further exasperating WV WORKS' financial difficulties.

In May 2002, West Virginia's state legislature provided an additional $20 million in state funds to help cover the anticipated $90 million deficit. DHHR was asked to find innovative ways to deal with the remaining $70 million deficit problem. The Department had already announced that it would scale back supportive services provided to those on and off welfare. In a letter to the United States Department of Health and Human Services, DHHR announced that it planned to reduce supportive services, limit lifetime eligibility for certain supportive services, and tighten income eligibility guidelines for services (DHHR 2002). DHHR also created a "revamp committee," comprised of DHHR staff and welfare advocates, to find administrative efficiencies to help deal with the projected deficit. The committee issued a report in May 2002 that not only suggested ways to save money but also stressed the need to improve case management practices. The committee recommended additional training for case managers, smaller caseloads for front line workers, more follow-up activities with families that have left the rolls, and more effective means of granting extensions to families that exhaust their sixty-month eligibility limit (Miller 2002).

In 1997, the Director of the Office of Family Support described the relationship between DHHR's Charleston office and the district offices with an analogy regarding house building. She explained, "We [the state office] do the framework on the house, and they [the district offices] can decorate as necessary." Using another metaphor, she said that a "cookie-cutter" approach won't work when implementing the new welfare program in West Virginia. Instead, district offices needed to stay within the framework, but innovate and push the boundaries. In her expression, "we are in a box" made up of federal and state laws. The idea is to push the sides of the box as much as possible to successfully meet the law's objectives (Plein and Williams 1997).

A better metaphor for WV WORKS implementation is, "someone has moved the goal line." DHHR was unable to follow a sustained and planned path for reorganizing its field offices. Instead, new and changing demands and pressures from federal and state policymakers, advocacy groups, and clients forced the Department to adjust and adapt its strategies. Over time, the idea of reinventing field offices into employment centers evolved into the need to close cases as quickly as possible. The political and practical consequences of case closure then led to a reorientation toward more responsive district level operations aimed at assisting WV WORKS recipients, leavers, and those at risk of being enrolled in WV WORKS. More recently, budgetary constraints have forced DHHR to refocus again, concentrating its resources on those enrolled in WV WORKS.

West Virginia's experience with welfare reform reinforces the widely held belief that fundamental reform is often blunted by organizational problems encountered during program implementation as well as by factors that are largely outside of the organization's control (Lindblom 1979). DHHR's lack of administrative capacity (low salaries, high turnover, differential caseloads, etc.) contributed to its abandonment of its initial goal of reinventing local field offices as employment centers. However, federal rules and regulations, largely beyond DHHR's control, also played a role. The mandated work participation rates and the threat of federal sanctions (and the political fallout that would have occurred if DHHR were sanctioned) led DHHR to reconsider its initial strategy. Given the state's anemic economy, DHHR correctly reasoned that the most efficient means of avoiding federal sanctions was to focus on case closure and to use the federal case closure credit to meet the work requirements. Ironically, this was exactly what federal welfare reform advocates wanted to avoid. They wanted states to focus on job placement. DHHR's focus on case closure was also influenced by the federal government's delay in issuing rules and regulations that clarified nuances of the 1996 welfare reform law. Lacking any clear signals concerning what was allowed, DHHR took the conservative route when spending money. Finally, DHHR had little control over the slowdown in the national and state economies, which has exacerbated the Department's financial problems, forcing it to reduce its expenditures on supportive services for WV WORKS recipients and, especially, on those currently enrolled in the program.

References

Barnow, Burt S., Thomas Kaplan, and Robert A. Moffitt, Editors. 2000. *Evaluating Comprehensive State Welfare Reform: The Wisconsin Works Program.* Albany, NY: Rockefeller Institute Press.

Boehnen, Elisabeth and Thomas Corbett. 2000. "Process Analysis—The Neglected Child in Evaluations: The Wisconsin Works W-2 Case Study." *Evaluating Comprehensive State Welfare Reform: The Wisconsin Works Program*, 165–190. ed. Burt S. Barnow, Thomas Kaplan, and Robert A. Moffitt. Albany, NY: Rockefeller Institute Press.

Breaux, David A., Christopher Duncan, C. Denise Keller, and John C. Morris. 2002. "Welfare Reform, Mississippi Style: Temporary Assistance for Needy Families and the Search for Accountability." *Public Administration Review* 62(1): 92-103.

Dilger, Robert Jay, Eleanor Blakely, Melissa Latimer, Barry Locke, Carson Mencken, L. Christopher Plein, Lucinda M. Potter, and David Williams. 2001. "WV WORKS: The Recipients Perspective." *The West Virginia Public Affairs Reporter* 18(3): 2-19.

_____, Eleanor Blakely, Karen V.H. Dorton, Melissa Latimer, Barry Locke, Carson Mencken, L. Christopher Plein, Lucinda M. Potter, David Williams, and Dong Pil Yoon. 2000. "West Virginia Case Closure Study." *The West Virginia Public Affairs Reporter* 17(1): 2-15.

_____, Eleanor Blakely, Karen V.H. Dorton, Melissa Latimer, Barry Locke, Carson Mencken, L. Christopher Plein, Lucinda M. Potter, David Williams, and Dong Pil Yoon. 1999. *West Virginia Case Closure Study*. Presented to the West Virginia Department of Health and Human Resources. Charleston, West Virginia. December.

Liebschutz, Sarah F., Editor. 2000a. *Managing Welfare Reform in Five States: The Challenge of Devolution*, 1-24. Albany, NY: Rockefeller Institute Press.

_____, Sarah F. 2000b. "Public Opinion, Political Leadership, and Welfare Reform." *Managing Welfare Reform in Five States: The Challenge of Devolution*, 1-24. ed. Sarah F. Liebschutz. Albany, NY: Rockefeller Institute Press.

Lindblom, Charles. 1979. "Still Muddling, Not Yet Through." *Public Administration Review* 39(6): 527-531.

Lurie, Irene. 2001. "Changing Welfare Offices." *Welfare Reform & Beyond, Policy Brief No.* 9. Washington, D.C.: The Brookings Institution.

Miller, Dawn. 2002. "Welfare Needs New Focus, Report Says." *Charleston Gazette.* May 3, 10A.

_____. 1997. "Social Service Money Shortage Not as Big as Originally Predicted." *Charleston Gazette.* October 15, 7A.

Nathan, Richard and Thomas Gais. 1999. *Implementing the Personal Responsibility Act of 1996: A First Look.* Albany, NY: Nelson A. Rockefeller Institute of Government.

Plein, L. Christopher. 2001a. "Welfare Reform in a Hard Place: The West Virginia Experience." *Rockefeller Report No. 13.* November. Albany, NY: Nelson A. Rockefeller Institute of Government.

_____. 2001b. *Field Report Form: West Virginia Medicaid Take-Up and Welfare Reform State Capacity Study.* Albany, NY: Nelson A. Rockefeller Institute of Government.

_____. 2001c. "The Use of Federal Rulemaking Process to Shape the Implementation of New Welfare Law." Paper presented at the 43rd Annual Meeting of the Western Social Science Association. Sparks, NV. April 19.

Plein, L. Christopher and David G. Williams. 2000. "State Capacity Study: Second Round Study on TANF and Social Service Programs in West Virginia." State Capacity Study. Albany, NY: Nelson A. Rockefeller Institute of Government.

_____. 1997. *West Virginia's Welfare Reform Experience: First Report.* State Capacity Study. Albany, NY: Nelson A. Rockefeller Institute of Government.

Portz, John H., Matthew Reidy, and David Rochefort. 1999. "How Managed Care is Reinventing Medicaid and Other Health-Care Bureaucracies." *Public Administration Review* 59(5): 400-409.

Riccucci, Norma M. and Irene Lurie. 2001. "Employee Performance Evaluation in Social Welfare Offices." *Review of Public Personnel Administration* 21(1): 27-37.

TANF Advisory Council. 2001. *Report and Recommendations.* Charleston, West Virginia. December 7.

Tickamyer, Ann, et al. 2000. "Where all the Counties are Above Average: Top Down versus Bottom-Up Perspectives on Welfare Reform." Paper presented at the Rural Dimensions of Welfare Reform, a research conference on poverty, welfare, and food assistance. Washington, D.C. May 5.

Tweedie, Jack. 2000. "From DC to Little Rock: Welfare Reform at Mid-Stream." *Publius: The Journal of Federalism* 30(1-2): 69-97.

United States Department of Health and Human Services, Administration for Children and Families (DHHS). 2000. *Temporary Assistance for Needy Families (TANF) Program. Third Annual Report to Congress.* Washington, D.C.: Office of Planning, Research, and Evaluation. August.

United States Department of Health and Human Services, Administration for Children and Families (DHHS). 1999. *Temporary Assistance for Needy Families (TANF) Program. Second Annual Report to Congress.* Washington, D.C.: Office of Planning, Research, and Evaluation. August.

West Virginia Department of Health and Human Resources (DHHR). 2002. "Letter to David J. Lett Re: Revisions to the WV WORKS Program." March 7. http://www.wvdhhr.org/ofs (accessed March 2002; link no longer maintained).

_____. 2000. *WV WORKS, West Virginia's Welfare Reform Program: 2000 Annual Report.* Charleston, WV: West Virginia Department of Health and Human Resources. October.

West Virginia Office of Legislative Auditor. 1997. *West Virginia Works: Welfare Reform Pilot Program.* Special Report. Charleston, WV: West Virginia Office of Legislative Auditor.

Chapter 6

Welfare Reform's Consequences for West Virginia's Safety Net System

L. CHRISTOPHER PLEIN

As noted in previous chapters, welfare reform was enacted because it was believed that existing institutional arrangements and policy directions needed to be improved. Indeed, welfare reform's rallying cry was the system is broken (Nathan and Gais 1999; Tweedie 2000; Weaver 2000). Solutions were fashioned from popular ideas at hand: decentralization and delegation of program authority to states, expectations of citizen obligation and reciprocity manifested in welfare-to-work, paternalistic state arrangements to encourage moral behavior, and culture change in welfare bureaucracies to focus on outcomes and results rather than procedures and protocols (Mead 1997; Nathan and Gais 1999; Heclo 2001). In the 1990s, the momentum of reform reached beyond welfare to include other programs making up the social policy safety net. The *Personal Responsibility and Work Opportunity Reconciliation Act of 1996* not only altered cash assistance by replacing Aid to Families with Dependent Children (AFDC) with Temporary Assistance for Needy Families (TANF), it also reformed Food Stamps and Supplemental Security Income (SSI). Throughout the decade, Medicaid was reformed in the hope of making the program more cost effective while, at the same time, extending healthcare insurance to new target populations (Plein 1999). Taken as a whole, all of these reforms were part of a general movement to "reinvent government" that offered change by adjusting intergovernmental relations, revising program purposes, and reconsidering government's role in providing and delivering public goods and services (Melnick 1994; Mead 1997; Plein 1999; Portz et al. 1999; Weaver 2000).

While this book focuses on welfare reform's effect on West Virginia, reform was afoot in other areas of social policy as well. Although cash assistance programs serve fewer people than some other safety net programs, such as Food Stamps and Medicaid, reforming welfare systems and practices had significant effects on these other programs. The story of welfare reform is, in large part, about health and human service systems adapting and adjusting to change. For example, across the nation, and in West Virginia, changes in front line management practices during TANF's initial implementation contributed to declining enrollment among those eligible for Food Stamps and Medicaid (U.S. General Accounting Office [GAO] 1999a, 1999b; Thompson and Gais 2000). Recognizing this trend, compensatory efforts were undertaken to connect and reconnect eligible families to these programs. Federal authorities encouraged states to step-up Medicaid enrollment efforts by allowing more flexibility in eligibility procedures and providing additional funds for outreach. New federal policies and procedures were developed to do the same for Food Stamps (Thompson and Gais 2000; Fossett et al. 2001; Thompson 2003).

This chapter explores West Virginia's safety net system of health and human services during a time of reform, focusing on three essential programs: Food Stamps, Medicaid, and SSI. Welfare reform's implementation affected all three programs, disturbing existing program arrangements and prompting the state to take corrective action. At the same time, each program was subject to its own reforms, which also altered policy and priorities. Yet, within this dynamic, the safety net system has proven to be resilient. Decades of development and use have contributed to sustained participation in the programs by those eligible for their services.

Welfare Reform's Consequences

Food Stamps, the Personal Responsibility and Work Opportunity Reconciliation Act, and the Consequences of Reform

> This, for example, is how one reporter saw the independent yeomanry, the family farmers, and the laid-off industrial workers in the Appalachians: 'Whole communities are precariously held together by a flour-and-dried-milk paste of surplus goods. The school lunch program provides many children with their only decent meals. Relief has become a way of life for a once proud and aggressively independent mountain people. The men who are no longer needed in the mines and the farmers who cannot compete with the mechanized agriculture of the Midwest have themselves become surplus commodities in the mountains.'
>
> – Michael Harrington (1962, 45)

Although the above quotation from Michael Harrington's *The Other America* is more than forty years old, it remains relevant to a discussion concerning the Food Stamp program's legacy in West Virginia. Harrington and others helped to put the needs of the rural poor in bold relief as the decade of the 1960s got underway. The specter of rural poverty gained considerable attention at this time, especially as it existed in Appalachia. Although the paradoxes and contradictions of rural poverty and dependency were sometimes overdrawn by references to cultural archetypes rooted more in myth than reality – images of a self-sufficient yeomanry and independent mountaineers immediately come to mind – attention to the matter helped to raise awareness that resulted in policy change. West Virginia figured prominently in these depictions (Harrington 1962; Tunley 1960). Responding to this portrait of poverty and delivering on campaign and presidential promises that he had made in West Virginia and elsewhere, President John F. Kennedy (D, 1961-63) set into motion a series of programs aimed at assisting the poor. One of these was the Food Stamp program. Acting on previous legislative efforts to advance Food Stamp program development, President Kennedy assigned the U.S. Department of Agriculture (USDA) the task of launching a pilot program (Finegold 1988). West Virginia was the initial demonstration site. In 1961, the first food stamps were distributed in McDowell County (West Virginia Department of Health and Human Services [DHHR] 2002a). Three years later, the program was formally set into law by the *Food Stamp Act of 1964*.

The West Virginia experience reveals how Food Stamps evolved over time to reach more and more people. Through the 1960s and 1970s, Food Stamp enrollment increased significantly. A number of factors account for this growth. First, the program's design provided choices for clients, an important difference from the commodity programs that preceded Food Stamps. Only a limited range of staples were provided under the commodities programs (Chafin and Sherwood 1994). In the 1970s, important steps were taken to reduce the transaction costs associated with program participation. In 1970, West Virginia became the first state to mail food stamps to recipients rather than requiring in-person visits to local welfare offices to pick up coupon allotments (Mabin 1999). The decade also saw the elimination of the "purchase requirement," which created a barrier to participation by imposing what was essentially a matching contribution on recipients (Finegold 1988). Under this arrangement, participating households had to pay 30 percent of their monthly net income to receive a month's worth of Food Stamps (Melnick 1994). According to state administrators, eliminating the purchase requirement did more than anything else to expand Food Stamp participation in West Virginia (Plein 2002a). Another important development was the adoption of practices that adjusted food stamp allotments to reflect for changes in inflation. Previously, the relative value of Food Stamps declined to such a degree that many receiving limited allotments opted to forego the benefit (Plein 2002a). During the late 1980s and early 1990s, federal reforms broadened participation by easing eligibility requirements and increasing benefits (Melnick 1994).

Because the Food Stamp program's reach is so extensive, it forms the backbone of state health and human service arrangements for low-income assistance programs and influences the structure and character of front line practices. Because a large number of those encountering the welfare system do so because they are seeking or receiving food stamps, administrative arrangements are shaped to accommodate this source of demand. Further strengthening the program's influence are federal regulations for eligibility determination and case management that are seen as more stringent than those associated with other programs, such as Medicaid and TANF (Plein 2002a). In practical terms, this means that application forms, front line procedures, and case management practices for programs, such as Medicaid and WV WORKS, must take into account Food Stamp regulations and requirements. Other states have also noted the influence the rule-bound Food Stamp program has on health and human services systems (Riccucci and Lurie 2001; Fossett and Gais 2002; Wiseman 2002).

States operate Food Stamp programs amidst conflicting policy signals. On one hand, states are encouraged to maximize program participation. Indeed, the USDA regularly conducts and commissions studies to gauge state performance in this regard. On the other hand, states have traditionally been under significant pressure to limit eligibility determination errors (Fossett et al. 2001). This discouraged states from promoting application and enrollment among those who are on the periphery or margins of income eligibility. Eligibility determination errors result when the state provides either too much or too little benefit amounts to enrolled recipients. Until recently, the practice was to peg performance to a benchmark - the median measure of state error rates. By using the median, the federal government guaranteed that in any single year one-half of the states were out of compliance.

In 2002, federal legislation changed error rate practices. While preserving the method of determining the error rate, a more permissive approach has been taken that minimizes the chances of federal sanction. States are allowed a greater margin of error, and penalties are to be applied only after two years of poor performance (USDA 2002a). This new policy is viewed as crucial to improving administrative practices that focus on providing rather than withholding Food Stamp benefits. These steps are aimed at correcting an old system of error rate determination that increasingly was viewed as counterproductive. As Dean and Rosenbaum noted (2002, 75), the error rate regime created a situation where "the Food Stamp quality control system exerted an inappropriate influence on state policy," and resulted in increased paperwork for families applying for benefits as well as short redetermination cycles that required frequent Food Stamp reapplication. In Dean and Rosenbaum's (2002, 75) view, "These policies appeared to have significantly reduced Food Stamp participation, especially among the working poor."

Although administrators perceive the Food Stamp program to be complex and rule-bound, it has grown into the first line of assistance for those requiring public aid. This is because Food Stamp income eligibility thresholds tend to be more permissive than other programs, allowing many low-income families and individuals to qualify for benefits. Benefit amounts vary according to family size and income, thus providing a primary source to cover food expenses or a useful supplement to the household budget. Nationwide, Food Stamp enrollment crested in March 1994 at 28 million and then began to decline. A combination of factors, including a better economy, changes in eligibility requirements, and TANF reform's effect in contributing to families exiting the health and human resources system, contributed to the downward trend (USDA 2003). By July 2000, the number of people receiving Food Stamps fell to 16.9 million (USDA 2002a). Starting in 2000, the caseload began to grow once again. By FY 2002, monthly average enrollment was approximately 19 million individuals (Schrim and Castner 2002a).

West Virginia's Food Stamp enrollment trends share both similarities and differences with national enrollment patterns. During the mid-1990s, approximately 300,000 West Virginians (17 percent of the state's population) were enrolled in the Food Stamp program in any one month (Plein 2002a). In state FY 1994, Food Stamp enrollment crested at approximately 327,000 individuals per month. In state FY 1997, on the eve of WV WORKS implementation, Food Stamp enrollment fell to approximately 272,000 cases per month. By 1999, average monthly enrollments had fallen to around 225,000 (DHHR 2003a). Between federal FY 1994 and 1999, West Virginia's Food Stamp enrollment fell 23 percent, compared to 33 percent nationally (U.S. Department of Health and Human Services

[DHHS] 2002a). By 2002, West Virginia's average monthly Food Stamp enrollment stood at approximately 227,000 individuals per month (13 percent of the state's population).

Welfare Reform and Food Stamps

> The reasons that lie behind a change in Food Stamp participation hold implications for the well-being of low-income families and the success of welfare policies.
> – USDA (2001, 1)

Declining Food Stamp enrollment coincided with welfare reform. Many policymakers, practitioners, and welfare advocacy groups viewed the relationship between declining Food Stamp enrollment and falling welfare enrollment as a cause for concern. Early critics of federal welfare reform warned that TANF's tougher program requirements would lead to families becoming disconnected from the social welfare safety net (Edelman 1997). For example, they argued that families leaving the welfare rolls might not be aware, might be reluctant, or might be dissuaded from applying for other benefits, such as Food Stamps. These possibilities became the focus of numerous studies and analyses (GAO 1999a, 2001; Thompson and Gais 2000; Czajka et al. 2001; USDA 2001; Wiseman 2002). One study noted that up to 60 percent of the decline in the Food Stamp program enrollment nationwide consisted of those recently leaving the welfare rolls (GAO 2002a). The USDA (2001) found that 56 percent of the total caseload decline occurred among those who were eligible but not participating in the program. Their study cited three reasons for a lack of participation in the program: 1) welfare implementation may have created barriers to participation due to new TANF application and front line practices, 2) a lack of understanding about new program rules leading to a perception among qualified individuals that they were no longer eligible for Food Stamps, and 3) personal decisions among those eligible to leave the program for reasons ranging from optimism regarding their employment prospects to concerns associated with the stigma of receiving the benefit (USDA 2001). With all of these factors, health and human resource systems can play a role in either exacerbating enrollment declines or promoting participation.

The participation rate, a measure of those *eligible* for Food Stamps who are actually *enrolled* in the program, has become important in gauging state program performance in an age of welfare reform. The nationwide decline in participation during the late 1990s suggested that TANF was having a negative effect on Food Stamp participation rates. Between 1994 and 1998, the participation rate among those eligible for the program fell from 71 to 59 percent. Since 1998, it has held steady at approximately 60 percent (Schrim and Castner 2002a, 2002b). In West Virginia, which has traditionally experienced very high participation rates, the decline in participation over time has not been as great. Between 1994 and 1997, the participation rate remained constant at approximately 90 percent. Between 1998 and 2000 the rate remained steady at approximately 83 to 89 percent (Schrim and Castner 2002a, 2002b). Faced with a declining participation rate at the national level, policymakers and administrators at the federal level have encouraged improved state performance in outreach and enrollment to correct the apparent disconnects that occurred with TANF implementation.

Aggregate statistics do not tell the whole story in understanding the effects of WV WORKS' implementation on the Food Stamp program in West Virginia. Initial implementation of welfare reform created considerable disruption and confusion in client-system relations (Plein 2001a; Dilger et al. 2000). From 1998 to 2000, TANF caseloads fell dramatically. Although it is difficult to ascertain the effect this had on other programs, it is safe to say that it had consequences for Food Stamp enrollment. For example, program administrators acknowledge that implementation of the state's TANF program in 1998 likely led to a decline in West Virginia's Food Stamp rolls (Plein 2002a). Surveys conducted in 1999 and 2000 within West Virginia also supported this conclusion (Dilger et al. 1999b, 2000, 2001). A survey of West Virginians who left TANF in 1998 indicated that only 52 percent of them were receiving Food Stamps when surveyed in the summer of 1999. Also, approximately 43 percent reported that their families had experienced circumstances when they could not afford to buy food since leaving the welfare rolls (Dilger et al. 1999b). Given that the survey found that approximately

83 percent of the respondents reported household income of $10,000 or less during 1998, many, no doubt, were still eligible for Food Stamps (Dilger et al 1999b).

At the national level, many analyses and studies suggested that one of welfare reform's greatest dangers was that individuals leaving the rolls would either have their Food Stamp benefits reduced, or they would be severed from the program even though they remained otherwise eligible. There was concern that this would impose hardship on these families and might also hasten their return to the welfare rolls (GAO 1999a). In West Virginia, the difficulties encountered when leaving welfare are revealed in responses to a survey of those who had spent time off the rolls, but returned to WV WORKS (Dilger et al. 2000). Some of their open-ended responses to questions show concerns and confusion associated with new program arrangements. When asked what policy changes DHHR should make, one TANF recipient commented, "Do not cut people totally off when they first start working, sometimes things do not work out or other things happen. You feel like a high wire act working without a safety net." Another commented, "After you get a job, they shouldn't take your Medicaid, Food Stamps, and your checks, right away. [They should] let you keep them for a few months until you have some money saved up. As soon as you tell them you have a job they want to take everything." Yet another said, "Don't take your Food Stamps immediately after you get a job because you have a job and still you're not able to buy food" (Dilger et al. 2000).

The *Personal Responsibility and Work Opportunity Reconciliation Act of 1996* not only disturbed the Food Stamp program by helping to alter front line management of welfare systems, it also changed the program by imposing a work requirement on "able-bodied" adults without children under the age of eighteen as a condition for receiving Food Stamps. Although the work requirements under the Food Stamp reforms were more flexible and lenient than those under TANF, the potential consequences were significant for adults without dependents. It limited receipt of Food Stamps to those not engaged in work to three months in any thirty-six month period. However, provisions allowing the requirement to be waived due to poor economic conditions blunted this policy's effect. By March 2000, approximately 45 percent of those who would otherwise be required to work resided in waived areas (Czajka et al. 2001).

West Virginia has been relatively untouched by the Food Stamp work requirement. The state received waivers for most of its counties due to chronically high unemployment or insufficient jobs. In 1997, the USDA allowed waivers in forty-eight of the state's fifty-five counties. In 1998, thirty-seven counties were granted waivers. In 2002, the same number of counties received waivers, three because of high unemployment and the remainder for insufficient jobs (USDA 2002c). According to an analysis conducted for the USDA's Food and Nutrition Service, 87 percent of those "able-bodied" adults in West Virginia who would otherwise be subject to the work requirement were waived from participation. Only 967 able-bodied recipients lived in non-waived areas of West Virginia and were subject to work requirements (Czajka et al 2001). Because of this, the state has invested relatively few administrative resources in the Food Stamp work program. As of October 2002, only eighteen case workers were assigned to this function in the entire state (Plein 2002a).

Food Stamp Case Management in the Reform Era

> According to their charts I make too much in one area but am just above poverty level on another. Yet they cut off my Food Stamps over a hundred and some dollars. I have rent and utilities to pay, car in[surance] so I can work, gas and normal living expenses and they expect me to buy groceries too.
>
> – WV WORKS Recipient
> (Dilger et al. 2000)

The transition from AFDC to TANF had a significant effect on the state's Food Stamp program arrangements. In West Virginia, as in most other states, the same agency administers welfare and Food Stamps. When the Bureau for Children and Families reorganized front line practices as part of WV WORKS' program implementation, eligibility determination and case management procedures changed not only for cash assistance programs but for other programs, such as Food Stamps. Food Stamp administration would henceforth distinguish between those receiving and those not receiving cash assistance. Caseworkers, now called Family Support Specialists, were assigned to specific WV WORKS families. Each family's caseworker was responsible for administering and coordinating all benefits, such as Medicaid and Food Stamps, for which the family was qualified. For those families outside of the TANF system, benefit and case management arrangements proceeded much as before. A corps of income maintenance workers would be responsible for processing applications, determining benefits, and case management for non-TANF benefits and services (Plein 2001a, see also Chapters 4 and 5). Those subject to work requirements under Food Stamps would also be assigned to Food Stamp Employment and Training workers once those in an "assistance group" were deemed eligible for Food Stamps and determined to be required to work for the food stamp benefit. As already noted, this is a little used provision given that so many are exempted from the requirement.

Two problems quickly became apparent during WV WORKS' implementation. First, DHHR's attempt to clear the welfare rolls by using diversion tactics resulted in an obvious disconnect with the Food Stamp program for those who left TANF. These initial diversion tactics focused on dissuading and discouraging application for cash assistance under the new WV WORKS system, not referring individuals to alternative sources of support, such as Food Stamps. Second, there was a lack of case management coordination for families leaving WV WORKS as they secured other sources of income, such as from employment. By early 2000, the state attempted to correct these problems by providing more supportive diversion arrangements, including referral to the Food Stamp program, and by providing transitional case management supports for those leaving the rolls. In addition, West Virginia took advantage of new federal guidelines allowing more state discretion and flexibility in program administration.

Like most other states, West Virginia used federal options and waivers that minimized administrative burdens associated with eligibility determination and redetermination. Developed in response to concerns about declining enrollment in the wake of welfare reform, these policies were designed to ease administrative burdens for both clients and the state. Included among the new provisions was a longer period between initial determination and redetermination of client eligibility. It is now common for a year to pass before a redetermination is required. New regulations also allow clients to inform caseworkers about changes in their income or family status by telephone rather than in face-to-face interviews (Plein 2002a). In a comparative sense, a review of recent national level analyses suggests that West Virginia is more "liberal" than other states in extending coverage and in minimizing the effects of sanctions on Food Stamp recipients (Gabor and Botsko 1998; Schirm and Castner 2002b; GAO 2002a).

Apart from the disruptive effects of WV WORKS' implementation in the late 1990s, West Virginia has maintained relatively high participation rates in its Food Stamp program without relying, as other states have, on any concerted outreach or promotional campaigns to increase numbers. There is little incentive to do so when the difference between those eligible and those participating is so small (Plein 2002a). There are several reasons why West Virginia has been able to maintain its historically high participation rates. For example, there is a broad social awareness and acceptance of the Food Stamp program within the state. Approximately 13 percent of the state's population is enrolled in the program at any one time, creating a relatively high level of informal communication and education about the availability of Food Stamp benefits. The incremental and piecemeal changes and developments in the state's administration of the Food Stamp program also have lowered the transaction costs involved in application and enrollment. Steps taken long ago, such as eliminating the purchasing requirement and allowing Food Stamp coupons to be mailed to recipients, helped shape the program's development. More recent steps, such as longer redetermination cycles and more permissive criteria for the "categorically" eligible, such as those receiving SSI, have also contributed to these high participation rates.

Welfare Reform's Consequences

Medicaid in West Virginia: Revisiting Purposes in a Time of Reform

A number of significant policy decisions were made by state officials and the West Virginia Legislature over the past several years resulting in significant growth in the State's Medicaid program. State Policy during this period has resulted in increased access to health care services for large numbers of West Virginians and a shifting of costs to the federal government in order to increase available financing for public services in the areas of health, social services, and education.

– West Virginia Governor's Cabinet for Children and Families (Heasley 1995, 3)

Government did not undertake the provision of health care to the poor in order to benefit health-care providers any more than government builds roads to benefit contractors.

– West Virginia Governor's Commission on Fair Taxation (quoted in Nyden 1998)

Since the 1960s, Medicaid has been crucial to improving health care access and quality in West Virginia. By leveraging Medicaid dollars through a generous three-to-one federal-state match, West Virginia has been able to expand health coverage to the medically needy and the working poor, compensate hospitals that serve a disproportionate share of indigent cases, and help sustain rural clinics and public health departments. In short, Medicaid has helped to build the state's health care infrastructure (Plein 1998, 2000). As the previous quotations illustrate, this capacity-building function has been viewed from different perspectives. Clashing views on program expansion and cost containment have shaped Medicaid policy debates for decades. Recently, Medicaid reform efforts have sought to address these goals simultaneously. And, as these reforms have been pursued, West Virginia's health and human resource system has had to adjust not only to these changes, but to welfare reform's spillover effects as well.

Medicaid is not simply a program for those on welfare. It covers many working families with children. In the 1980s, coverage was extended to many pregnant women through more lenient economic criteria. In addition, the program provided a safety net for those with catastrophic illness and for the elderly who exhaust financial resources while in long-term care. In short, by moving beyond a welfare program, state health and human services have had to adjust to new populations, program demands, and methods of providing enrollment and outreach for the many different individuals who may qualify for Medicaid (Selden et al. 1998; Ku et al. 2000; Lykens and Jargowsky 2002; Plein 2002b). In any one month, Medicaid covers between 15 and 16 percent of West Virginia's population. In 1997, on the eve of welfare reform, Medicaid enrollment stood, on average, at 298,386 individuals per month. In state FY 2000, average monthly enrollment had fallen to 269,246, and by 2002, it had grown to 294,661 (DHHR 2003b).

Medicaid serves many eligibility groups. In addition to its traditional "cash assistance" base, Medicaid beneficiaries include those receiving SSI, children and pregnant women who qualify under expanded income eligibility guidelines, those designated as medically needy, and many of the elderly who rely solely, or in part, on Medicaid benefits to cover long-term care and other health-related costs.

Medicaid is especially important to the state's children. Between 1988 and 1994, Medicaid covered 49.9 percent of the births in West Virginia (West Virginia Office of Maternal and Child Health 1996). Since the advent of welfare reform, with some exceptions, there has been relatively little slippage in child enrollment in Medicaid. Benefits continue to be widely provided to those who qualify under expanded income eligibility guidelines for low-income children and pregnant women. In 2001, Medicaid provided insurance coverage to approximately 26 percent of West Virginia's children. The more recently adopted Child Health Insurance Program (CHIP) extends insurance coverage to an additional 4.4 percent of the state's children (Richardson et al. 2002a). Recent estimates suggest that children now comprise approximately 50 percent of the Medicaid enrollment base (Atkins 2002).

Indirectly, Medicaid serves thousands more West Virginians because program dollars have helped build the state's health care delivery system and infrastructure. By compensating charity care and providing some of the financial underpinning of local health departments and rural clinics, Medicaid extends support to the uninsured. This is important because relatively few able-bodied, low-income working age adults in West Virginia qualify for Medicaid. This, along with a poor insurance market, means that a significant portion of West Virginians aged 18 through 64 lack health insurance. A recent study found that approximately 20 percent of non-elderly adults in West Virginia lack health insurance. For those with income levels 200 percent or below the federal poverty level, this rises to 53.1 percent – much higher than the 34.4 percent national average (Richardson et al. 2002b). These figures confirm a long-term trend in lack of insurance coverage for low-income families (see Chapter 2 for further details).

In West Virginia, two bureaus within the Department of Health and Human Resources (DHHR) share Medicaid program management. The Bureau for Medical Services is responsible for establishing the state's Medicaid plan, which outlines covered services, eligibility criteria, and reimbursement rates for health care providers. The Bureau for Children and Families is responsible for eligibility determinations, enrollment, and many aspects of case management. In recent years, some case management functions have been shared with a private contractor responsible for implementing a Medicaid managed care program for some TANF recipients (Plein 1998; Plein 2000). In more simple terms, the Bureau for Children and Families is primarily responsible for dealing with those individuals and families Medicaid covers. The Bureau for Medical Services is primarily responsible for dealing with health care providers and others who provide Medicaid services.

For the past decade, DHHR has had to cope with a series of reforms aimed at both reducing program costs and expanding coverage to new target populations. Cost-cutting priorities are reflected in laws and regulations that restrict state discretion in shifting non-medical service costs to Medicaid, allow states to lower reimbursement rates for long-term care, and provide states greater flexibility to devise managed care and non-institutional care for various Medicaid populations. The desire to extend coverage is reflected in policies that preserve expanded eligibility criteria for the working poor and in the development of the Children's Health Insurance Block grant. This gives states the option of providing health insurance coverage to children in low-income families that would not otherwise qualify for Medicaid. The conflicted nature of cost-containment and program expansion was perhaps best epitomized in the passage of the *Balanced Budget Act of 1997*, which in many ways was to Medicaid what the *Personal Responsibility and Work Opportunity Reconciliation Act of 1996* was to welfare. As noted at the time, this major program overhaul contained objectives to both cut spending and expand coverage (Schneider 1997). As in the case of welfare reform, Medicaid reform prompted significant attention in academic and policy circles (Fossett et al. 2000; Hackey and Rochefort 2001; Lykens and Jargowsky 2002). While adjusting to these changes, administrators also had to contend with the effects welfare reform had on the Medicaid system.

Welfare Reform and Medicaid

> Moreover, recent reports of welfare and Medicaid enrollment declines have raised questions about the unintended consequences of welfare reform for Medicaid and the viability of the federal and state protections to ensure continued Medicaid eligibility for low-income families and children.
> – U.S. General Accounting Office (1999b, 1)

> I really need a medical card [Medicaid] so I can get some [relief] from the pain my body endures from working as a waitress, because being a cashier I could not get enough hours to make it. So, I had to become a waitress also.
> – Former West Virginia AFDC/TANF Recipient (Dilger et al. 1999b)

The 1996 welfare reforms raised questions about how changes in cash assistance programs might affect Medicaid enrollment. Under the old law, AFDC eligibility all but guaranteed Medicaid status. Under TANF, the eligibility link between the two programs was eliminated. Delinking cash assistance from Medicaid provided some advantages for welfare recipients. Medicaid eligibility could be preserved even in the face of cash assistance's tougher eligibility requirements. Also, Medicaid eligibility was not tied to the sixty-month TANF limit, allowing for unlimited enrollment. Welfare recipients could also receive transitional Medicaid benefits for a short period after leaving welfare. TANF also guaranteed Medicaid eligibility for those meeting AFDC income guidelines as of July 1996, regardless of their current status on the welfare rolls (DHHS 1997). However, welfare advocacy groups warned that the disadvantages of delinking cash assistance from Medicaid outweighed its advantages. They argued that individuals might not be aware that they were still eligible for Medicaid even though they no longer received welfare benefits. Worse yet, front line workers might not be aware of this and fail to inform recipients of their Medicaid eligibility (Rosenbaum and Darnell 1996; Ku and Coughlin 1997; National Governors Association 1997; Schott and Mann 1998).

Recent research suggests that these concerns were justified. Nationally, there was a substantial decline in Medicaid enrollments for low-income populations once the transition to TANF was fully underway (GAO 1999b; Burke and Abbey 2002). In West Virginia, Medicaid enrollment among the low-income population as a whole, excluding those receiving SSI and those age 65 and older, declined 11.2 percent between 1995 and 2000 (Burke and Abbey 2002). Medicaid enrollment among low-income children fell approximately 2 percent between 1995 and 2000 (Burke and Abbey 2002).

National trends suggest that delinking cash assistance from Medicaid had a significant effect on Medicaid enrollment among the very poor. The evidence suggests that those low-income families receiving Medicaid who were not on welfare at the time of reform were less effected by change than those receiving welfare. Kronebusch (2001) found enrollment trends for children varied significantly by income level. For example, for families with no income, those likely to be on public assistance, the probability of Medicaid enrollment fell from 81 to 68 percent between 1995 and 1998 at the national level. At the same time, the probability for Medicaid enrollment among families at one half of the federal poverty rate fell from 61 to 53 percent (Kronebusch 2001). During the same period in West

Virginia, the probability of enrollment for families with no income fell from 92 percent to 74 percent (Kronebusch 2001).

In West Virginia, the statewide implementation of WV WORKS in 1998 created abrupt changes in the relationship between the cash assistance population and the Medicaid system. Low-income enrollment fell from 198,863 to 174,774 between state FYs 1997 and 1999 (Burke and Abbey 2002). This drop-off was significant among low-income children. Approximately 20,000 fewer children received Medicaid in 1999 than in 1997 (Burke and Abbey 2002). Findings from a survey of those who left the rolls in 1998 found that 58 percent of the respondents reported that they or their children no longer received Medicaid coverage. Given that 80 percent of respondents reported incomes of $10,000 or less in 1998, it is likely that the vast majority of these individuals qualified for Medicaid (Dilger et al. 2000).

For low-income adults, Medicaid enrollment declined 28 percent in West Virginia (Burke and Abbey 2002). Compared to other states, it is difficult for working-age adults to qualify for Medicaid in West Virginia. While their children may qualify for publicly-funded health insurance because of the expanded coverage under Medicaid and the new CHIP program, the income threshold for adult eligibility is set relatively high. For example, while Medicaid covers 26.3 percent of state's children and 15.1 percent of those 65 and older, it covers only 7.5 percent of the non-elderly adult population (Chambers et al. 2003). One study estimated that a working family in West Virginia could make no more than $342 per month, after disregards and deductions, to qualify for Medicaid coverage, compared to a national median average of $666 (Guyer and Mann 1999). More recent analysis confirms this and notes that strict income eligibility criteria remain (Chambers et al. 2003).

National data and survey results from studies conducted in West Virginia strongly suggest that serious disconnects in Medicaid eligibility and enrollment occurred during the initial stages of welfare reform implementation in 1998 and 1999. Since then, there has been marked improvement in program performance in enrolling qualified individuals for Medicaid. These changes have been accomplished, in part, through improved front line case management practices and new administrative resources. Greater emphasis is now placed on helping not only those who remain on welfare but also the working poor and uninsured. Front line practices, at least in some districts, now focus on more flexible verification and review standards. An administrative structure that allows for program coordination between Charleston and state-run district field offices appears to have facilitated the development of new policies and front line procedures that place greater emphasis on smoothing the application and redetermination process for those in need of Medicaid. Improvements in the state's RAPIDS management information system has made eligibility determination quicker and less error prone (Plein 2001b). To maximize coverage, the state has also adopted the twelve month "continuous eligibility" provision allowed under federal law. By lengthening the redetermination cycle, more integrated care can be provided and less administrative burden is placed on clients and front line workers. The state has also stepped up efforts to ensure that transitional Medicaid benefits are provided to those who leave WV WORKS (Plein 2001b).

CHIP was crucial to connecting and reconnecting West Virginia families to Medicaid. It requires all applicants to be screened for Medicaid eligibility. This bodes well for Medicaid enrollment in West Virginia. Although WV CHIP initially enrolled a fairly small number of children, approximately 19,000 in a typical month in 2001, it serves as a vehicle for extending Medicaid coverage to children. Since 2000, West Virginia has pursued WV CHIP outreach and enrollment efforts with great fanfare and effort. For example, West Virginia's Governor Robert Wise (D, 2001-2005) participated in numerous door-to-door outreach campaigns. Various nonprofit and governmental institutions not previously engaged in Medicaid outreach also promote WV CHIP. This has helped to expand Medicaid's enrollment base. Because the Bureau for Children and Families is primarily responsible for both Medicaid and WV CHIP eligibility determination and enrollment functions, it has coordinated application procedures. Both programs now use a combined application form, and both programs offer similar benefits in terms of services covered and length of time allowed between initial eligibility determination and redetermination. In the past few years, many states have pursued strategies similar to West Virginia's, and West Virginia is recognized for smoothing the barriers to both Medicaid and CHIP program participation (Plein 2002b; Thompson 2003; Burke 2003).

Supplemental Security Income: Welfare Reform and Substitution Effects?

> I think people who are on SSI should not be disqualified from benefits.
> – Former West Virginia TANF/AFDC Recipient
> (Dilger et al. 1999b,)

> I think that just because a person receives SSI or social security income in the home that people should not be cut off from their AFDC check.
> – Former West Virginia TANF/AFDC Recipient
> (Dilger et al. 1999b,)

SSI is a federally funded and administered program that serves disabled children and adults with little, if any, employment experience. Established more than thirty years ago, SSI was fashioned from a collection of existing state and federal programs that provided assistance to the aged, blind, and disabled. A variety of programs established under the *Social Security Act of 1935* delegated implementation to states and required state matches for program funding. By the 1960s, substantial variation in state eligibility and benefit practices created concerns about the equity and consistency of program delivery and benefit distribution among states. This led to reforms focusing on better program coordination and cohesiveness (Quadagno 1988). In 1972, these programs were federalized when they were combined into the SSI program (U.S. Social Security Administration [SSA] 2002). Rather than being implemented by states, since 1974 the Social Security Administration has administered the program.

The U.S. Social Security Administration (2002, 4) characterizes SSI as "assistance of the last resort" aimed at supplementing rather than supplanting other forms of assistance. The SSI application process requires both medical and non-medical reviews of the applicant's circumstances. Adults "must have a medically determinable physical or mental impairment that is expected to last (or has lasted) at least 12 continuous months or to result in death" and "prevents him or her from doing any substantial gainful activity" (SSA 2002, 2). Even though the eligibility bar is set quite high, SSI has grown to become an essential component of public assistance support in the United States. Its eligibility criteria was broadened during the 1970s and 1980s to include a wider range of disabilities associated with mental health. In addition, administrative law procedures evolved allowing applicants more opportunities to contest negative determinations. Over time, SSI enrollments grew, especially among children.

As its name implies, SSI provides supplemental income to individuals to help cover living and medically-related expenses not covered by other programs or income. Monthly payments have traditionally been modest, given the many expenses associated with disability. In 2001, for example, the national average monthly SSI benefit was $423. In West Virginia, the average monthly payment was $373 (SSA 2002). Perhaps more important than receiving the benefit is the role SSI plays as a gateway to Food Stamps and Medicaid. It acts as an "if, then" program that conveys "categorical eligibility" to other programs when individuals qualify for the SSI benefit. Medicaid and Food Stamp income-related criteria do not apply to those deemed categorically eligible, thus easing access to both programs.

In the early 1990s, the perception that SSI eligibility criteria had become too flexible and that benefits were extended to many undeserving individuals gained some degree of acceptance in the policy arena (Karoly et al. 2001; Weaver 2000). Provisions in the *Personal Responsibility and Work Opportunity Reconciliation Act of 1996* were intended to restrict SSI enrollment by tightening eligibility criteria. For example, adults who were disabled due to alcohol or drug addiction were excluded from the program. The *Personal Responsibility and Work Opportunity Reconciliation Act* also tightened children's eligibility requirements to mirror those established for adults so that a disability might be more demonstrable (U.S.

Congress 1996). Some welfare advocacy groups argued that because of categorical eligibility links to Medicaid, these new provisions might cause disabled children to lose medical coverage. Continued coverage was guaranteed only until July 1997. Under the original provisions of the new law, children were required to be redetermined under these tighter eligibility standards by January 1, 1998 (DHHS 1997). Some 283,000 children were slated for redetermination nationwide, including approximately 2,500 West Virginians (SSA 1996). In 1997, child welfare advocates in West Virginia estimated that approximately 61 percent of SSI children could lose benefits under the new eligibility requirements (Michaels 1997). Mounting criticism to this provision led to policy corrections later that year. Provisions in the *Balanced Budget Act of 1997* restored Medicaid eligibility for many children who did not meet the new criteria (Karoly et al. 2001).

SSI enrollment in West Virginia has grown in recent years - especially among working-age adults. SSI is a particularly important part of West Virginia's safety net system. In December 2001, approximately 73,000 state residents received SSI benefits. Of these, approximately 72 percent were between the ages of 18 and 64 (SSA 2002). West Virginia's SSI enrollment rates have traditionally been higher than the national average, and the trend has continued since the 1996 welfare reform law was adopted. National summary statistics vary on the degree of this difference but confirm the trend. According to the U.S. Department of Health and Human Services (2002a), 3.9 percent of West Virginia's adult population received SSI benefits in 2000, compared to 2.3 percent nationally. Most notably, the SSI enrollment rate for adults (aged 18 to 64) in West Virginia was 4.5 percent, compared to 2.2 percent nationally. U.S. Bureau of the Census (2002) statistics reveal an even higher SSI enrollment rate in the state (see Chapter 2).

The percentage of working-age West Virginians that receive SSI has grown appreciably over the years, both in absolute terms and compared to national trends. In 1992, the rate grew to 3.5 percent, up from 2.9 percent in 1990. Since then, the rate has steadily increased (DHHS 2002a). The SSI enrollment rate varies within the state as well. For example, Latimer and Mencken (2003) note that the prevalence of SSI receipt is higher in coal-dependent counties in Appalachia than elsewhere in the region. They suggest that SSI benefits may substitute for unemployment and other benefits.

The temptation to substitute SSI benefits for cash assistance welfare payments has long been recognized and reflected in policy arrangements. Because SSI benefits are fully funded and administered with federal dollars, states have an incentive to shift the cost of public assistance from state-supported arrangements to federal ones. This dimension has created some tension between states and the federal government (Keiser 1999). Prior to 1996, when AFDC was in effect, federal regulations prohibited individuals, but not households, from receiving both AFDC and SSI. It was common for welfare workers to encourage eligible individuals to enroll in SSI rather than AFDC. Under these circumstances, the recipient's family might still qualify for AFDC assistance because SSI income was excluded from cash assistance eligibility determinations (DHHS 2002a). The *Personal Responsibility and Work Opportunity Reconciliation Act* removed the prohibition against individuals receiving both SSI and cash assistance (DHHS 2002a). West Virginia was one of the few states that elected to maintain this separation as a substitution strategy. Initially, the state further strengthened the separation by also including SSI income in cash assistance eligibility determinations for families, thus essentially excluding all families with one or more SSI recipient from WV WORKS.

SSI, Welfare Reform, and the Safety Net

> In the development of WV WORKS, many policy decisions were made to avoid replication of the inequities in the old system. One of those changes was to treat Supplemental Security Income (SSI) as any other unearned income.
> – *WV WORKS 1997 Annual Report* (DHHR 1998, 11)

> I can not work. I am too sick. I get SSI, but the welfare took my little girl's check for $149. If I could get it back, that would help because I only get $500 a month to live on.
> – Former West Virginia AFDC/TANF Recipient
> (Dilger et al. 1999b)

There are important connections between SSI and TANF in the West Virginia welfare reform experience. As discussed in previous chapters, when WV WORKS was first implemented, DHHR counted SSI benefits as income in TANF eligibility determination. As this provision was implemented, many families on AFDC left the program. Welfare advocacy groups criticized the new policy and numerous editorials opposing the policy appeared in the state's leading newspapers (Miller 1997; Bundy 1997; Sharlip 1998). During the first eight months of statewide WV WORKS implementation (January through August 1998), approximately 30 percent of all case closures (3,303 cases) were due to the state's SSI income policy (Dilger et al. 1999a).

DHHR argued that it was simply correcting an "inequity" of the AFDC system that allowed SSI income to be excluded in cash assistance determinations. It also went to great lengths to emphasize that families where one or more members received SSI payments were likely to be eligible for both Medicaid and Food Stamps (DHHR 1998). However, welfare reform advocacy groups and others interpreted DHHR's effort to count SSI income as a means to remove individuals from TANF. As controversy over DHHR's SSI policy mounted, action shifted to the courts and the legislative arena. Eventually, legislative action forced a policy reversal (Plein 2001a).

West Virginia's practice of counting SSI as income in eligibility determinations was a not too subtle method of trying to hold down TANF caseloads by using the SSI program as a substitute for cash assistance. Although abandoning the practice of counting SSI as income, DHHR has continued to seek ways to divert adult SSI recipients from TANF. One practice is to exclude adults from assistance groups so that their families might be considered "child-only" cases. This signals a return to AFDC-era practices when individual SSI recipients in a household were otherwise excluded from the "assistance group" receiving cash assistance benefits. These child-only cases, comprising approximately 30 percent of the state's TANF caseload in any given month, are excluded from both federal work requirements and time limits. West Virginia has not been alone in this practice.

Nationwide, as of FY 2000, approximately 46 percent of all child-only cases had a parent present in household. In such circumstances, the parent is not subject to the TANF work requirement. In West Virginia, only 9 percent of child-only cases have a parent present. However, like many other states, a very high percentage of these parents are SSI recipients. While the national average for a parent receiving SSI in a child-only household is 41.5 percent, in West Virginia this rate is greater than 90 percent. In other states where there is a high incidence of parents receiving SSI, the prevalence of parental presence in child-only case composition amplifies the effect of this practice. For example, in Wisconsin, more than 50 percent of all child-only families have a parent present, and the rate of parents within these families receiving SSI is more than 90 percent. In Mississippi, the corresponding rates are 61 and 99 percent respectively, and in Massachusetts 68 and 85 percent respectively (DHHS 2002b). The U.S. General Accounting Office (2002c), has recognized the emergence of this trend in TANF management practices, noting that the use of SSI is one of the options that states have to relieve the pressures work requirements and time limits have on the TANF population.

One does not need a legal or administrative determination to be disabled. For example, only 40 percent of those leaving TANF who reported having physical or mental "impairments" were receiving SSI (GAO 2002d). Many individuals who are or have recently relied on cash assistance may have disabilities, but the extent of impairment may not satisfy SSI eligibility criteria. This may lead to long-term welfare dependency under a time-limited cash assistance program (Sweeney 2000). Or, it may lead to difficulties once separated from the welfare system. In a study of those leaving the welfare rolls in West Virginia during 1998, one-third of the recipients cited illness or disability as the reason they were unable to find employment (Dilger et al. 1999b). The rate of disability appears to be higher for those on or recently off the rolls than for the general population. For example, federal surveys reveal that approximately 9.1 percent of the general population between the ages of 18 and 64 consider themselves to have a disability (DHHS 2002a).

L. Christopher Plein

Recent downturns in state finances are forcing states to reexamine how they fund their TANF programs and how they might assist those with substantial barriers to leaving TANF. The advent of child-only cases that include parents on SSI and assessment initiatives to convert TANF cases to SSI cases are examples of recent steps states have taken to address these concerns. Recent state responses also reveal the fluidity of the reform experience. A short time ago, when state coffers were relatively flush, a group of scholars noted that, "Given the currently robust economy and states' relative fiscal largesse, the motivation for cross-program shifting since [the 1996 welfare reform law was adopted] has diminished." They hastened to add that poor economic conditions would create a new situation where "states may face a greater fiscal pressure to move as many recipients as possible from TANF to SSI" (Karoly et al. 2001, 493). It is now apparent that many states have moved in this direction. West Virginia was one of the first states to experiment with substitution when it implemented its controversial policy of counting SSI income in TANF eligibility determination. It continues to pursue this strategy with a more nuanced approach of utilizing the child-only case option for those households where one or more adults have a disability.

Faced with federal time limits and long-term dependency, some states are investing resources into client assessment efforts to help adults move from TANF to SSI. States are looking at ways to facilitate SSI enrollment for those on TANF who have disabilities. In FY 2001, Georgia's welfare system budgeted approximately $3 million in comprehensive assessments for this purpose (Ellen-Duke and Rich 2001). In West Virginia, DHHR has contracted with legal aid organizations to help individuals on TANF apply for SSI benefits.

The Safety Net in an Age of Reform: An Assessment

There are programs such as Food Stamps, Medicaid, WIC, Housing Programs and others that help families. Welfare reform will change them too. But the changes will be different in each case. It just depends on the situation of the individual or family. You may be able to receive some benefits and not others.
– *Welfare Reform and You*
(WV Welfare Reform Coalition 1997)

Give us more food stamps to last for a full month and stop taking food stamps from us every time I get a couple of dollars raise on my SSI check. Your [sic] starving us.
– WV WORKS Recipient (Dilger et al. 2000)

The twin forces of frustration and opportunity inspire reform. Frustration is the product of believing that the "way things are" just will not work any more and that change is needed. Opportunity is the product of seizing on the problem to advance a preferred solution or program. In such an environment, different strategies and remedies emerge. Some may be complementary, others may be contradictory, and invariably a contest ensues to see which answer prevails. This is the path of policy change, and generations of social scientists have detailed its contours (Schattschneider 1960; Cobb and Elder 1972; Kingdon 1984; Baumgartner and Jones 1993). Amidst complex and embedded policy arrangements that are the product of decades of development and practice, the desire to fashion fundamental, stark changes that cut through ingrained practices and attitudes is appreciable. It is little wonder that complex and entrenched welfare systems have so frequently been the target for reform. However, such solutions may be pursued at the expense of appreciating the dynamics of system adjustment, the resiliency of existing bureaucratic and programmatic arrangements, and the complexities of implementing new policy. In short, the fortunes and consequences of fundamental policy change are highly uncertain and contingent in an environment that is inherently incremental (Lindblom 1979). This point has not been lost on those studying the reform experience in health and human services (Fossett et al. 2001; Riccucci and Lurie 2001; Weil 2001; Plein 2002b).

The *Personal Responsibility and Work Opportunity Reconciliation Act of 1996* was advanced with fundamental reform in mind and offered as a correction for failed or underperforming past reforms. But even with a strong intent to change "welfare as we know it," reform's architects and administrators had to reshape welfare within the constraints of existing health and human services systems and the management and implementation of other major safety net programs. In the 1990s, welfare wasn't the only program on the reform agenda. Medicaid, Food Stamps, and SSI also were reformed. The result was to complicate an already complex network of programs, institutions, intergovernmental relations, administrative arrangements, and public welfare needs. Reform in any one area is challenging enough, but when other related programs are undergoing change, the demands are difficult and the risks of failure high.

As the various chapters of this book spell out, implementation of welfare reform was neither smooth nor easy in West Virginia. It caused frustration and friction for policymakers and administrators, but more importantly, it was caused hardship for many of the state's most needy. West Virginia's experience is not exceptional. Other states have experienced similar circumstances (Nathan and Gais 1999, Tweedie 2000). When TANF was created in 1996, there were many warnings that the new welfare law would have harmful spillover effects in the form of declining enrollment among those eligible for Food Stamps and Medicaid. Extensive analysis conducted by many researchers across the country suggests that this did come to pass. In West Virginia, enrollment decline was not as deep, or as long lasting, but it was certainly apparent in the initial phases of WV WORKS implementation in 1998 and 1999. Since then, many have recognized the need to correct the deficiencies and problems associated with the 1996 welfare reform law's implementation. For example, both the state and federal government have created programs to encourage those leaving WV WORKS who remain eligible for Medicaid and/or Food Stamps to apply for those benefits.

The state has also adopted programs to encourage low-income households never before connected with the welfare system to apply for Food Stamps, Medicaid, and CHIP.

Welfare reform has also encouraged states to rely more on safety net programs than on cash-assistance arrangements under TANF. States increasingly are diverting applicants to programs that are not time-limited, such as Food Stamps and Medicaid. And some states, including West Virginia, look at SSI as a substitute for TANF for at least some of the adult welfare population.

Some lessons can be drawn from West Virginia's experiences with welfare reform. First, those who implement reform operate in a political environment that is often rife with conflicting and contradictory policy signals. As Thompson and Gais (2000, 122) have observed, "Programs such as Medicaid and Food Stamps always had enrollees who were not on cash assistance. With greater delinkage, the proportion of enrollees in this noncash-assisted group promised to grow. Whether states could slam on the brakes with respect to TANF while simultaneously accelerating in respect to the other safety-net programs loomed, of course, as an open question." In other words, the contradiction posed by reform is that program changes in welfare encourage shrinking the rolls and deterring enrollment through work-first strategies. At the same time, states were encouraged to promote Food Stamp enrollment, and new policy changes associated with the Medicaid and CHIP programs placed a premium on expanding coverage to new clients.

Fossett et al. (2001, 210) describe these contradictions as "dissonant spillover," noting that this occurs when "implementing agents in the same general sphere (e.g., providing various safety net benefits to 'low-income' people) are expected to pursue conflicting objectives, depending on the particular program and benefit involved." Policy priorities and signals tend to converge and place pressure on state health and human services. In states like West Virginia, a relatively few administrators are given the task of addressing multiple demands for reform (Plein 1999). Since the mid-1990s, the West Virginia experience has been characterized by senior level administrators juggling many, and often competing, demands. The challenges involve not only implementing new and sometimes conflicting policy directives, but include maintaining current program arrangements. As detailed in Chapter 4, these competing demands displace attention from reform efforts, such as WV WORKS, and focus instead on mundane, but immediate issues, such as minimizing Food Stamp error rates. Health and human service systems can be characterized as a patchwork quilt of programs with different origins and purposes, which share a common trait of disjointed and incremental development. The complexities of reform mean that intra-departmental efforts do not always mesh well.

Second, there has been an enduring level of intergovernmental conflict in health and human service program implementation in the United States. This conflict led to the eventual development of a nationally-centered system of welfare and human services programs largely funded and directed by the federal government (Weir et al. 1988). Subsequent reform efforts undertaken in the 1960s, 1970s, 1980s, and 1990s centered on revising welfare reform arrangements between the state and federal government (Weaver 2000; Heclo 2001). Differences between state and federal interests continue to shape program implementation and design today. More recently, debates surrounding TANF reauthorization have been framed in an intergovernmental context reflecting tensions that often exist between federal and state authorities. One of the more contentious issues involves state flexibility in using federal TANF dollars for safety net systems. Until recently, many states used their TANF surpluses to support programs state general revenue dollars traditionally funded. As noted in the preceding chapter, West Virginia used TANF dollars to fund various social service programs and soon found its welfare system in dire fiscal condition. Recent economic circumstances have forced states to move away from this practice. In the future, federal law may further constrain state discretion to spend TANF dollars on other safety net programs.

Third, reform begets reform, and proposed changes are modeled on enduring concerns and objectives. TANF's reauthorization debate has focused on President George W. Bush's desire to tighten state performance standards, especially regarding mandated state work participation rates, and imposing increased work requirements on those receiving cash assistance (Plein 2002c). Beyond the immediate scope of TANF reauthorization, there have been other reforms associated with the welfare reform experience, and still others are currently on the policy agenda. For example, CHIP was a response, in part, to what many saw as a concern about the plight of working families and children who had left the welfare rolls during the initial phases of TANF implementation. One of CHIP's primary architects, Senator Jay Rockefeller (D-WV), recently proposed further extending publicly-funded health insurance to 18 to 24 year olds. As for Food Stamps, legislative changes were incorporated in the national farm bill, adopted in 2001, that reflect the practical realities of program implementation and administration in a post-AFDC world. These changes allow greater coordination of enrollment and eligibility determination practices with TANF administration.

Fourth, undergirding reform efforts is a quest for creating integrated health and human service systems. For decades, there has been an expressed policy and professional preference toward creating coordinated, integrated, and "seamless" arrangements that provide for the efficient administration and use of the range of programs and services that make up the health and human services system. Attaining this has been likened to the holy grail of health and human services policy (Agranoff 1991). Because programs are an agglomeration of state and federal initiatives developed over many years, such an objective is likely beyond the realm of possibility. But no doubt, many clients, administrators, policymakers, and advocates would settle for at least complementarity in program operations.

In West Virginia, the concentration of most services and programs within DHHR's Bureau for Children and Families as well as direct state administration of programs through field offices reflects a desire for integrated services. However, the separate origins and authorities involved in federal programs can frustrate arrangements, even when administered under one roof. With welfare reform moving out in front of changes in other programs, disconnects in program coordination became apparent. One of the positive consequences of the reform era has been a move to better coordinate eligibility procedures, case management, and information systems. Unfortunately, these improvements were often drawn from hard lessons where those that the safety net is intended to serve bore much of the burden. Among states, progress has varied in correcting the disruptions and fragmentation of health and human service systems in an era of welfare. Compared to many other states, West Virginia has made significant strides to correct and improve past practices (Plein 2001a, 2002b; Bryner 2002; Thompson 2003; Burke 2003).

Fifth, West Virginia's reform experiences transit an arc from confusion, to cohesion, to uncertainty. Welfare reform in West Virginia, as elsewhere, was a seismic event that sent shock waves radiating across the expanse of health and human services. At the same time, other forces of reform were disturbing the environment as well. Whether it was developing managed care arrangements for Medicaid recipients, developing and implementing WV CHIP, or adjusting to new demands and opportunities in the Food Stamp program, reforms have altered the landscape of policy and administration. After stumbling in the initial phases of welfare reform implementation, West Virginia refined program management and practices to facilitate enrollment in Food Stamps, Medicaid, and other programs. The evolution of front line practices discussed in Chapter 5 as well as the development of more integrated application procedures using an upgraded management information system helped to improve service delivery. In addition, CHIP outreach efforts brought more people into the Medicaid system (Plein 2002b). The state's health and human services reform experience as a whole parallels that described in Chapters 4 and 5 regarding the state's response to welfare reform. Although confusion and discord characterized the initial stages of reform, with experience a second phase of responsiveness and cohesion emerged. Now, economic difficulties and ambiguity surrounding the next phase of reforms associated with a reauthorized TANF law are creating new uncertainty.

Sixth, economics changes both the capacity of systems and the demands placed upon them. In the short time that welfare reform has been implemented and new developments encountered by cash assistance and other health and human services programs, the national and state economy have seen significant changes. The economy has faltered. At present, the most apparent effect of this has been a decline in fiscal capacity across states. Economists and public finance specialists have sought to distinguish the various structural and cyclical factors contributing to and compounding state fiscal stress. In regard to health and human services, the consequences, if not the causes, are easy to discern. Medicaid budget deficits across the United States began to grow in 2001 (Fossett and Burke 2003). By mid-2002, West Virginia faced budget problems with its program on a scale not experienced since the early 1990s (Plein 2002d). The primary stressors on the program are found not in services to the poor, but in drug costs and long-term health care costs, primarily associated with services to the elderly. As for TANF, states are facing significant shortfalls in funding that effects spending for both cash assistance and non-cash assistance services. This situation has forced West Virginia to begin to withdraw benefits and programs serving those no longer on WV WORKS.

In West Virginia, the percent of those eligible for cash assistance and other federally-funded safety net programs who are enrolled in these programs has, for many years, been much higher than the national average. It is tempting to offer a "cultural" explanation for West Virginia's apparent success in program enrollment. But, it is a mistake to fall back on the Appalachian appellation of dependency, which is characterized by an image of rustic, rural, individualistic families who make the most of what is available to them. As various authors have noted, this is a common theme in framing Appalachian culture, which does little to help understand the complexities of this, or any other, "culture" (Harrington 1962; Stewart 1996). Yet, this perceptual framework has been advanced for decades (Tunley 1960; Caudill 1963; Ball 1970; Fetterman 1970). It continues to be perpetuated today (Spald 1997). The picture, of course, is much more complex. Other non-Appalachian states have demonstrated high levels of program enrollment. For example, Alaska, Hawaii, Maine, Michigan, Missouri, and South Carolina have experienced Food Stamp participation rates of 70 percent or better in recent years (USDA 2002b; Schrim and Castner 2002a). One possible explanation for West Virginia's relatively high program enrollment rate is that West Virginians generally do not attach a negative social stigma to program participation (Plein 2002a).

It is beyond the scope of this chapter to examine the reasons why individuals are connected to the welfare system, but as the other chapters in this book illustrate, most who use the system do so episodically. They access services and programs as need dictates. The safety net metaphor is apt, for there are an array of programs to turn to when in need. Dependency is less the rule than the exception. For many, work is contingent on forces beyond their control, and families must cope with a host of challenges imposed by economic, medical, and psychological need. The capriciousness of seasonal and low-wage employment and the uncertainties of family situations and health appear to be contributing factors to service use, rather than a long-term dependency on the welfare system. Duncan (1992) and Tickamyer (1992) reached this same conclusion after conducting surveys of low-income individuals in rural Appalachia and elsewhere. Program enrollment's episodic nature is further evidence by fluctuations in welfare rolls, where enrollment typically peaks during the last months of winter when those employed in seasonal jobs are most likely to be laid off (Plein 2001a). It is also evidenced when economic conditions worsen and needs deepen. This played out all too clearly during the recession in 2001 and 2002. Between June 2001 and December 2002, WV WORKS' caseload grew 11.2 percent (DHHR 2003c).

Because of the vagaries of economics, it is important for safety-net programs to be counter-cyclical instruments that address the consequences of economic downturns. Traditionally, federally-funded programs have helped to provide this support. Today, the counter-cyclical functions are harder to ascertain. The general thrust of reform has been to limit federal expenditures and shift more burden to states, but there appear to be both constraints and opportunities in the current environment. Food Stamps remains an open-ended grant to states. The program's work requirements are relatively weak and can be easily waived in poor labor markets. The *Personal Responsibility and Work Opportunity Reconciliation Act* sought to restrict access to SSI, but states continue to view the program as a substitute benefit for those with disabilities who would otherwise not be able to leave the welfare rolls. Medicaid has undergone reforms that often have contradictory purposes, limiting federal funding on the one hand and expanding coverage to newly eligible populations of the near and working poor on the other. The opportunities these safety net programs provide become even more important as the counter-cyclical effectiveness of federally funded cash assistance programs become suspect. Now that the *Personal Responsibility and Work Opportunity Reconciliation Act* has replaced AFDC's open-ended funding with TANF's set funding, programs such as Food Stamps, Medicaid, and SSI play an even more crucial role than in the past in serving those in need.

References

Agranoff, Robert. 1991. "Human Services Integration: Past and Present Challenges in Public Administration." *Public Administration Review* 54(6): 457-464.

Atkins, Nancy. 2002. "West Virginia Medicaid. Presentation of Nancy Atkins, Commissioner of the Bureau for Medical Services." Summer Institute on Aging. Morgantown, West Virginia. June 12.

Ball, Richard. 1970. "The Southern Appalachian Folk Subculture as a Tension-Reducing Way of Life." *Change in Rural Appalachia: Implications for Action Programs*. ed. John Photiadis and Harry K. Schwarzweller, 69- 79. Philadelphia: University of Pennsylvania Press.

Baumgartner, Frank and Bryan Jones. 1993. *Agendas and Instability in American Politics*.Chicago: University of Chicago Press.

Bryner, Gary. 2002. "The Relationship Between Medicaid and Welfare Agencies." *Managing Medicaid Management Take-Up Brief*. Albany, NY: Nelson A. Rockefeller Institute of Government. November.

Bundy, Jennifer. 1997. "Welfare Cases Drop in Pilot Counties." *The Charleston Gazette*. August 17:1C, 5C.

Burke, Courtney. 2003. "The Complexity of Simplifying the Medicaid Application Process." *Managing Medicaid Management Take-Up Brief*. Albany, NY: Nelson A. Rockefeller Institute of Government. January.

_____, and Craig Abbey. 2002. "Medicaid Enrollment Trends:

1995 -2000." *Managing Medicaid Management Take-Up Brief.* Albany, NY: Nelson A. Rockefeller Institute of Government. August.

Caudill, Harry. 1963. *Night Comes to the Cumberlands: A Biography of a Depressed Area.* Boston: Little, Brown.

Chafin, Raymond and Topper Sherwood. 1994. *Just Good Politics.* Pittsburgh: University of Pittsburgh Press.

Chambers, Sonia, Melissa McCormick, and Johnna Beane. 2003. "Health Care Coverage in West Virginia." A presentation to the West Virginia Health Care Advisory Council, Charleston, West Virginia. February 3.

Cobb, Roger and Charles Elder. 1972. *Participation in American Politics: The Dynamics of Agenda Building.* Baltimore: The Johns Hopkins Press.

Czajka, John L., Sheena McConnell, Scott Cody, and Nuria Rodriguez. 2001. *Imposing a Time Limit on Food Stamp Receipt: Implementation of the Provisions and Effects on Food Stamp Participation. Volume 1, Final Report.* Prepared for the USDA Food and Nutrition Service by Mathematica Policy Research, Inc. Washington, D.C. September.

Dean, Stacy and Dorothy Rosenbaum. 2002. *Implementing New Changes to the Food Stamp Program: A Provision by Provision Analysis of the Farm Bill.* Washington, D.C.: Center on Budget and Policy Prioroities. August. http://www.cbpp.org/8-27-02fa.pdf.

Dilger, Robert Jay, Eleanor Blakely, Melissa Latimer, Barry Locke, Carson Mencken, L. Christopher Plein, Lucinda Potter, David Williams. 2001. "WV WORKS 2000: The Recipients' Perspective." *West Virginia Public Affairs Reporter* 18(3): 2-19.

_____, Eleanor Blakely, Melissa Latimer, Barry Locke, Carson Mencken, L. Christopher Plein, Lucinda Potter, David Williams. 2000. *WV WORKS 2000: The Recipients' Perspective.* Presented to the West Virginia Department of Health and Human Resources, Charleston, WV. December 14.

_____, Eleanor Blakely, Karen Dorton, Melissa Latimer, Barry Locke, Carson Mencken, L. Christopher Plein, Lucinda Potter, David Williams, and Dong Pil Yoon. 1999a. *Phase 1 Report: TANF/WV WORKS Case Closure Study*. Presented to the West Virginia Department of Health and Human Resources, Charleston, West Virginia. February 18.

_____, Eleanor Blakely, Karen Dorton, Melissa Latimer, Barry Locke, Carson Mencken, L. Christopher Plein, Lucinda Potter, David Williams, and Dong Pil Yoon. 1999b. *WV WORKS Case Closure Study*. Presented to the West Virginia Department of Health and Human Resources, Charleston, West Virginia. December 7.

Duncan, Cynthia. 1992. "Persistent Poverty in Appalachia: Scarce Work and Rigid Stratification." *Rural Poverty in America*. ed. Cynthia Duncan, 111-133. Westport, CT: Auburn House.

Edelman, Peter. 1997. "The Worst Thing Bill Clinton has Done." *The Atlantic Monthly*. (March): 43-58.

Ellen-Duke, Amy and Michael Rich. 2001. "Georgia Field Report Medicaid Take-Up and Welfare Reform Study." Albany, N.Y.: Rockefeller Institute of Government.

Fetterman, John. 1970. *Stinking Creek: A Portrait of a Small Mountain Community in Appalachia*. New York: E.F. Dutton and Co.

Finegold, Kenneth. 1988. "Agriculture and the Politics of U.S. Social Provision: Social Insurance and Food Stamps." *The Politics of Social Policy in the United States*. ed. Margaret Weir, Ann Shola Orloff, and Theda Skocpol, 199-234. Princeton, NJ: Princeton University Press.

Fossett, James W. and Courtney Burke. 2003. "Is Medicaid Retrenching? State Budgets and Medicaid Enrollment in 2002." *Managing Medicaid Take-Up Management Brief*. Albany, NY: Nelson A. Rockefeller Institute of Government. February.

_____, and Thomas Gais. 2002. "A New Puzzle for Federalism: Different State Responses to Food Stamps and Medicaid."

Paper Presented at the Annual Meetings of the American Political Science Association, Boston, Massachusetts. September.

_____, Thomas Gais, and Frank Thompson. 2001. "Federalism and Performance Management: Health Insurance, Food Stamps, and the Take-Up Challenge." *Quicker, Better, Cheaper? Managing Performance in American Government.* ed. Dall Forsythe, 207-244. Albany, NY: Rockefeller Institute Press.

_____, Malcolm Goggin, John Hall, Jocelyn Johnston, L. Christopher Plein, Richard Roper, and Carol Weissert. 2000. "Managing Medicaid Managed Care: Are States Becoming Prudent Purchasers?" *Health Affairs* 18(4): 36-49.

Gabor, Vivian and Christopher Botsko. 1998. "State Food Stamp Choices Under Welfare Reform: Findings of 1997 50-State Survey." Report prepared by Health Systems Research, Inc. for U.S. Department of Agriculture, Food and Nutrition Service. May. http://www.fns.usda.gov/oane/menu/Published/FSP/FILES/ProgramDesign/finsum.pdf.

Guyer, Jocelyn and Cindy Mann. 1999. "Employed But Not Insured." Report. Washington, D.C.: Center on Budget and Policy Priorities. March.

Hackey, Robert and David Rochefort, Editors. 2001. *The New Politics of State Health Policy.* Lawrence, KS: University Press of Kansas.

Harrington, Michael. 1962. *The Other America: Poverty in the United States.* Baltimore: Penguin.

Heasely, Steven. 1995. *Medicaid Policy Considerations for Children: Issue Brief 1(2).* Charleston, WV: West Virginia Governor's Cabinet for Children and Families.

Heclo, Hugh. 2001. "The Politics of Welfare Reform." *The New World of Welfare.* ed. Rebecca Blank and Ron Haskins, 169-200. Washington, D.C.: Brookings Institution Press.

Karoly, Lynn, Jacob Klerman, and Jeannette Rogowski. 2001. "Effects of the 1996 Welfare Reform Changes on the SSI Program."

in *The New World of Welfare.* ed. Rebecca Blank and Ron Haskins, 482-495. Washington, D.C.: Brookings Institution Press.

Keiser, Lael. 1999. "State Bureaucratic Discretion and the Administration of Social Welfare Programs: The Case of Social Security Disability." *Journal of Public Administration Research and Theory* 9(1): 87-106.

Kingdon, John. 1984. *Agendas, Alternatives, and Public Policies.* Boston: Little, Brown.

Kronebusch, Karl. 2001. "Medicaid for Children: Federal Mandates, Welfare Reform, and Policy Backsliding." *Health Affairs* 20(1): 97-111.

Ku, Leighton, Marilyn Ellwood, Shiela Hoag, Barbara Ormond and Judith Wooldridge. 2000. "Evolution of Medicaid Managed Care Systems and Eligibility Expansions." *Health Care Financing Review* 22(2): 7-25.

_____, and Teresa A. Coughlin. 1997. "How the New Welfare Reform Law Affects Medicaid." Briefing Paper. Washington D.C.: Urban Institute.

Latimer, Melissa and F. Carson Mencken. 2003. "Socioeconomic Trends in Mining Dependent Counties in Appalachia." *Communities of Work: Rural Restructuring in Local and Global Contexts.* ed. William Falk, Michael Schulman, and Ann R. Tickamyer, 79–103. Athens, OH: Ohio University Press.

Lindblom, Charles. 1979. "Still Muddling: Not Yet Through." *Public Administration Review* 39(6): 527-531.

Lykens, Kristine A. and Paul A. Jargowsky. 2002. "Medicaid Matters: Children's Health and Medicaid Eligibility Expansions." *Journal of Policy Analysis and Management* 21(2): 219-238.

Mabin, Connie. 1999. "Are People Better Off?" *Charleston Sunday Gazette-Mail.* August 8: 1A, 5A.

Mead, Lawrence, Editor. 1997. *The New Paternalism: Supervisory Approaches to Poverty.* Washington, D.C.: Brookings Institution Press.

Melnick, R. Shep. 1994. *Between the Lines: Interpreting Welfare Rights*. Washington, D.C.: Brookings Institution Press.

Miller, Dawn. 1997. "The Case of Jerry Good, Jobless Father, Five Children Feel the Pinch of Welfare Reform." November 29. http://library.cnpapers.com.

Michaels, Daleen. 1997. "Disabled Kids Face Losing SSI." *The Dominion Post*. July 30: A1.

Nathan, Richard and Thomas Gais. 1999. *Implementing the Personal Responsibility Act of 1996: A First Look*. Albany, NY: Rockefeller Institute of Government.

National Governors Association. 1997. "MCH Update 1997: State Medicaid Coverage of Pregnant Women and Children." Washington, D.C.: National Governors Association. http://www.nga.org/center/divisions/1,1188,C_ISSUE_BRIEF^D_635,00.html.

Nyden, Paul J. 1998. "Tax Cut Could Hurt State's Medicaid Recipients." *The Charleston Gazette*. July 27. http://library.cnpapers.com.

Plein, Christopher. 2002a. "Food Stamp Report: West Virginia." Albany, NY: Rockefeller Institute of Government.

_____. 2002b. "Building Administrative Capacity for CHIP and Medicaid: Image, Outreach, and Organization." *Managing Medicaid Take-Up Management Brief*. Albany, NY: Nelson A. Rockefeller Institute of Government. December.

_____. 2002c. "Welfare Reform in the South: Considering Work Participation Rates on the Eve of Reauthorization." Paper presented at the Welfare Reform Reauthorization, National and Southern Perspectives Conference. Sponsored by the Brookings Institution of Government. Atlanta, Georgia. November.

_____. 2002d. *Medicaid Sustainability: Budgetary and Administrative Actions in 2002. West Virginia Field Report*. Albany, NY: Nelson A. Rockefeller Institute of Government.

_____. 2001a. "Welfare Reform in a Hard Place: The West Virginia

Experience." *Rockefeller Report* No. 13. November.

———. 2001b. "Medicaid Take-Up Study: West Virginia." Albany, NY: Nelson A. Rockefeller Institute of Government. October.

———. 2000. *Getting More Than What's Bargained For: The Hidden Administrative Costs of West Virginia's Mountain Health Trust Program*. Case Studies in Medicaid Managed Care. Albany, NY: Nelson A. Rockefeller Institute of Government.

———. 1999. "The Administrative Burdens of Change: The Convergence of Multiple Paths of Reform." Paper presented at the 21st Annual Conference of the Association for Public Policy Analysis and Management. Washington, D.C. November 5, 1999.

———. 1998. "Uncertain Prospects: West Virginia and Medicaid Reform." in *Medicaid Reform and the American States*. ed. Mark Daniels, 275-291. Westport, CT: Auburn House.

Portz, John, Matthew Reidy, and David A. Rochefort. 1999. "How Managed Care is Reinventing Medicaid and Other Public Health-Care Bureaucracies." *Public Administration Review* 59(5): 400-409.

Quadagno, Jill. 1988. "From Old-Age Assistance to Supplemental Security Income: The Political Economy of Relief in the South, 1935-1972." *The Politics of Social Policy in the United States*. ed. Margaret Weir, Ann Shola Orloff, and Theda Skocpol, 235-264. Princeton, NJ: Princeton University Press.

Riccucci, Norma M. and Irene Lurie. 2001. "Employee Performance Evaluation in Social Welfare Offices." *Review of Public Personnel Administration* 21(2): 27-37.

Richardson, Sally, Raymond Goldsteen, Robert Fulda, and Karen Goldsteen. 2002a. *Health Insurance in West Virginia: The Children's Report*. Morgantown, WV: West Virginia University, Institute for Health Policy Research. April.

———. 2002b. *Health Insurance in West Virginia: The Non-Elderly*

Adult Report. Morgantown, WV: West Virginia University, Institute for Health Policy Research. July.

Rosenbaum, Sara and Julie Darnell. 1996. "An Analysis of the Medicaid and Health-Related Provisions of the Personal Responsibility and Work Opportunity Reconciliation Act of 1996." *Health Policy & Child Health* 3(3): 1-8.

Schattschneider, E. E. 1960. *The Semi-Sovereign People.* New York: Holt, Rinehart and Winston.

Schirm, Allen L. and Laura A. Castner. 2002a. "Reaching Those in Need: State Food Stamp Participation Rates in 2000." Washington, D.C.: United States Department of Agriculture. Prepared by Mathematica Policy Research, Inc. December.

———. 2002b. "Reaching Those in Need: State Food Stamp Participation Rates in 1999." Washington, D.C.: United States Department of Agriculture. Prepared by Mathematica Policy Research, Inc. June.

Schneider, Andy. 1997. "Overview of the Medicaid Provisions of the Balanced Budget Act of 1997, P.L. 105-33." Washington, D.C.: Center for Budget and Policy Priorities. http://www.cbpp.org/908mcaid.htm.

Schott, Liz and Cindy Mann. 1998. "Assuring that Eligible Families Receive Medicaid when TANF Assistance is Denied or Terminated." Briefing Paper. Center for Budget and Policy Priorities. November 5. http://www.cbpp.org/11-5-98mcaidhtm.

Selden, Thomas M., Jessica S. Banthin, and Joel W. Cohen. 1998. "Medicaid's ProblemcChildren: Eligible but Not Enrolled." *Health Affairs* 17(3): 192-200.

Sharlip, Carol. 1998. "Cash Aid and SSI Pay Off in Potential of State's Citizens." *Charleston Gazette.* September 9, p. 7A.

Spald, Elizabeth Levitan. 1997. "The Test of Welfare Reform Lies in Appalachia," *Christian Science Monitor* (February 10).

Stewart, Kathleen. 1996. *A Space on the Side of the Road: Cultural Poetics in an "Other" America.* Princeton, NJ: Princeton University Press.

Sweeney, Eileen. 2000. "Recent Studies Indicate That Many Recipients Who are Current or Former Welfare Recipients Have Disabilities or Other Medical Conditions." Briefing Paper. Washington, D.C.: Center on Budget and Policy Priorities. February 29.

Thompson, Frank. 2003. "Children and the Take-Up Challenge: Renewal Processes in Medicaid and CHIP." *Managing Medicaid Take-Up Management Brief.* February.

_____, and Thomas Gais. 2000. "Federalism and the Safety Net: Delinkage and Participation Rates." *Publius* 30(1-2):119-142.

Tickamyer, Ann. 1992. "The Working Poor in Rural Labor Markets: The Example of the Southeastern United States." *Rural Poverty in America.* ed. Cynthia Duncan, 41-61. Westport, CT: Auburn House.

Tunley, Roul. 1960. "The Strange Case of West Virginia." *Saturday Evening Post* (February 6): 19-21, 64-66.

Tweedie, Jack. 2000. "From D.C. to Little Rock: Welfare Reform at Mid-term." *Publius* 30(1-2): 69-97.

U.S. Bureau of the Census, U.S. Department of Commerce. 2002. *Statistical Abstract of the United States, 2002.* http://www.census.gov/statab/www/

U.S. Congress, House of Representatives. 1996. *Personal Responsibility and Work Opportunity Reconciliation Act of 1996: Conference Report to Accompany H.R. 3734.* Washington, D.C.: U.S. Government Printing Office.

U.S. Department of Agriculture [USDA]. 2003. *Characteristics of Food Stamp Households: Fiscal Year 2001.* Washington, D.C.: U.S. Department of Agriculture. Prepared by Randy Rosso, Mathematica Policy Research, Inc. http://www.fns.usda.gov/OANE/menu/Published/FSP/FILES/Participation/2001CharReport.pdf.

_____. 2002a. "Characteristics of Food Stamp Households: Fiscal Year 2001." Washington, D.C.: U.S. Department of

Agriculture. Prepared by Christina Tuttle, Mathematica Policy Research, Inc. July. http://www.fns.usda.gov/OANE/menu/Published/FSP/FILES/Participation/2001advrpt.pdf.

———. 2002b. "Food Stamp Program: Average Monthly Participation." Washington, D.C.: U.S. Department of Agriculture. http://www.fns.usda.gov/pd/fsfypart.htm.

———. 1997, 1998, 1999, 2002c. *Waiver Requests – Section 824 of PROWRA (ABAWDS), Montana - Wyoming*. Washington, D.C.: U.S. Department of Agriculture. http://www.fns.usda.gov/fsp/rules/waivers/default.htm

———. 2001. "The Decline in Food Stamp Participation: A Report to Congress." Nutrition Assistance Research Report Series, The Office of Analysis, Nutrition, and Evaluation. July. Report No. FSP-01-WEL. http://www.fns.usda.gov/OANE/menu/Published/FSP/FILES/Participation/PartDecline.pdf.

U.S. Department of Health and Human Services (DHHS). 2002a. *Indicators of Welfare Dependence: Annual Report to the Congress*. Washington, D.C.: U.S. Department of Health and Human Services. http://aspe.hhs.gov/hsp/indicators02/.

———. 2002b. *Temporary Assistance for Needy Families, Fourth Annual Report to Congress*. Washington, D.C.: U.S. Department of Health and Human Services. April.

———. 1997. *Personal Responsibility and Work Opportunity Reconciliation Act: A Compilation of Implementation Materials*. Washington, D.C.: U.S. Department of Health and Human Services. April.

U.S. General Accounting Office (GAO). 2002a. *Food Stamp Program: States' Use of Options and Waivers to Improve Program Administration and Promote Access*. GAO-02-409 Washington, D.C.: U.S. General Accounting Office. February. http://www.gao.gov.

———. 2002b. *Food Stamp Program: Implementation of Electronic Benefit Transfer Systems*. GAO-02-332. Washington, D.C.: U.S. General Accounting Office. January. http://www.gao.gov.

———. 2002c. *Welfare Reform: With TANF Flexibility, States Vary in How They Implement Work Requirements and Time Limits.* GAO-02-770. Washington, D.C.: U.S. General Accounting Office. July.

———. 2002d. *Welfare Reform: Former TANF Recipients with Impairments Less Likely to Be Employed and More Likely to Receive Federal Supports.* GAO-03-210. Washington, D.C.: U.S. General Accounting Office. December.

———. 2001. "Food Stamp Program: Program Integrity and Participation Challenges, Statement of Robert E. Robertson, Director Education, Workforce, and Income Security Issues." GAO-01-881T. Washington, D.C.: U.S. General Accounting Office. June 27. http://www.gao.gov.

———. 1999a. "Food Stamp Program: Various Factors Led to Declining Participation." RCED-99-185. Washington, D.C.: U.S. General Accounting Office. July. http://www.gao.gov.

———. 1999b. "Welfare Reform: Information on Former Recipients' Status." HEHS-99-48. Washington, D.C.: U.S. General Accounting Office. April. http://www.gao.gov.

U.S. Social Security Administration (SSA). 2002. *SSI Annual Statistical Report, 2001.* Office of Policy and Office of Research, Evaluation, and Statistics. Washington, D.C.: U.S. Social Security Administration. http://www.ssa.gov/policy/docs/statcomps/ssi_asr/2001/

———. 1996. "SSI Childhood Disability Cases Requiring Reevaluation" Briefing Document. Washington, D.C.: U.S. Social Security Administration. August.

Weaver, R. Kent. 2000. *Ending Welfare as We Know It.* Washington, D.C.: Brookings Institution Press.

Weil, Alan. 2001. "Increments Toward What? Incremental Steps Taken Today Affect the Options Available to Future Coverage Expansions." *Health Affairs* 20(1): 68-81.

Weir, Margaret, Ann Shola Orloff, and Theda Skocpol. 1988. "Introduction: Understanding American Social Politics."

L. Christopher Plein

    The Politics of Social Policy in the United States. ed. Margaret Weir, Ann Shola Orloff, and Theda Skocpol, 3-27. Princeton, NJ: Princeton University Press.

Welfare Reform and You. 1997. Brochure published by the West Virginia Welfare Reform Coalition, Charleston, West Virginia.

West Virginia Department of Health and Human Resources [DHHR], Office of Audits, Analysis and Research. 2003a. "Food Stamps - Cases, Recipients, and Expenditures, Monthly Average for State Fiscal Years 1997 - 2003." Charleston, WV: West Virginia Department of Health and Human Resources. http://www.wvdhhr.org/oamr/DAMRreports.htm.

_____. 2003b. "Medicaid Cases and Recipients by County, Monthly Average for State Fiscal Years 1997 - 2003." Charleston, WV: West Virginia Department of Health and Human Resources. http://www.wvdhhr.org/oamr/DAMRreports.htm.

West Virginia Department of Health and Human Resources (DHHR). 2002. "Food Stamp Program" Website. Charleston, WV: West Virginia Department of Health and Human Resources. http://www.wvdhhr.org.

_____. 1998. *WV WORKS: West Virginia's Welfare Reform Program, 1997 Annual Report*. Charleston, WV: West Virginia Department of Health and Human Resources. February.

West Virginia Office of Maternal and Child Health. 1996. *Maternal and Child Health Block Grant Application, Fiscal Year 1997*. Charleston, WV: West Virginia Department of Health and Human Resources, Bureau for Public Health. July.

Wiseman, Michael. 2002. "Food Stamps and Welfare Reform." *Brookings Institution Welfare Reform and Beyond Policy Brief*. No. 19 (April). Washington, D.C.: The Brookings Institution.

Chapter 7

Training Opportunities and Outcomes for WV WORKS Recipients

MELISSA LATIMER

Since the late 1960s, there have been attempts to formally institutionalize the expectation that welfare recipients, including mothers with children, work or participate in a job training activity as a condition for receiving benefits. For example, during the late 1960s, the *Work Incentive Program* provided welfare recipients job training and placement services, and states implemented "workfare" programs that placed welfare recipients into community service jobs. During the early 1970s, the *Comprehensive Employment and Training Act* provided welfare recipients and others with job training and job readiness programs. More recently, the *Family Support Act of 1988* increased the emphasis on work-first strategies by requiring states to implement a Job Opportunities and Basic Skills (JOBS) program. Although states had to place only 20 percent of their caseload into employment situations, the *Family Support Act of 1988* clearly stated that, with a few exceptions, able-bodied adult welfare recipients were expected to work or participate in an activity leading to work. The *Personal Responsibility and Work Opportunity Reconciliation Act of 1996* went even farther. It required states to place at least half of their single-parent family caseload and 90 percent of their two-parent family caseload in a work activity, defined to include both education and job training activities. States failing to meet the work participation rates were subject to fiscal sanctions (see Chapter 3).

Melissa Latimer

This chapter uses data from the authors' 1999 comprehensive statewide survey of WV WORKS leavers to identify significant factors affecting recipient access to education and training programs, skill acquisition, and employment outcomes (Dilger et al. 2000). It is important to remember that West Virginia is a rural state with limited economic diversity and viability. Its economic difficulties made the task of finding employment for recipients difficult. Not only were jobs relatively scarce in many areas within the state, but the state's rural nature, coupled with the lack of an extensive public transportation system, meant that even if a job were available, it was often difficult for the recipient to reach it. Also, as detailed in Chapters 4 and 5, West Virginia's Department of Health and Human Resources (DHHR) intended to reinvent itself from a bureaucracy that focused primarily on determining eligibility into an employment and training center. However, for a host of reasons, especially federal rules that allowed states to count closed cases against the federal work participation requirements, DHHR abandoned that strategy. Instead, it focused on creating administrative barriers to new applicants to keep enrollment and cost as low as possible. And, for those in the program, it embraced a work-first strategy where job training and human capital development were offered only as a "last resort" (Plein 2001).

This chapter examines the effectiveness of West Virginia's education, vocation, and job training programs in promoting job preparation. Specifically, it examines recipient access to education, vocation, and job training programs; factors affecting recipient completion of training programs; the skills recipients learn while in training programs; the recipient's assessment of West Virginia's training programs' usefulness in finding a job; and factors affecting the recipient's employment status after leaving welfare.

Background

Many scholars have studied education and job training programs to determine their effect on the employability of welfare recipients. However, this task has proven to be difficult because states and localities have implemented a large variety of programs

(Gueron and Pauly 1991). For example, some states have focused on classroom instruction and basic skill acquisition while others have emphasized job training (Hagen and Davis 1995; Koon 1997). Also, most states offer a combination of services and often place welfare recipients in programs with little evaluation of their current skills and job readiness status (Orr et al. 1996). This wide variation in programs offered, the skills taught, and the characteristics of the participants complicates the evaluation process and limits the researcher's ability to draw clear cut conclusions about the relationship between training and employment.

One major consequence of this variety is that "evaluations of education and training programs for welfare recipients have shown mixed results" (Relave 1999, 4). For example, the Manpower Demonstration Research Corporation evaluated the most comprehensive welfare-to-work initiatives in the United States and found that the most expensive training programs led to both higher levels of employment and earnings because these programs most directly affected the participant's skill levels. Less expensive work programs led to higher levels of employment (but not higher earnings) by increasing the number and type of jobs for which participants applied (Burtless 1995). Overall, most research studies have found that education and training programs are worthy investments, but have a limited effect on welfare recipient employment and earnings (Bassi 1995; Haveman 1995; Cohen 1998; Relave 1999). As Burtless (1995, 94) argued, "None of it suggests that education and training alone can eliminate the job market problems faced by long-term welfare recipients."

The method chosen to assess program effectiveness (i.e., experimental research designs compare results to a nonparticipating control group while non-experimental research designs do not compare results to a nonparticipating control group) have also provided contradictory results (Porter 1990; Gueron and Pauly 1991; Friedlander and Burtless 1995; Koon 1997). For example, Gueron and Pauly (1991) conducted a comprehensive analysis of thirteen major studies using an experimental research design. They found that voluntary training programs resulted in higher earnings, but not higher levels of employment than mandatory ones. Porter (1990) and Hagen and Davis (1995) did not utilize an experimental research design and reached slightly different conclusions. Porter (1990) found that voluntary training programs attracted more participants than mandatory ones. Hagen and Davis (1995) found that welfare recipients who volunteered for the JOBS program often assessed the program itself and their own ability to learn skills necessary to obtain and keep employment more highly than those who were required to participate.

The *Personal Responsibility and Work Opportunity Reconciliation Act of 1996* further complicated the assessment of education and job training programs by (1) granting states unprecedented responsibility and flexibility to design their own programs, (2) sending contradictory messages to state program designers concerning the relative importance of skill acquisition, work, and caseload reduction, and (3) minimizing reporting requirements. For example, although states were provided additional flexibility to design their own programs, the law required these programs to "end the dependence of needy parents on government benefits by promoting job preparation, work, and marriage" (Public Law 104-193, 1996, 2113). This language suggests that skill acquisition was one of the law's main goals. At the same time, federal guidelines pressure states to "focus on work by attaching both penalties and rewards to program outcomes related to work" (Tweedie 2000, 72). As Tweedie (2000, 72) has noted, "No state had ever managed to achieve participation rates anywhere near those that were required by 2002."

In an effort to avoid federal sanctions, state policymakers across the nation initially increased their "emphasis on work, resulting in immediate and near-universal work requirements and strengthened enforcement" (Tweedie 2000, 72). Thanks in large part to the caseload reduction credit (see Chapter 3), West Virginia, and all other states, were able to avoid significant federal sanctions. However, the federal government's mixed messages concerning which strategy should take precedence, work-first or train-first, resulted in significant state variations in who had access to and who participated in training programs. This variation further complicated efforts to measure the program's efficacy in improving job readiness.

Factors Affecting Participation and Completion

A number of studies predating the *Personal Responsibility and Work Opportunity Reconciliation Act of 1996* identified several variables that affect welfare recipients' participation in education or job training programs, their completion of those programs, and their employment outcomes. For example, the selection of participants and the nature and duration of training varies from state-to-state, with some states defining education and training programs as a "way to increase earnings capacity" (Cohen 1998, 2). States that do this offer education and job training programs only to the most employable welfare recipients so they can find better paying jobs. This strategy is supported by research that found that unemployed workers with at least a high school degree or its equivalent were more likely than those with less education to receive training from their employers (Brown 1998). This employer training, in turn, led to overall higher earnings and less susceptibility to layoffs.

Other states define education and training programs "as an option of last resort for people who cannot find a job without further preparation" (Cohen 1998, 2). Under this scenario, states consider the recipient's age, marital status, education, and his or her children's ages when determining who participates in their training programs. Preference was given to those considered least employable (recipients who are young, never-married, high school dropouts, and/or have preschool aged children) (Edin, Harris, and Sandefur 1998).

Research on Missouri's JOBS program found that (1) slightly older welfare recipients were more likely to complete JOBS than younger recipients, (2) recipients with high educational attainment were more likely to complete JOBS than recipients with low educational levels, and (3) recipients with fewer children and who had delayed child bearing longer were among those most likely to complete JOBS (Koon 1997). In contrast, research on a Title III job retraining program found that, with the exception of race, demographic characteristics were unrelated to program completion (Stewart 1998).

Melissa Latimer

Factors Affecting Employment

A number of pre-welfare reform studies identified education, childcare constraints, and local labor market conditions as the three key factors that determine who works and who does not work, who leaves welfare when they begin to work, and who remains on welfare even though they work. One study found that "education is more important than work experience in helping women leave welfare, helping women to leave welfare more quickly, and helping women stay off welfare once they leave" (Harris 1998, 7). Specifically, it concluded that "a high school education reduced the chance that a woman would return to welfare by 39 percent and education beyond high school reduced the chance of welfare return by 41 percent, compared to those who drop out" (Harris 1998, 8). Another pre-welfare reform study had similar results. It found that Aid to Families with Dependent Children (AFDC) recipients with high educational attainment were more likely than recipients with low educational levels to find employment after completing their JOBS program. Also, slightly older AFDC recipients were more likely than younger recipients to find employment after participating in JOBS (Koon 1997).

Harris (1998, 8) also found that work experience "did not help women stay off welfare. Women who worked prior to their welfare spell were no more likely to remain off of welfare than the women who had no work experience." She concluded that "job placement by itself will not improve the economic situation of women and children on welfare" (Harris 1998, 8).

Although states have tried a variety of work and training programs for welfare recipients over the years, the relationship between training program participation and employment remains unclear (Burtless 1995). Most research findings suggest that welfare recipients who complete their training programs have better earnings and employment outcomes than those who do not. However, one study found that individuals who did not complete the Title III job-retraining program had better post-program outcomes than those who completed the program (Stewart 1998).

Previous research also suggests that childcare affects low-income adults' ability to leave and remain off welfare. According to Harris (1998, 9) "Childcare constraints consistently show significant effects in slowing women's exit from welfare and in causing women to return to welfare." Another study found that AFDC recipients with fewer children and who had delayed childbearing longer were among the most likely to find employment after participating in JOBS (Koon 1997).

Labor market conditions, especially unemployment and wage rates, also affect low-income adults' ability to leave and remain off welfare (Harris 1998). Of particular interest to West Virginia is that rural areas typically have higher unemployment and underemployment rates, higher poverty rates, and they are more likely to experience persistent poverty than urban areas (Lichter 1987; Findeis 1993; Findeis et al. 2001).

After carefully examining the efficacy of job and education training programs for welfare recipients, Gueron and Pauly (1991, 28) concluded that "Employment and earnings impacts did not occur when resources per eligible individuals were too low to provide employment-directed assistance or when programs were operated in a rural, very weak labor market." Several other studies also found that residing in a rural area with high unemployment rates has a negative impact on the efficacy of job and education training programs (Johnson and Stromsdorfer 1990; Maynard 1995; Bischak 1997).

The Research Design

This chapter presents the results of a logistic regression analysis of data from the authors' 1999 survey of 962 WV WORKS recipients whose cases were closed during 1998 (see Chapter 1 for a description of the data gathering process and tests of the sample's representativeness). The analysis (1) determines if WV WORKS leavers had the same opportunity to participate in a vocation, education, or job training program when they were on welfare, (2) identifies the significant factors that affect the recipient's chances of completing a training program, (3) identifies the skills recipients learned in their training program(s), (4) determines their assessment of how helpful the training program was in securing employment, and (5) determines the significant factors that affect WV WORKS leavers' ability to become employed.

Each research questions is identified in the following tables as a dependent variable. For example, 38 percent of respondents to the WV WORKS leaver survey reported that they had participated in a vocation, education, or job training program when they were on welfare. The RECEIVED TRAINING dependent variable was created to indicate if the respondent had received training in any of the following programs while on welfare: JOBS (29.8%), Job Training Partnership Act (JTPA) (29.1 %), Community Work Experience Program (15.4%), Joint Opportunities for Independence (2.6%), Summer Youth Employment Program (6.8%), State Government Rehabilitation (1.5%), Adult Basic Education (11.3%), General Educational Development (GED) class (25.2%), Vocational Training (computers, beauty school, etc.) (15.3%), community college (13.4%), four year college (9.5%), and other programs (7.8%). Respondents could mark multiple responses if necessary. Also, the TRAINING COMPLETION dependent variable was created to indicate if respondents reported that they had completed their training program (28.5%).

Respondents were also asked if they had learned any of the following skills in their training program: job readiness skills (interviewing, resume writing, grooming) (26.3%); childcare or adult care skills (5.5%); computer training (repair, programming) (6.9%); skilled trade (truck driver, machinist, mechanic, welding) (4.1%); food service (food preparation, cook, server) (5.5%); office skills (secretary, receptionist, data entry) (15.7%); health care skills (home health aide) (5.8%); advanced medical training (LPN, RN, EMT, rehab) (3.9%); custodial skills (janitor, housekeeper) (6.9%); personal service skills (beautician, barber, manicurist) (3%); none (14.8%); and other (4.4%). Respondents could mark multiple responses. Dummy, dependent variables were created to indicate if the respondent reported that they had learned any of the three most cited skills (i.e., JOB READY for learning job readiness skills, OFFICE SKILLS for learning office skills, and NO SKILLS for not learning any skills).

Respondents were also asked to evaluate their training program as being: very helpful (27.3%); somewhat helpful (24.1%); they would have helped, but there were no jobs available (19.7%); and not helpful (28.9%) in getting a job. The dichotomous dummy, dependent variable HELPFUL was created to indicate if the respondent reported that the training program was either very helpful or somewhat helpful in getting a job (51.4%).

Finally, respondents were not asked directly if they were employed. However, the survey offered a series of questions under a section marked "Please Complete This Section If You Are Currently Working." This section of the survey included a series of questions about the nature of the respondent's employment. For example, they were asked if their current job was temporary (21%), permanent (75%), or seasonal (4%). The dependent variable EMPLOYED was created to indicate if the respondent marked any of these three responses. Respondents who skipped the survey's working section legitimately (this was determined by examining the respondent's answers to surrounding questions) were coded as not working.

Independent Variables

Previous research has determined that a number of individual (e.g., age, gender, education, etc.), household (e.g., family size, age of children, etc.), and local labor market measures (e.g., unemployment rates, wage rates, labor force participation rates, etc.) are related to poverty, human capital accumulation, and employment. The logistic regression models presented in the following tables include these factors as independent variables. For example, the independent variable NO HIGH SCHOOL (30.4%) measures the respondent's educational attainment, THIRTYONE OR OLDER (49.9%) measures the respondent's age, and FEMALE (82.2%) measures the respondent's sex.

Two additional individual characteristics were included in the models as independent variables. TOTALON measures welfare use. It indicates that the respondent reported that they had received monthly cash assistance for three or more years (40.4%). DISABILITY measures the respondent's assessment of their physical condition as it relates to working. It indicates that they reported that they found it difficult to find a job because they have a physical disability (15%).

Several household characteristics were also used in the models. MARRIED measures marital status. It indicates if the respondent reported having a spouse or partner in the home (38.7%). GT TWO KIDS measures the number of children in the household. It indicates if the respondent reported having three or more children in their household (24%). CCARE ASSISTANCE measures the need for childcare. It indicates if the respondent reported receiving state childcare assistance while on WV WORKS (26%). OWN CAR measures access to reliable transportation. It indicates if the respondent reported that they owned a car or motorcycle (68.8%). PHONE measures access to a working telephone. It indicates if the respondent reported having a working telephone in their home (64.9%).

ARC DISTRESSED and RURAL were created to measure the economic viability of the respondent's local labor market. ARC DISTRESSED indicates if the respondent lived in a county designated by the Appalachian Regional Commission (ARC) as economically distressed (45%). RURAL indicates if the respondent reported living in a rural or a very rural/isolated area (38.1%).

JOBS and JTPA were created to measure the effectiveness of these two training programs. JOBS indicates if the respondent reported that they had participated in a Job Opportunities and Basic Skills program while on welfare (23.1%). JTPA indicates if the respondent reported that they had participated in the Job Training Partnership Act program while on welfare (20.7%).

Finally, the independent variable DHHR was created to measure how the respondent heard about the training program (i.e., from a newspaper, friend or acquaintance, state employment service, or DHHR)/welfare office). It indicates if the respondent reported that they heard about the training program from the DHHR/welfare office (49.2%).

The Data Analysis

Table 7.1 contains the results from the logistic regression for the RECEIVED TRAINING model. The results indicate that when

WV WORKS leavers were on welfare they were not equally likely to participate in a vocation, education, or job training program. For example, the results indicate that recipients who live in a rural area are 1.46 times less likely to participate in a training program than recipients who live in a city/suburb or a small town (i.e., "urban areas"). Also, living in an economically distressed county increases the odds of participating in a training program by 42 percent. In addition, long-term recipients (on welfare for three years or more) are 1.76 times more likely than shorter-term recipients (on welfare for less than three years) to participate in a training program, older recipients (31 years or older) are 1.78 times more likely than younger recipients (18-30 years old) to participate in a training program, and those who received state childcare assistance are almost three times (2.94) more likely than those who did not receive state childcare assistance to participate in a training program. The recipient's sex, marital status, number of children, education, having a physical disability, access to transportation, and access to a working telephone are not significant predictors of receiving vocation, education, or job training in West Virginia.

Table 7.2 contains the results from the logistic regression for the TRAINING COMPLETION model. The results indicate that neither of the labor market measures (ARC DISTRESSED and RURAL) are significant predictors of completing a vocation, education, or job training program. As expected, the recipient's marital status and the number of children in their household affects their chances of completing a training program. Married recipients are 1.54 times more likely than unmarried recipients to finish a training program, and recipients with three children or more are 1.62 times less likely than those with fewer children to complete a training program. Also, recipients with at least a high school degree or GED are 4.94 times more likely than those without a high school degree or GED to complete a training program; long-term recipients (on welfare for three years or more) are 2.64 times more likely than shorter-term recipients to complete a training program; older recipients (31 years or older) are 1.70 times more likely than younger recipients to complete a training program; and those who received state childcare assistance are 2.75 times more likely than those who

	B [1]	S.E. [2]	O/R [3]
ARC Distressed County	.3524**	.1780	1.42
Rural Area	-.3788*	.1856	.6847 [1.46]
Married	.0582	.1960	—
Three Kids or More	.0709	.2121	—
Working Phone	.2408	.1902	—
Own Car/Motorcycle	.2284	.2025	—
No High School	-.0912	.2104	—
Female	.2417	.2627	—
31 Years or Older	.5661**	.1942	1.78
Received Welfare 3 Years Or More	.5661**	.1851	1.76
Physical Disability	-.0401	.2657	—
Received State Assistance With Childcare	1.08***	.2022	2.94

Intercept   -1.59***
-2 Log Likelihood   777.442
Chi-Square   67.136***

* p ≤ .05   ** p ≤ .01   *** p ≤ .001

[1] Standardized coefficients. [2] Standard errors. [3] Odds ratios.

Table 7.1: *Logistic Regression of RECEIVED TRAINING on Labor Market, Household, and Individual Variables (N = 620)*

did not receive state childcare assistance to complete a training program. Once again, the recipient's sex, having a physical disability, access to transportation, and access to a working telephone are not significant predictors of completing a vocation, education, or job training program. It is interesting to note that WV WORKS leavers who participated in a JTPA program while on welfare were

	B	S.E.	O/R
ARC Distressed County	.1015	.1950	—
Rural Area	.3230	.2028	—
Married	.4348*	.2147	1.54
Three Kids or More	-.4832*	.2409	.6168 (1.62)
Working Phone	-.1341	.2120	—
Own Car/Motorcycle	.3099	.2280	—
No High School	-1.589***	.2878	.2023 (4.94)
Female	.3763	.2947	—
31 Years or Older	.5295**	.2121	1.70
Received Welfare 3 Years Or More	.9709***	.2056	2.64
Physical Disability	-.1484	.3018	—
Received State Assistance With Childcare	1.10***	.2133	2.75
Intercept	-2.03***		
-2 Log Likelihood	664.850		
Chi-Square	113.370***		

* $p \leq .05$ ** $p \leq .01$ *** $p \leq .001$

Table 7.2: Logistic Regression of TRAINING COMPLETION on Labor Market, Household, and Individual Variables (N = 620)

more likely than those participating in other training programs to complete their training. Also, those who heard about their training program through the DHHR/welfare office are 98 percent more likely than those who heard about the training programs from another source to complete a training program. Table 7.3 contains the results from the logistic regression for the three skills learned models: JOB READY, OFFICE SKILLS, and NO SKILLS. The results indicate that a variety of variables significantly affect the type of skills recipients learn in their vocation, education, and job training programs. For example, recipients with at least a high school degree or GED are 2.95 times more likely than recipients without a high school degree or GED to learn job readiness skills; recipients who heard about the training program through the DHHR/welfare office are 73 percent more likely than those who heard about the training through another source to learn job readiness skills; and recipients who had participated in a JOBS or JTPA program are, respectively, 2.57 and 1.72 times more likely than those who did not participate in JOBS or JTPA programs to learn job readiness skills. Also, recipients who completed a training program are 2.71 times more likely than those who did not complete a training program to learn job readiness skills.

Education, JTPA participation, and training completion are also significant predictors of learning office skills. Once again, recipients with at least a high school degree or GED are 2.74 times more likely than recipients without a high school degree or GED to learn office skills; JTPA participants are 2.33 more likely than nonparticipants to learn office skills; and recipients who completed a training program are 78 percent more likely than those who did not complete a training program to learn office skills. In addition, female recipients are almost nine times more likely than male recipients to learn office skills.

The type of training program and how recipients heard about the training program were the only significant predictors in the learned-no-skills model. Recipients who heard about the training program through the DHHR are 89 percent more likely than those who heard about the training program from other sources to learn no skills. In contrast, those who did not participate in JOBS are 2.11 times more likely than those who did participate in JOBS to learn no skills.

Table 7.4 contains the results from the logistic regression for the HELPFUL model. The results indicate that recipients who live in a county that has not been designated economically distressed are 74 percent more likely than those living in an economically distressed county to report that their training program was helpful in finding a job, recipients with at least a high school degree or GED

	JOB READY		OFFICE SKILLS		NO SKILLS	
	B	O/R	B	O/R	B	O/R
ARC Distressed County	.103	—	-.314	—	.132	—
Rural Area	-.099	—	.240	—	-.537	—
Married	-.379	—	.061	—	.300	—
Three Kids or More	.134	—	-.126	—	.204	—
Working Phone	.066	—	.733*	2.08	-.153	—
Own Car/Motorcycle	-.304	—	-.109	—	-.467	—
No High School	-1.08***	.339 (2.95)	-1.02*	.362 (2.74)	.460	—
Female	.179	—	2.14**	8.87	.178	—
31 Years or Older	.030	—	-.157	—	.216	—
Welfare > 2 Years	.209	—	.171	—	-.183	—
Physical Disability	-.179	—	.043	—	.468	—
Completed Training	.996***	2.71	.574*	1.78	-.533	—
Heard Thru DHHR	.550*	1.73	.184	—	.635*	1.89
Participated in JOBS	.943***	2.57	.279	—	-.746*	.474 (1.89)
Participated in JTPA	.543*	1.72	.848**	2.33	-.046	—
Intercept	-1.99***		-4.60***		-1.71**	
-2 Log Likelihood	476.288		378.035		379.296	
Chi-Square	91.550***		59.546***		28.121*	

* p ≤ .05   ** p ≤ .01   *** p ≤ .001

Table 7.3: Logistic Regression of JOB READY, OFFICE SKILLS, and NO SKILLS on Labor Market, Household, and Individual Variables (N = 485)

are 59 percent more likely than those without a high school degree or GED to report that their training program was helpful in finding a job, and recipients who learned office skills in their training program are 2.07 times more likely than those who did not learn office skills in their training program to report that their training program was helpful in finding a job.

Melissa Latimer

Living in an economically distressed county and sex are the only significant predictors when type of skills is deleted from the HELPFUL model. In this new model, female recipients are 2.11 times more likely than male recipients to report that their training program was helpful in finding a job.

	B	S.E.	O/R
ARC Distressed County	-.553*	.263	.575 (1.74)
Rural Area	-.063	.278	——
Married	.238	.306	——
Three Kids or More	-.146	.320	——
Working Phone	.155	.283	——
Own Car/Motorcycle	.310	.305	——
No High School	-.765*	.372	.466 (1.59)
Female	.631	.422	——
31 Years or Older	-.032	.285	——
Welfare > 2 Years-	.044	.273	——
Physical Disability	-.411	.404	——
Completed Training	-.135	.286	——
Heard Thru DHHR	.140	.295	——
Participated in JOBS	.000	.337	——
Participated in JTPA	-.238	.318	——
Job Readiness Skills	.266	.303	——
Office Skills	.726*	.377	2.07
Intercept	-.246		
-2 Log Likelihood	352.490		
Chi-Square	29.884*		

 * $p \leq .05$ ** $p \leq .01$ *** $p \leq .001$

Table 7.4: Logistic Regression of HELPFUL on Labor Market, Household, and Individual Variables (N = 342)

Training Opportunities and Outcomes

Table 7.5 contains the logistic regression for the EMPLOYED model. The results indicate that WV WORKS leavers are not equally likely to be employed. Surprisingly, living in a rural area or an economically distressed county are not significant predictors of employment. Marital status, access to transportation, education, having a physical disability, and state assistance with childcare are the key predictor variables in this model. For example, married leavers are 2.30 times less likely than non-married leavers to be employed. Those who own a car or motorcycle are 2.41 times more likely than those who do not own a car or motorcycle to be employed.

Leavers who have not completed high school or its equivalent are twice as unlikely than those with a high school degree to be employed. Leavers who report having a physical disability are approximately eight times less likely than those without a physical disability to be employed. Leavers who received state assistance for childcare are 1.82 times more likely than those without this assistance to be employed. The number of children in the household, access to a working telephone, length of time on welfare, age, gender, completion of a training program, type of skills learned in the program, and how they heard about the training programs are not significant predictors of leaver employment status.[1]

It is interesting to note that when all the training variables are eliminated from this model (decreasing the sample size to 585) the only change in what predicts employment is that leavers with a working telephone in their home are 67 percent more likely than those without access to a working telephone to be employed. This finding suggests that West Virginia's Link-Up America program, which subsidizes telephone installation in low-income households, may have a beneficial effect on the employability of the state's low-income population.

	B	S.E.	O/R
ARC Distressed County	.247*	.249	1.28
Rural Area	-.392	.259	—
Married	-.833*	.284	.435 (2.30)
Three Kids or More	.014	.296	—
Working Phone	.269	.259	—
Own Car/Motorcycle	.879**	.284	2.41
No High School	-.695*	.335	.499 (2.00)
Female	.058	.380	—
31 Years or Older	.355	.264	—
Welfare > 2 Years-	.101	.260	—
Physical Disability	-2.074***	.447	.126 (7.96)
Completed Training	.338	.263	—
Heard Thru DHHR	.266	.262	—
Participated in JOBS	.136	.324	—
Participated in JTPA	.119	.312	—
Job Readiness Skills	.030	.303	—
Office Skills	-.228	.352	—
State Assistance with Childcare	.598*	.272	1.82

Intercept   -.410
-2 Log Likelihood   693.968
Chi-Square   116.807***

* $p \leq .05$ ** $p \leq .01$ *** $p \leq .001$

Table 7.5: Logistic Regression of EMPLOYED on Labor Market, Household, and Individual Variables (N = 372)

Training Opportunities and Outcomes

Conclusion

One of this chapter's primary goals was to identify significant factors affecting recipient skill acquisition. The fact that only 38 percent of the survey's respondents participated in a vocation, education, or job training program while on welfare was the first indication that West Virginia's welfare recipients are not equally likely to have access to training. The logistic regression analyses presented in Tables 7.1 - 7.5 provided further empirical support for this conclusion.

The TRAINING PARTICIPATION model was the only one in which both labor market variables (ARC DISTRESSED and RURAL) have significant effects on the dependent variable. These results indicate that "place" affects access to training programs. Recipients who live in the state's more rural areas are significantly less likely to participate in training programs than recipients in more urban areas. Tickamyer and Duncan (1990) argue that, nationally, one of the problems of living in rural areas is that rural areas have a less developed "public infrastructure" than urban areas. They argue that rural areas have a more restricted institutional and financial base than urban areas and that these restrictions adversely affect the availability, effectiveness, and delivery of public programs. This analysis supports that conclusion. WV WORKS rural recipients clearly have less access than their urban counterparts to training programs designed to increase employment and income.

This analysis also revealed that WV WORKS recipients who live in an economically distressed county are more likely than those living in a non-economically distressed county to participate in a training program. Although WV WORKS has a "work first/training last" orientation, the stagnant economic situation in economically distressed counties limits recipient employment options. It appears that caseworkers in West Virginia's economically distressed counties are more likely than caseworkers in other counties to place recipients into vocation, education, and job training programs.

It is interesting to note that older recipients and long-term recipients are more likely than younger and shorter-term recipients to receive training in West Virginia. These results reinforce the notion that WV WORKS offers training as a last resort to the least employable welfare recipients. The data suggest that long-term recipients have literally worked their way through the system into these training programs. Educational level is not significant in this model because "training" was broadly defined to include adult basic education programs, GED programs, job training, and vocational training programs. In fact, when the definition of training is restricted to participation in a JTPA program, individuals with at least a high school degree or GED are twice as likely as those without a high school degree or GED to participate in this type of training.

The finding that recipients who received state childcare assistance are more likely than those who did not receive state childcare assistance to participate in training programs suggests that West Virginia's efforts to increase recipient childcare services is warranted. The empirical evidence indicates that providing recipients financial assistance for childcare services reduces barriers to programs that help recipients move toward economic self-sufficiency.

Access to a training program is the first step toward skill acquisition. The second step is completing the training program. Only 28 percent of the respondents to the WV WORKS leaver survey reported that they had completed a training program when they were on welfare. Surprisingly, place did not have a significant effect on training completion. Some researchers argue that welfare recipients in more economically viable labor markets leave training programs early when job openings occur. This was not the case in West Virginia. One possible explanation for this is that, with only a few exceptions, West Virginia's economy is so weak that there is relatively little difference in the job opportunities available to welfare leavers in counties designated by ARC as economically distressed and in those without that label.

As expected, household variables have a significant effect on training completion. Several national studies have suggested that being married limits women's labor market opportunities. This was not the case in West Virginia. Being married increased the probability of completing a training program. One possible explanation for this is that having a spouse or partner provides additional social

Training Opportunities and Outcomes

and economic support, and this support translated into a higher completion rate. Several national studies also found that the number of children in the household, the recipient's age, and the recipient's education had a significant effect on training completion (Koon 1997). This was also true in West Virginia. Recipients with three or more children in the household were less likely than recipients with fewer children to complete a training program, older recipients (31 years old and older) were more likely than younger recipients to complete a training program, and recipients with at least a high school degree or GED were more likely than recipients without a high school degree or GED to complete a training program.

The analysis revealed that recipients who received state childcare assistance are more likely than those who did not receive state childcare assistance to complete a training program. This finding suggests that the state's efforts to enhance its childcare assistance programs was warranted. The empirical evidence indicates that providing state childcare assistance helps recipients to receive the training necessary to move them toward economic self-sufficiency.

Another of this chapter's goals was to identify training outcomes for West Virginia's welfare recipients. One way to assess training outcomes is to examine the actual skills learned in the training programs. One of the most distressing findings in this research is that the three skills recipients learned most frequently in their training programs are job readiness skills (26.3%), office skills (15.7%), and no skills (14.8%). These "skills" do little to help recipients leave and stay off welfare, and they do relatively little to reduce poverty.

As in the previous model, the more employable recipients (i.e., those having more education) are more likely to receive job readiness and office skills in their training program than the least employable recipients. Also, participation in JOBS and/or JTPA has significant positive effects on "skill" acquisition. Unfortunately, both of these programs have been eliminated (JOBS was eliminated by the *Personal Responsibility and Work Opportunity Reconciliation Act of 1996* and JTPA was eliminated by the *Workforce Investment Act of 1998*). In addition, it is important to note that recipients who complete a training program are more likely than recipients who do not complete a training program to gain both job readiness and office skills. Finally, recipients who heard about their training program from the DHHR/welfare office are more likely than those who heard about their training program from another source to learn no skills. One possible explanation for this is that going through the DHHR/welfare office increases the probability that the recipient's participation in the training program was mandatory. Hagen and Davis (1995) found that recipients who volunteer for training programs often assess the programs and their own ability to learn skills more favorably than those required to participate.

Another way to assess training outcomes is to examine the recipient's assessment of the training programs in which they participated. Only about half (51.4%) of the respondents to the WV WORKS leavers' survey who participated in an education, vocation, or job training program in West Virginia reported that the program was "helpful" in helping them find a job. Unfortunately, the data suggest that West Virginia's training programs promote job preparation for only some recipients (i.e., those living in an economically distressed county and those with at least a high school degree or GED).

The final way to assess training outcomes in West Virginia is to examine the employment status of WV WORKS leavers. Approximately 46 percent of the respondents to the WV WORKS leavers survey reported that they were employed at the time they completed the survey. Obviously, WV WORKS leavers are not equally likely to be employed. Several national studies have found that education, vocation, and job training programs' effect on recipients' annual earnings depends largely upon the recipient's job readiness (i.e., educational attainment, absence of physical and mental disability, absence of childcare needs, etc.) (Gueron and Pauly 1991; Harris 1998; Koon 1997). This analysis supports this conclusion. For example, having at least a high school degree or GED and lacking a physical disability are both significant predictors of WV WORKS leaver employment. The negative effect having a physical disability has on finding employment in West Virginia is worth special mention. West Virginia has a relatively high worker disability rate, especially among male recipients. Although work disability is a prevalent health problem throughout rural Appalachia, West Virginia's work disability rates, most likely related to the state's relatively heavy reliance on the mining and natural resource extraction industries, are among the highest in the nation (Burkett 1994).

Finally, WV WORKS leavers who own a car or motorcycle are significantly more likely than those who do not own a vehicle to be employed. This finding provides empirical support for continuing DHHR's efforts to provide recipients subsidized vehicle leases to help them find and retain employment and take advantage of training opportunities.

Participation in and completion of an education, vocation, or job training program also has a positive effect on employment outcomes (i.e., once state assistance for childcare is removed from the model). This finding provides additional support for the argument that training programs are worthy investments for helping recipients move toward economic self-sufficiency (Burtless 1995). Surprisingly, the measures of labor market conditions are not significant predictors of employment. This finding is a testament, once again, to the relatively dire economic conditions WV WORKS recipients and leavers face in most areas within the state.

In sum, the key to designing education, vocation, and job training programs that enhance the skills of welfare recipients is understanding the types of programs available, the type of skills taught within those programs, the characteristics of participants in those programs, and the outcomes of these programs. Developing efficient, cost-effective training programs is particularly crucial for an economically disadvantaged state like West Virginia. The empirical analysis of the data from the WV WORKS leaver survey indicates that West Virginia is far from reaching this goal. Moreover, in most instances, the most disadvantaged WV WORKS recipients (those with the least job skills and education) are the least likely to participate in a training program, the least likely to complete a training program, the least likely to acquire skills from a training program, and the least likely to find employment. The data cannot tell us if DHHR engages in "creaming," a process where front line workers purposely avoid placing the least job ready recipients into a job or into an education, vocation, or job training program. It is possible that the more job ready recipients self-selected themselves for more training opportunities than those who have been less successful at school and work. Regardless of the cause, this pattern of not providing training to the least job ready is disheartening and the consequences of this pattern must be fully understood. Previous research has shown that even though long-term recipients and those with low educational attainment, minimal job experience, and low skill levels are the least job ready, they receive the greatest benefit from education, vocation, and job training programs (Koon 1997; Porter 1990). The only way most of these least job ready recipients are ever going to leave welfare and move toward economic self-sufficiency is to provide them access to West Virginia's education, vocation, and job training programs. Unfortunately, that has not been the case in West Virginia.

Notes

1. Completion of a vocation, education, or job training program is a significant positive predictor of employment once received state assistance with childcare is removed from this model.

References

Bassi, Laurie J. 1995. "Stimulating Employment and Increasing Opportunity for the Current Work Force." *The Work Alternative: Welfare Reform and the Realities of the Job Market*. ed. Demetra Smith Nightingale and Robert H. Haveman, 137-156. Washington, D.C.: The Urban Institute.

Bischak, Greg. 1997. "Briefing Paper: Welfare Reform and its Potential Impact on Appalachia." Washington, D.C.: Appalachian Regional Commission.

Brown, Charles. 1989. "Empirical Evidence on Private Training." *Labor Economics and Public Policy*. ed. Laurie Bassi and David Crawford. Greenwich, CT: JAI Press.

Burkett, Gary L. 1994. "Status of Health in Appalachia." *Sowing Seeds in the Mountains: Community-Based Coalitions For Cancer Prevention and Control*. ed. Richard Couto, Nancy K. Simpson, and Gale Harris, 43-61. Washington D.C.: The

National Cancer Institute.

Burtless, Gary. 1995. "Employment Prospects of Welfare Recipients." *The Work Alternative: Welfare Reform and the Realities of the Job Market*. ed. Demetra Smith Nightingale and Robert H. Haveman, 71-108. Washington, D.C.: The Urban Institute.

Cohen, Marie. 1998. "Education and Training Under Welfare Reform." *Welfare Information Network Issue Note* (Vol. 2): 2. http://www.financeprojectinfo.org/Publications/edissue.htm.

Dilger, Robert Jay, Eleanor Blakely, Karen V.H. Dorton, Melissa Latimer, Barry Locke, Carson Mencken, L. Christopher Plein, Lucinda M. Potter, David Williams, and Dong Pil Yoon. 2000. "West Virginia Case Closure Study." *The West Virginia Public Affairs Reporter* 17(1): 2-15.

Edin, Kathryn, Kathleen Mullan Harris, and Gary D. Sandefur, Editors. 1998. *Welfare to Work: Opportunities and Pitfalls*. Washington, D.C.: American Sociological Association.

Findeis, Jill L. 1993. "Utilization of Rural Labor Resources." *Economic Adaptation: Alternatives for Nonmetropolitan Areas*. ed. David Barkley. Boulder, CO: Westview Press.

Findeis, Jill L., Mark Henry, Thomas Hirschl, Willis Lewis, Ismael Ortega-Sanchez, Emelie Peine, Julie Zimmerman. 2001. "Welfare Reform in Rural America: A Review of Current Research." Rural Policy Research Institute. P2001-5. Columbia, MO: University of Missouri.

Friedlander, Daniel and Gary Burtless. 1995. *Five Years Later*. New York: Russell Sage Foundation.

Gueron, Judith M. and Edward Pauly. 1991. *From Welfare to Work*. New York: Russell Sage Foundation.

Hagen, Jan L. and Liane V. Davis. 1995. "The Participants' Perspective on the Job Opportunities and Basic Skills Training Program." *Social Service Review* 69 (December): 656-678.

Harris, Kathleen Mulan. 1998. "Presentation." *Welfare to Work:*

Opportunities and Pitfalls. ed. Kathryn Edin, Kathleen Mullan Harris, and Gary D. Sandefur, 6-9. Washington, D.C.: American Sociological Association.

Haveman, Robert H. 1995. "The Clinton Alternative to 'Welfare as We Know It': Is It Feasible." *The Work Alternative: Welfare Reform and the Realities of the Job Market.* ed. Demetra Smith Nightingale and Robert H. Haveman, 185-202. Washington, D.C.: The Urban Institute.

Johnson, Terry R. and Ernst W. Stromsdorfer. 1990. "Evaluating Net Program Impact." *Evaluating Social Programs at the State and Local Level: The JTPA Evaluation Design Project.* ed. Ann Bonar Blalock, 43-131. Kalamazoo, MI: W. E. Upjohn Institute.

Koon, Richard L. 1997. *Welfare Reform: Helping the Least Fortunate Become Less Dependent.* New York: Garland Publishing, Inc.

Lichter, Daniel. 1987. "Measuring Underemployment in Rural Areas." *Rural Development Perspectives* 3: 11-14.

Maynard, Rebecca A. 1995. "Subsidized Employment and Non-Labor Market Alternatives for Welfare Recipients." *The Work Alternative: Welfare Reform and the Realities of the Job Market.* ed. Demetra Smith Nightingale and Robert H. Haveman, 109-136. Washington, D.C.: The Urban Institute.

Orr, Larry L, Howard S. Bloom, Stephen H. Bell, Fred Doolittle, Winston Lin, George Cave. 1996. Does Training for the Disadvantaged Work?: Evidence from the National JTPA Study. Washington, D.C.: The Urban Institute Press.

Plein, Christopher. 2001. *Welfare Reform in a Hard Place: The West Virginia Experience.* Report No. 13. Albany, NY: The Nelson A. Rockefeller Institute of Government.

Porter, Kathryn H. 1990. *Making JOBS Work: What the Research Says About Effective Employment Programs for AFDC Recipients.* Washington, D.C.: Center on Budget and Policy Priorities.

Relave, Nanette. 1999. "Moving from Welfare-to-Work: An Overview of Work Participation Issues: Compiled from the WIN Web site." Welfare Information Network Issue Note Volume 3, Issue 7. http://www.welfareinfo.org/nanetteissue.htm.

Stewart, James B. 1998. "Worker Re-Training and Labor Market Outcomes: A New Focus for Labor Research." *The Review of Black Political Economy* 25(4): 55-75.

Tickamyer, Ann R. and Cynthia Duncan. 1990. "Poverty and Opportunity Structure in Rural America." *Annual Review of Sociology* 16(1): 67-86.

Tweedie, Jack. 2000. "From D.C. to Little Rock: Welfare Reform at Mid-term." *Publius: The Journal of Federalism* 30(1-2): 69-97.

West Virginia Department of Health and Human Resources (DHHR). 2001. *Report to the Legislative Oversight Commission on Health and Human Resources Accountability*. Charleston, WV: West Virginia Department of Health and Human Resources.

Chapter 8

Is Work the Solution?

LUCINDA A. POTTER

It is increasingly clear that the only way for families to break the cycle of dependency and escape poverty is through work ... welfare reform has brought unprecedented success as millions of Americans now know the value and reward of hard work.
– Tommy Thompson, Secretary, U.S. Department of Health and Human Services (DHHS 2002)

The *Personal Responsibility and Work Opportunity Reconciliation Act of 1996* fundamentally changed American welfare policy. It replaced Aid to Families with Dependent Children (AFDC), an open-ended reimbursement categorical grant that provided states 50 percent to 80 percent of their expenses (inversely related to the state's per capita income), with Temporary Assistance for Needy Families (TANF), a block grant with fixed annual expenditures. It also changed the "rules of the game" for both recipients and states. With very few exceptions, recipients now must work in exchange for their benefits, and they are subject to a sixty-month lifetime limit on the receipt of benefits. States were required to place an increasing percentage of their adult recipients into an approved work activity (at least half of their total caseload and 90% of two-parent households by FY 2002) or be subject to fiscal sanctions (5% of their federal TANF funds during the first year of non-compliance, and an additional 2% of funding for each consecutive year they continue in noncompliance, up to a maximum of 21%). This new emphasis on work, often referred to as the work-first strategy, assumed that paid employment was universally positive, that jobs were available, and that individuals, not government, were ultimately responsible for their social and economic circumstances and for changing those circumstances. Given these assumptions, it makes sense to ask if the emphasis on work-first has improved the lives of the poor. Specifically, this chapter addresses three questions:

- Does work enhance TANF recipients' ability to leave and remain off welfare?

- Does work lead to a significant improvement in household income or expectations concerning future household income?

- Does work influence recipients' assessment of their own well-being?

Requiring the Able-bodied to Work: The Work Requirement Is No Surprise

Much of the current rhetoric concerning work requirements is a continuation of a subtle shift in explicit policy goals that began in earnest in 1967. However, associating work with the receipt of welfare benefits dates back much farther (Weir et al. 1988; Gordon 1994; Handler and Hasenfeld 1997). Requiring work has its roots in the earliest social welfare policies that evolved in Elizabethan times. For example, the Statute of Laborers enacted in the mid-1300s forced beggars to work by forbidding the giving of alms to the able-bodied. Given the acute labor shortage at that time, largely due to widespread famine and the Black Death, the Statute of Laborers also fixed wages, restricted travel among the unemployed, and literally "compelled jobless persons to work for any employer willing to hire them" (Trattner 1999, 8). In 1536, the *Henrician Poor Law*, also known as the *Act for the Punishment of Vagabonds and Beggars*, strengthened penalties for begging as a means to reduce dependence and sloth. However, it also established the precedent of limited government responsibility for addressing the poor's needs by appropriating public funds to create work for the able-bodied.

The emphasis on work continued with the passage of the *Elizabethan Poor Law* in 1601. Further reinforcing government's interest in supporting and maintaining a strong economy, it created two categories of "needy": the deserving and non-deserving. Those deemed unable to care for themselves (the deserving) were provided locally financed and administered relief. Able-bodied adults (the non-deserving) were required to participate in "work-relief" programs. Able-bodied children were apprenticed. To discourage the migration of undesirables to their communities, and to keep local taxes as low as possible, local governments typically imposed stringent residency requirements for the receipt of benefits.

Prior to the Great Depression, aid to the poor in the United States, following the English tradition, was primarily a state and local government responsibility, and most of those programs were targeted toward deserving populations (those deemed unable to help themselves). During the Great Depression, unemployment and poverty, previously thought to reflect an individual failing rather than a systematic condition, were so pervasive that many began to reconsider this basic assumption. This opened a policy window of opportunity that resulted in the passage of the *Social Security Act of 1935*. Its five programs, Old-Age Insurance (OAI), Old-Age Assistance (OAA), Unemployment Insurance, Aid to the Blind (AB), and Aid to Dependent Children (ADC), ushered in a new era, with the national government playing an increasingly important role in providing assistance to the poor. Nevertheless, funding for these programs, at least initially, remained relatively modest, and the amount of assistance provided recipients purposely fell short of the level necessary to escape poverty. The intent was to provide recipients enough assistance to get by, but not enough to discourage work. As a result, although none of these programs required recipients to work, many recipients were forced to work to make ends meet.

From its very beginnings, America's "welfare state" has really been the equivalent of a "work ethic state" because most public assistance programs were tied to work. For example, workers' compensation is conditioned on prior participation in the workforce.

Social security pensions are for those who have paid into the system during their working lifetimes. Even the Earned Income Tax Credit, a program that has received bipartisan support, is, by definition, available only to those with earned income (Kaus 2001).

Attitudes about the nature of welfare and work began to change following the publication of *The Other America* in 1962 (Harrington 1962). This book focused on the plight of the impoverished in the United States, a population that had been largely invisible since World War II. Harrington argued that despite being the most affluent nation in the world, nearly one out of every four Americans were living in poverty (Segal and Brzuzy 1998). Moreover, he argued that there were pockets of economic hardship that would prove particularly difficult to erase: the rural poor located in the Appalachian mountains and in the deep South, and the urban poor located in the ghettoes of America's largest cities. Coupled with intense interest group activity in areas, such as civil rights, voting rights, and women's rights, Harrington's book helped set the stage for a new policy discourse on poverty in America. For the first time since the 1930s, social welfare policy development ranked high on the national government's political agenda. President Lyndon Johnson's subsequent War on Poverty led to a proliferation of legislation during the 1960s that created a myriad of programs, services, and agencies designed to help the poor escape poverty. For example, Food Stamps addressed hunger, Community Action was created to ameliorate poverty on the local level, Medicare and Medicaid addressed the nation's health care needs, and Head Start provided services to poor preschool children. It was a time of great optimism: the national government would and could address all of the nation's social and economic problems (Segal and Brzuzy 1998).

Almost immediately, there were efforts to return to the long-standing commitment to work as the primary means to ameliorate poverty. For example, the Work Incentive (WIN) amendments to Title IV of the *Social Security Act of 1967* provided funding for job training and job placement services for welfare recipients. Although it moved relatively few recipients into work, WIN marked the beginning of a shift away from the education-first and job training-first strategies underlying many of the War on Poverty programs back toward encouraging recipients to work (Edwards et.al. 1997). Women's changing role in society (i.e., more women entered the workforce) helped to legitimize this expectation. As more middle and upper income mothers entered the workforce, they began to wonder why welfare mothers were not required to do the same (Weil and Finegold 2002).

Subsequent reforms continued to erode welfare's entitlement status. In 1972, President Richard Nixon proposed a federal guaranteed minimum income to replace Aid to Families With Dependent Children (AFDC), OAA, AB, and Aid to the Permanently and Totally Disabled (APTD) program. His "Family Assistance Plan" failed to win congressional approval, but it established a political dialogue that resulted in major changes in OAA, AB, and APTD. These three programs were federalized under a new program, Supplemental Security Income (SSI). States no longer determine eligibility requirements, nor directly administer these programs. In essence, these programs became subject to minimum national standards, thereby separating their populations from AFDC recipients (DiNitto and Dye 1987). This segmentation made it possible to explicitly redefine AFDC recipients as "undeserving" without having to deem the aged, blind, and disabled populations as undeserving. More importantly, from a policy perspective this move left welfare recipients politically exposed and vulnerable (Helco 2001).

The *Family Support Act of 1988* further increased the emphasis on work and work readiness preparation by requiring states to establish a Job Opportunities and Basic Skills (JOBS) program. With only a few exceptions, able-bodied, adult AFDC recipients who were not already working thirty or more hours a week were required to participate in a JOBS program. States had to place an increasing percentage of their adult caseload (starting at 7% in FY 1990 and rising to 20% in FY 1995), or lose a portion of their AFDC funds. Because states were having difficulty meeting the work participation requirements, many of them requested, and were granted, federal waivers that allowed them to experiment with innovative programs designed to encourage recipients to find and retain work. By the early 1990s, most states operated under federal waivers rather than under the JOBS provisions. The *Personal Responsibility and Work*

Lucinda A. Potter

Opportunity Reconciliation Act of 1996 continued the shift back to a work-first strategy for addressing poverty by requiring states to place an increasing percentage of their adult recipients into an approved work activity (increasing the mandated work participation threshold from 20% under *The Family Support Act of 1988* to at least half of the state's total caseload and 90% of its two-parent family caseload by FY 2002).

Solving the Poverty Problem: Competing Values and Policy Assumptions

Economists use human capital theory to explain poverty. They argue that the poor are poor because they lack the knowledge, skills, training, work habits, and abilities employers seek in a free market. Because the private economy has no general role for such people, they become government's responsibility (Dye 1987). Since the 1960s, national, state, and local governments have spent tens of billions of dollars annually on job training and educational programs designed to enhance the poor's human capital. Despite countless studies, the efficacy of these programs remains unclear. Advocates of the train-first strategy for addressing poverty point to studies that indicate that the best way to enhance the poor's human capital is to provide them job-readiness and job training programs. Advocates of the education-first strategy for addressing poverty point to other studies that indicate that the poor's long-term earning power increases as their educational attainment increases. Advocates of the work-first strategy point out that despite spending tens of billions of dollars each year on job training and educational programs, there is little evidence to suggest that these programs have had a significant effect on the nation's overall poverty rate. They argue that the best way to enhance the poor's human capital is to put them into a job, any job.

Advocates of the human capital development strategy for addressing poverty have historically advocated government funding for both job training and educational programs. They then rely on caseworkers to decide, in consultation with recipients, the best strategy for enhancing that particular recipient's human capital (Michalopoulos and Schwartz 2000; Gueron and Hamilton 2002). Some recipients, they argue, need educational assistance followed by job training assistance, and some need job training or job search assistance only. However, despite their continued support for additional government funding for welfare and related support programs, advocates of the human capital development strategy have struggled with at least three "helping conundrums" (Ellwood 1988; Berlin 2001). The assistance-family structure conundrum recognizes that welfare threatens the sanctity of the traditional family structure because recipients often lose their benefits after getting married (because the spouse's income is counted toward the program's eligibility requirements). The targeting-isolation conundrum recognizes that public assistance programs stigmatize, label, and isolate people, making it more difficult for them to find and retain work. Most importantly, the security-work conundrum recognizes that reducing the pressure to work decreases both the incentive to work and the rewards of working. The worry is that freely giving benefits can lead to idleness, lack of responsibility, and deterioration of society's moral fabric (Gordon 1994; Handler and Hasenfeld 1997).

Advocates of the work-first strategy for addressing poverty have pointed to these "helping conundrums," especially the security-work conundrum, as further evidence of the need to place recipients into work or work-related activities. Advocates of the human capital development strategy counter these claims by pointing to studies that have demonstrated that the typical welfare recipient maintains a strong orientation toward work. In fact, recipients are very uncomfortable with notions of dependency, but many of them report multiple employment barriers (lack of education, lack of appropriate training, lack of childcare, lack of available jobs, lack of transportation, etc.) that prevent them from obtaining and retaining a job (Rank, 1994; Henly and Danzinger 1997). Numerous studies have indicated that poor people, including welfare recipients, dislike welfare and would much rather be economically self-sufficient. They derive dignity from paid work, even if the wages are low and advancement opportunities are limited (Cherlin and Wilson 2002). Americans who leave welfare for work gain the respect society reserves for workers (Kaus 2001). As such, recipients view work as the means to higher self-esteem, full participation in the economic system, and acceptance as responsible, productive, self-reliant citizens.

Lucinda A. Potter

Research Design

This chapter presents the results of a logistic regression analysis of data from the authors' 1999 survey of 962 WV WORKS recipients whose cases were closed during 1998 (see Chapter 1 for a description of the data gathering process and tests and tests of the sample's representativeness). The analysis tests the assumption underlying the enactment of the *Personal Responsibility and Work Opportunity Reconciliation Act of 1996* that emphasizing a work-first strategy is the best solution for addressing poverty in America. Specifically, it determines if paid employment (i.e., the work-first strategy) (1) improves the recipient's ability to leave and stay off welfare, (2) increases household income and expectations about household income, and (3) improves the recipient's notion of well-being (several studies have indicated that individuals with fatalistic attitudes and poor self-worth have lower employment and earnings histories than those with more positive attitudes and images of self-worth).

Each of these research questions is identified in the following tables as a dependent variable. For example, the survey asked respondents to indicate their involvement with WV WORKS. Most of the respondents (77.9%) reported that they had left WV WORKS and stayed off the program. The remainder either had left the program but were back on WV WORKS when they completed the survey (10.9%) or had left WV WORKS, returned to WV WORKS, and had left the program again (11.2%). The LEFT AND STAYED OFF WV WORKS dependent variable was created to indicate if the respondent had left and stayed off WV WORKS (see Table 8.1).

Respondents were also asked to report how much money their household received in 1998. Respondents chose from among six categories: Less than $5,000 (47.7%); $5,000 to $10,000 (35.2%); $10,001 to $15,000 (10.2%); $15,001 to $20,000 (3.4%); $20,001 to $25,000 (1.7%); and more than $25,000 (1.8%). The TOTAL HOUSEHOLD INCOME dependent variable was created to indicate if the respondent reported a 1998 total household income greater than $10,000 (17.1%) (see Table 8.2).

Respondents were also asked to report how much money they thought their household would receive in 1999. Respondents chose from among six categories: Less than $5,000 (30.3%); $5,000 to $10,000 (39.6%); $10,001 to $15,000 (15.9%); $15,001 to $20,000 (6.5%); $20,001 to 25,000 (3.5%); and more than $25,000 (4.3%). The TOTAL EXPECTED HOUSEHOLD INCOME dependent variable was created to indicate if the respondents reported that they expected a 1999 total household income greater than $10,000 (30.2%) (see Table 8.3).

Respondents who reported that they were not currently receiving WV WORKS were asked to respond to a general question about their personal circumstances. They were asked to complete the statement, "Personally, are you . . .": Much better off than when you were on WV WORKS, TANF or AFDC (28.2%); Better off than you were on WV WORKS, TANF or AFDC (18.1%); About the same as when you were on WV WORKS, TANF or AFDC (33.3%); Worse off than when you were on WV WORKS, TANF, or AFDC (12.4%); or much worse off than when you were on WV WORKS, TANF or AFDC (8%). The FEELING BETTER OFF NOW dependent variable was created to indicate if respondents reported that they were either much better off or better off now than when they were on welfare (46.3%) (see Table 8.4).

The Independent Variables

Previous research has suggested that local economic conditions are significantly associated with the ability to leave and stay off welfare, total household income, expectations about household income, and self-assessment of well-being (Knab et al. 2000; Michalopoulos and Schwartz 2000; O'Neill and Hill 2001; Gueron and Hamilton 2002; Kim 2002; Moffitt 2002a and 2002b; Patel 2002; and Sawhill and Haskins 2002). Respondents who live in an area with a relatively strong job market are expected to fare better all four outcome measures than those residing in areas with relatively weak job markets. The GOOD WAGE INDEX and JOB GROWTH RATE independent variables were included in the analysis to assess the influence of local economic conditions on the four dependent variables.

The GOOD WAGE INDEX (also known as the Job Pay Index)

is calculated each year by the West Virginia Bureau of Employment Program's Research, Information and Analysis Division for the West Virginia Prevention Resource Center's Mountain State Measures, a set of six desirable outcomes for West Virginia's children and families (West Virginia Prevention Resource Center 2001). The index measures the capacity of each county's job base to support its resident population. Specifically, in each county the average annual wage for each job within each industry is calculated. Each job in the county that has an average annual wage of at least 100 percent, but less than 150 percent of the poverty level for a family of four receives one point. Each job with an average annual wage of at least 150 percent, but less than 200 percent of the poverty level for a family of four receives two points. Each job with an annual salary of 200 percent or more of the annual poverty level for a family of four receives three points. The sum of these points in each county is then divided by the county's population and multiplied by 100 to produce that county's index score (West Virginia Bureau of Employment Programs, Research, Information and Analysis Division 2002). The index scores for 1998 (the year the respondents left WV WORKS) ranged from a high of 98.4 in Kanawha County to a low of 9.5 in Wirt County. The state's overall score was 54.8. A high index score indicates relatively good availability of jobs that provide an annual wage above poverty level. A low index score indicates relatively poor availability of jobs that provide an annual wage above poverty level.

The JOB GROWTH RATE independent variable indicates the percentage change in the number of jobs available in each West Virginia county in 1998 relative to 1997. The JOB GROWTH RATE ranged from a high of 4.1 percent in Upshur County to a low of –5.7 percent in Mingo County. The mean value was -.9 percent. A positive job growth value indicates that the number of jobs in the county increased. A negative job growth value indicates that the number of jobs in the county declined.

Previous research also suggests that three individual factors (educational attainment, access to transportation, and the presence of a physical or mental disability) are also significantly related to the ability to leave and stay off welfare, total household income,

Is Work the Solution?

expectations about household income, and self-assessment of well-being (Levenson et al. 1999; Loprest 1999a and 1999b; Tweedie et al.1999; Zedlewski 1999; Knab et al. 2000; Center on Fathers, Families, and Public Policy 2002; Holzer 2002;). Each of these independent variables is included in the analysis. EDUCATIONAL ATTAINMENT indicates if the respondent reported having a high school degree or General Educational Development credential (GED) (69.6%), ACCESS TO TRANSPORTATION indicates if the respondent reported that they own their own car or motorcycle (68.7%), and DISABILITY indicates if the respondent reported that they have a physical or mental disability that has made it hard for them to find a job (15.5%). Gender and marital status were also included in the analysis. GENDER indicates if the respondent reported that they were female (82.2%). MARITAL STATUS indicates if the respondent reported that they were married (38.8%).

Previous research has also indicated that three program factors (receipt of childcare assistance, receipt of job training, and receipt of other support services) are also significantly related to the ability to leave and stay off welfare, total household income, expectations about household income, and self-assessment of well-being (Loprest 1999a and 1999b; Zedlewski 1999; Tweedie et al.1999; Knab et al. 2000). Each of these independent variables is included in the analysis. The HELP WITH CHILDCARE independent variable indicates if the respondent reported receiving state-sponsored childcare assistance (12.7%). The COMPLETED JOB TRAINING independent variable indicates if the respondent reported completing a job training program while on welfare (30.9%). The NUMBER OF POST-TANF SUPPORT SERVICES independent variable indicates the number of public, private, and voluntary support service programs respondents reported that they or their family received services from since leaving welfare. The number of post-TANF support service programs received ranged from zero to thirty-two. The average number of post-TANF support services received was 3.46.

The focus of this chapter, paid employment, is also included in the analysis. The PAID EMPLOYMENT - RESPONDENT independent variable indicates if the respondent reported that they were engaged in paid employment when they completed the survey

Lucinda A. Potter

(44.1%). In addition, because previous research also indicates that a working spouse contributes significantly to household income, the independent variable PAID EMPLOYMENT - OTHER ADULT was included in the analysis (Moffitt 2002b). It indicates if the respondent reported the presence of another adult in the household who was engaged in paid employment (20.4%).

Data Analysis

Table 8.1 contains the results from the logistic regression for the LEFT AND STAYED OFF WV WORKS dependent variable. The results indicate that only two of the independent variables (EDUCATIONAL ATTAINMENT and PAID EMPLOYMENT - RESPONDENT) are significant determinants of a recipient's ability to leave and stay off welfare. Those having at least a high school degree or GED are 64 percent more likely than those without a high school degree or GED to leave and stay off welfare. Also, respondents with paid employment are 74 percent more likely than those without paid employment to leave and stay off welfare.[1]

Labor market variables (GOOD WAGE INDEX and JOB GROWTH RATE) and program variables (HELP WITH CHILDCARE, COMPLETED JOB TRAINING, and NUMBER OF POST-TANF SUPPORT SERVICES) were not significant factors. Other individual variables included in the analysis (MARITAL STATUS, ACCESS TO TRANSPORTATION, DISABILITY, and GENDER) were also not significant factors.

Table 8.2 presents the results from the logistic regression for the TOTAL HOUSEHOLD INCOME dependent variable. The results indicate that (1) married respondents are more than three and a half times as likely as unmarried respondents to have a total household income greater than $10,000 in 1998 (the year they left WV WORKS), (2) women are approximately twice as likely as men to report an annual household income greater than $10,000, (3) those with a physical or mental disability that interferes with their ability to get a job are significantly less likely than those without a physical or mental disability to report an annual household income greater than $10,000, (4) the more post-TANF services a respondent receives, the less likely they are to report an annual household income

Is Work the Solution?

	B¹	S.E.²	O/R³
LABOR MARKET VARIABLES			
good wage index	-.0075	.0049	_____
job growth rate	-.0221	.0619	_____
INDIVIDUAL VARIABLES			
educational attainment (High School)*	.4966	.2835	1.6431
marital status	-.1350	.2710	_____
access to transportation	.0251	.2832	_____
disability	-.2749	.3465	_____
gender	.2133	.3355	_____
PROGRAM VARIABLES			
help with childcare	-.2837	.3585	_____
completed job training	-.2489	.2582	_____
number of post-TANF support services	.0211	.0356	_____
EMPLOYMENT VARIABLES			
paid employment – respondent**	.5579	.2520	1.7471
paid employment – other adult	.0046	.0080	_____
constant	.7288	.7786	_____

model chi-square 16.844 w/12 df
PRE = 72%

¹Standardized coefficients. ²Standard errors. ³Odds ratios.

*.1>p>.05 **.05>p>.01 ***.01>p>.001 ****.001>p>.0001

Table 8.1: Logistic Regression of LEFT AND STAYED OFF WV WORKS and Individual Variables (N = 449)

	B	S.E.	O/R
LABOR MARKET VARIABLES			
good wage index	.0023	.0051	—
job growth rate	.0464	.0643	—
INDIVIDUAL VARIABLES			
educational attainment (High School)	.2808	.3430	
marital status****	1.2857	.2803	3.6171
access to transportation	-.1182	.3068	—
disability *	-.8988	.5055	.4071
gender *	.7105	.3883	2.0350
PROGRAM VARIABLES			
help with childcare	.2644	.3679	—
completed job training	-.1667	.2767	—
number of post-TANF support services *	-.0720	.0430	.9306
EMPLOYMENT VARIABLES			
paid employment – respondent**	.5432	.2683	1.7215
paid employment – other adult	-.0020	.0083	—
constant ****	-3.6439	.8972	—

model chi-square 38.990 w/12 df

PRE = 79%

*.1>p>.05   **.05>p>.01   ***.01>p>.001   ****.001>p>.0001

Table 8.2: Logistic Regression of TOTAL HOUSEHOLD INCOME and Individual Variables (N = 496)

greater than $10,000, and (5) respondents with paid employment are 72 percent more likely than respondents without paid employment to report an annual household income greater than $10,000.

Table 8.3 indicates the logistic regression results for the TOTAL EXPECTED HOUSEHOLD INCOME dependent variable. Seven of the independent variables significantly influence expectations about future household income: (1) married respondents are 184 percent more likely than unmarried respondents to expect their annual household incomes to exceed $10,000 in 1999 (the year they were surveyed), (2) respondents with access to transportation (who own their own car or motorcycle) are nearly twice as likely as those who lack access to transportation to expect their annul household income to exceed $10,000, (3) women are more than twice as likely as men to expect their annual household income to exceed $10,000, (4) those who have received state-sponsored childcare support are more likely than those who have not received state-sponsored childcare support to expect their annual household income to exceed $10,000, (5) those who have a physical or mental disability that interferes with their ability to get a job are significantly less likely than those without a disability to expect their annual household income to exceed $10,000, (6) the more services respondents receive, the less likely they are to expect their future annual household income to exceed $10,000, and (7) respondents in paid employment are nearly twice as likely as respondents not in paid employment to expect their future annual household income to exceed $10,000. Neither of the labor market independent variables (GOOD WAGE INDEX and JOB GROWTH RATE) had a significant influence on respondents' expectations concerning their future annual household income.

Table 8.4 indicates the logistic regression results for the FEELING BETTER OFF NOW dependent variable. Seven independent variables significantly affect respondents' personal assessment of their well-being now that they are off welfare. Two of the independent variables, the GOOD WAGE INDEX and DISABILITY, have a negative relationship. Living in a county with a relatively high availability of above average paying jobs and having a physical or mental disability have a negative influence on their personal assessment of their well-being since leaving welfare. The

	B	S.E.	O/R
LABOR MARKET VARIABLES			
good wage index	-.0032	.0045	_____
job growth rate	7.40E-5	.0566	_____
INDIVIDUAL VARIABLES			
educational attainment (High School)	.2908	.2966	
marital status****	1.0442	.2490	2.8411
access to transportation**	.6859	.2762	1.9855
disability **	-1.1469	.4456	.3176
gender **	.8990	.3492	2.4573
PROGRAM VARIABLES			
help with childcare*	.5199	.3124	1.6818
completed job training	-.2746	.2394	_____
number of post-TANF support services **	-.0773	.0357	.9256
EMPLOYMENT VARIABLES			
paid employment – respondent***	.6734	.2337	1.9608
paid employment – other adult	-.0022	.0076	_____
constant ****	-3.4400	.8167	_____

model chi-square 69.711 w/ 12 df

PRE = 63%

*.1>p> .05   **.05>p.>.01   ***.01>p>.001   ****.001>p>.0001

Table 8.3: Logistic Regression of TOTAL EXPECTED HOUSEHOLD INCOME and Individual Variables (N = 459)

Is Work the Solution?

	B	S.E.	O/R
LABOR MARKET VARIABLES			
good wage index**	-.0098	.0040	.9903
job growth rate	-.0066	.0515	___
INDIVIDUAL VARIABLES			
educational attainment (High School) **	.5953	.2558	1.8136
marital status	-.1073	.2212	___
access to transportation****	.8426	.2372	___
disability ***	-.9268	.3332	.3958
gender **	.7084	.2979	2.0307
PROGRAM VARIABLES			
help with childcare	.2406	.3002	___
completed job training	.1870	.2140	___
number of post-TANF support services *	-.0265	.0272	___
EMPLOYMENT VARIABLES			
paid employment – respondent**	.5135	.2048	1.6710
paid employment – other adult**	.0126	.0064	1.0127
constant	-2.2108	.6810	___

model chi-square 72.761 w/ 12 df
PRE = 53%

*.1>p>.05   **.05>p.>.01   ***.01>p>.001   ****.001>p>.0001

Table 8.4: *Logistic Regression of FEELING BETTER OFF NOW and Individual Variables (N = 495)*

remaining five independent variables have a positive influence on their personal assessment of their well-being since leaving welfare. Those with at least a high school degree or GED are 81 percent more likely than those without a high school degree or GED to have a positive assessment of their well-being since leaving welfare. Those with access to transportation are approximately one and a third times more likely than those without access to transportation to have a positive assessment of their well-being since leaving welfare. Also, women are more likely than men and those with paid employment are more likely than those without paid employment to have a positive assessment of their well-being since leaving welfare.

Conclusion

One of the most important assumptions underlying the *Personal Responsibility and Work Opportunity Reconciliation Act of 1996* was that the previous emphasis on education-first and training-first strategies to help recipients leave and stay off welfare, move toward economic self-sufficiency, and escape poverty did not live up to expectations and should be replaced by the work-first strategy. This analysis indicates that placing recipients into paid employment situations has a positive and significant influence on recipients' ability to leave and stay off welfare, their total household income, their expectations concerning future household income, and their assessment of their well-being since leaving welfare. However, the analysis also indicates that placing recipients into paid employment situations is only part of the solution to helping recipients leave and stay off welfare, move toward economic self-sufficiency, and escape poverty. Education also plays an important role. As shown on Table 8.1 and Table 8.4, having at least a high school degree or GED also has a positive and significant influence on the recipient's ability to leave and stay off welfare and their assessment of well-being since leaving welfare. Importantly, the data analysis indicates that paid employment and education go hand-in-hand. Paid employment in the absence of education and education in the absence of paid employment do not explain the recipient's ability to leave and stay off welfare. As a result, the work-first strategy can be effective, but only when used in conjunction with the education-first strategy. The data analysis suggests that a more holistic approach for helping recipients leave and stay off welfare, move toward economic self-sufficiency, and escape poverty is to emphasize both education and work.

The analysis also suggests that tailoring support services to meet individual needs is also warranted. For example, counting college education as a work activity makes sense given that educational attainment is positively related to leaving and staying off welfare. Also, paying special attention to the needs of those with a physical or mental disability is warranted given disability's negative relationship with household income, expectations about future household income, and assessment of well-being. In addition, many of the respondents who reported having a physical or mental disability that made it difficult for them to obtain a job are men (see Chapter 9) . This may help to explain why women were more likely than men to report higher household incomes, higher expectations concerning future household incomes, and more positive assessments concerning their well-being since leaving welfare.

It is not surprising to discover that the receipt of a relatively large number of post-TANF benefits did not have a significant and positive relationship with leaving and staying off welfare and their personal assessment of their well-being since leaving welfare and was negatively related to household income and future expectations concerning household income. Respondents well on their way to economic self-sufficiency no longer need a large number of post-TANF benefits. It was somewhat surprising that neither of the labor market variables, GOOD WAGE INDEX and JOB GROWTH RATE, positively influenced the respondent's ability to leave and stay off welfare, total household income, and expectations of future household income. The only significant relationship between these variables and any of the four dependent variables was that the GOOD WAGE INDEX was negatively related to FEELING BETTER OFF NOW. One possible explanation for this negative relationship is that respondents living in an area where good-paying jobs are relatively plentiful may find it easier to find employment, but are frustrated by their inability to get one of the above average paying jobs (the respondent's median wage was just $5.90 an hour).

In summary, this analysis suggests that emphasizing a work-first strategy to help recipients leave and stay off welfare, move toward economic self-sufficiency, and escape poverty has merit, but employing it as a "one size fits all" strategy for all recipients is a mistake. Paid employment and education go hand-in-hand.

Notes

1. Some social scientists, particularly those working with relatively small sample sizes, have used p values of .1 or less to determine statistical significance. The conventional measure of statistical significance is a p value of .05 or less. Education's p value in the LEFT AND STAYED OFF WV WORKS logistic regression analysis was .07, just missing the conventional p value of .05 or less for statistical significance. The p value of .1 or less to determine statistical significance is used here because, as demonstrated in Chapter 7, education is a significant predictor of paid employment. Therefore, part of education's explanatory value is captured by paid employment. If education's influence could be separated out, it is likely that its p value would fall under the more rigorous .05 level of significance.

References

Berlin, Gordon. 2001. "The Thirty-Year Tug-of-War: Can Reform Resolve Welfare Policy's Thorniest Conundrum?" *Brookings Review* (19): 34-38.

Center on Fathers, Families, and Public Policy. 2002. "Report Provides Critique of Marriage Promotion Efforts." *Policy Briefing* 4:2. http://www.cffpp.org/briefings/pdfs/brief_0203.pdf.

Cherlin, Andrew J. and William Julius Wilson. 2002. "Welfare Reform and the Current Recession." *News & Issues: Post 9/11 Environment for Low Income Families.* March. http://www.nccp.org/pub_win02b.html.

DiNitto, Diana M. and Thomas R. Dye. 1987. *Social Welfare Politics and Public Policy*. Englewood Cliffs, NJ: Prentice-Hall Publishers, Inc.

Dye, Thomas R. 1987. *Understanding Public Policy*. Englewood Cliffs, NJ: Prentice-Hall, Inc.

Edwards, Richard L., Philip W. Cooke, and P. Nelson Reid. 1997. "Social Work Management in an Era of Diminishing Federal Responsibility." *Social Policy: Reform, Research and Practice*. ed. Patricia A. Ewalt, Edith M. Freeman, Stuart A. Kirk, and Dennis L. Poole, 19-34. Washington, D.C.: National Association of Social Workers Press.

Ellwood, David. 1988. *Poor Support: Poverty in the American Family*. Chicago: Basic Books.

Gordon, Linda. 1994. *Pitied but Not Entitled: Single Mothers and the History of Welfare*. Cambridge, MA: Harvard University Press.

Gueron, Judith M. and Gayle Hamilton. 2002. "The Role of Education and Training in WelfareReform." *Welfare Reform and Beyond*. Policy Brief No. 20. April 2002. Washington, D.C.: The Brookings Institution. http://www.brookings.org/dybdocroot/es/wrb/publications/pb/pb20.htm.

Handler, Joel F. and Yeheskel Hasenfeld. 1997. *We the Poor People: Work, Poverty & Welfare*. New Haven, CT: Yale University Press.

Harrington, Michael. 1962. *The Other America: Poverty in the United States*. New York: Macmillan Press.

Helco, Hugh. 2001. "The Politics of Welfare Reform." *The New World of Welfare*. Ed. Rebecca Blank and Ron Haskins. Washington, D.C.: The Brookings Institution.

Henly, Julia R. and Sandra K. Danzinger. 1997. "Confronting Welfare Stereotypes: Characteristics of General Assistance Recipients and Postassistance Employment." *Social Policy: Reform, Research and Practice*. ed. Patricia A. Ewalt, Edith M. Freeman, Stuart A. Kirk, and Dennis L. Poole, 124-139. Washington,

D.C.: National Association of Social Workers Press.

Holzer, Harry J. 2002. "Do we need a stronger welfare policy for a weaker economy?" *Assessing the New Federalism Short takes on Welfare Policy No. 1.* Washington D.C.: The Urban Institute.

Kaus, Mickey. 2001. "TANF and "Welfare": Further Steps Toward the Work-Ethic State." *Brookings Review* (19): 43-47.

Kim, Anne. 2002. *Up the Ladder: The Role of Training & Education in Promoting Job Advancement for Welfare Recipients.* Washington, D.C.: The Progressive Policy Institute. http://www.ppionline.org/ppi_ci.cfm?knlgAreaID=114&subsecID =143&contentID=250289.

Knab, Jean Tansey, Johannes M. Bos, Daniel Friedlander and Joanna W. Weissman. 2000. *Do Mandates Matter? The Effects of a Mandate to Enter a Welfare-to-Work Program.* New York: Manpower Development Research Corporation. http://www.mdrc.org/publications/265/full.pdf.

Levenson, Alec R., Elaine Reardon and Stefanis R. Schmidt. 1999. *Welfare, Jobs and Basic Skills: The Employment Prospects of Welfare Recipients in the Most Populous U.S. Counties.* NCSALL Reports #10B. Cambridge, MA: The Nation Center for the Study of Adult Learning and Literacy at Harvard.

Loprest, Pamela. 1999a. *How Welfare Families that left Welfare are Doing: A National Picture.* Washington, D.C.: The Urban Institute. in *Assessing the New Federalism* Briefing Series, No. B-1. http://www.urban.org/UploadedPDF/anf_b1.pdf.

_____. 1999b. "Families Who Left Welfare: Who Are They and How Are they Doing?" *Assessing the New Federalism* Discussion Paper No. 99-02. Washington D.C.: The Urban Institute. http://www.urban.org/UploadedPDF/discussion99-02.pdf.

Michalopoulos, Charles and Christine Schwartz. 2001. *What Works Best for Whom: Impacts of 20 Welfare-to-Work Programs by Subgroup.* NY: Manpower Development Research

Corporation. http://www.mdrc.org/publications/34/full.pdf.

Moffitt, Robert A. 2002a. *The Temporary Assistance for Needy Families Program*. National Bureau of Economic Research Working Paper 8749. Cambridge, MA: National Bureau of Economic Research.

———. 2002b. "From Welfare to Work: What the Evidence Shows." *Welfare Reform and Beyond*. Policy Brief No. 13. Washington, D.C.: The Brookings Institution. http://www.brookings.org/dybdocroot/es/wrb/publications/pb/pb13.htm.

O'Neill, June E. and M. Anne Hill. 2001. "Gaining Ground? Measuring the Impact of Welfare Reform on Welfare and Work." *Civic Report* No. 17, July. New York: Center for Civic Innovation.

Patel, Nisha. 2002. *Workforce Development: Employment Retention and Advancement Under TANF*. Technical Paper DE3888. Washington, D.C.: W. K. Kellogg Foundation.

Rank, Mark Robert. 1994. *Living on the Edge: The Realties of Welfare in America*. New York: Columbia University Press.

Sawhill, Isabel and Ron Haskins. 2002. "Welfare Reform and the Work Support System." *Welfare Reform and Beyond* Policy Brief No. 17, March. Washington, D.C.: The Brookings Institution. http;//www.brookings.org/wrb/publications/pb/pb17.htm.

Segal, Elizabeth A. and Stephanie Brzuzy. 1998. *Social Welfare Policy, Programs, and Practice*. Itasca, IL: F.E. Peacock Publishers, Inc.

Trattner, Walter I. 1999. *From Poor Law to Welfare State: A History of Social Welfare in America*. New York: The Free Press.

Tweedie, Jack, Dana Reichert and Matthew O'Conner. 1999. "Tracking Recipients after They Leave Welfare." *National Conference of Sate Legislatures Magazine*. August. http://www.ncsl.org/statefed/welfare/leavers.htm.

U.S. Department of Health and Human Services (DHHS). 2002.

"HHS Study Shows Poverty, Welfare Dependence Drop." Press Release, June 3. Washington, D.C.: U.S. Department of Health and Human Services.

Weil, Alan and Kenneth Finegold. 2002. *Welfare Reform: The Next Act.* Washington, D.C.: The Urban Institute.

Weir, Margaret, Ann Shola Orloff, and Theda Skocpol. 1988. *The Politics of Social Policy in the United States.* Princeton, NJ: Princeton University Press.

West Virginia Bureau of Employment Programs, Research, Information, and Analysis Division. 2002. Good wage index definition. Faxed by Joseph Jarvis, West Virginia Bureau of Employment Programs. July 9.

West Virginia Prevention Resource Center. 2001. *Mountain State Measures-Outcomes and Indicators of Child and Family Well-Being.* http://www.prevnet.org/outcomes/

Zedlewski, Sheila R. 1999. "Work Related Activities and Limitations of Current Welfare Recipients." *Assessing the New Federalism* Discussion Paper No. 99-06. Washington D.C.: The Urban Institute. http://www.urban.org/UploadedPDF/discussion99-06.pdf.

Chapter 9

The Most At-Risk, Disadvantaged Populations in West Virginia

ROBERT JAY DILGER

The authors of the *Personal Responsibility and Work Opportunity Reconciliation Act of 1996* had at their disposal a wealth of information concerning the Aid to Families with Dependent Children program. Statistics concerning poverty rates, caseloads, program costs, out-of-wedlock births, living arrangements, and many other recipient demographic characteristics were provided by a host of government agencies and welfare advocacy groups. They also had at their disposal numerous evaluative research studies produced by government research organizations, such as the U.S. General Accounting Office (GAO), the Congressional Research Service, and the Congressional Budget Office; Washington, D.C.-based think tanks, such as the Urban Institute, the Brookings Institution, the Rand Corporation, the Cato Institute, and the Heritage Foundation; children's advocacy groups, such as the Children's Defense Fund; contract program evaluators, such as the Manpower Demonstration Research Corporation; and intergovernmental organizations, such as the National Governors Association, among others. During congressional hearings on welfare reform in 1995 and 1996, 338 policy experts testified before the House Ways and Means Committee (providing 4,049 pages of testimony), and sixty-two policy experts testified before the Senate Finance Committee (providing 1,138 pages of testimony) (Weaver 2000). Many of these studies reached contradictory conclusions concerning how to best address welfare dependency. However, there was a consensus in the literature that some families were more likely, or at-risk, than others to experience an especially difficult time making the transition from cash assistance to economic self-sufficiency (Bane and Ellwood 1994; Weaver and Dickens 1995; Weaver 2000). Because there was disagreement concerning how to define most at-risk, there was disagreement concerning the percentage of recipients that were likely to have an especially difficult time making the transition from cash assistance to economic self-sufficiency. Nevertheless, in recognition of these families' special circumstances, and in an attempt to avoid being perceived by the public as being insensitive to the poor's needs, when Senator Robert Dole (R-KS) introduced the Republican party's welfare reform proposal in the U.S. Senate in 1995, it included a "circuit breaker" provision. It allowed states to exempt up to 15 percent of their caseload from the proposed maximum, sixty-month limit on the receipt of benefits. The House's version of the bill also included a circuit breaker. It allowed states to exempt up to 10 percent of their caseload from the proposed time limit. Several organizations, including the Urban Institute, argued that those percentages were too low, especially for states where it might be more difficult to move recipients into jobs because of relatively high unemployment rates or limited funds for job training and employment assistance (Zedlewski et al. 1996). Also, many states, led by the National Governors' Association, lobbied hard to get the circuit breaker percentage increased. States worried that they would be forced to use their own resources to support these "difficult" cases should they fail to achieve self-sufficiency by the time they reached their state's limit on the receipt of benefits. Senator Dole later increased the circuit breaker exemption percentage in his proposal from 15 percent to 20 percent of each state's average monthly caseload. The 20 percentage figure was later incorporated into most other versions of welfare reform legislation that were subsequently discussed in the Senate, and was later included in the *Personal Responsibility and Work Opportunity Reconciliation Act of 1996* (Weaver 2000).

The 1996 welfare reform law allowed states to exempt up to 20 percent of their average monthly caseload from the state's time

The Most At-Risk, Disadvantaged Populations

limit on the receipt of benefits for hardship or if the family includes an individual who has been battered or subjected to extreme cruelty. They could also count state funding for families that needed assistance beyond the sixty-month time limit toward their state maintenance-of-effort requirement (states were required to spend at least 80 percent of previous state funding, or 75 percent if the state satisfied federally mandated work participation rate requirements). In 2003, thirty-eight states limited recipients to sixty cumulative monthly payments; seven imposed time limits as short as twenty-four cumulative months; and five, plus the District of Columbia, used their own resources to provide assistance past the sixty-month limit (DHHS 2002).

Scholars, practitioners, and policymakers have always been interested in the relative ease or difficulty in making the transition off cash assistance. This issue has become especially important now that many recipients across the nation have reached, or are nearing, their state's time limit on the receipt of benefits (Miller 2002a; Vallianatos 2002). For example, in 2002, 556 families were forced off welfare in West Virginia because they reached the state's sixty-month limit on the receipt of benefits (*State of West Virginia ex rel. K.M, vs. West Virginia Department of Health and Human Resources* 2002). During 2003, an additional forty to fifty families each month lost benefits for this reason (Boothe 2003).

States have several options when a family reaches its benefit time limit. If the state has not reached the federally imposed 20 percent cap, it can grant the family an exemption under the 1996 welfare reform law's circuit breaker provision. Under this scenario, the family continues to receive benefits and the state continues to receive the federal government's share of expenses for providing those benefits. The state can also use its own resources to provide the family with income support; it can commit additional state money for support services to assist the family in its effort to become self-sufficient; it can assist the family in other ways, such as providing information concerning the availability of other public and private programs; or it can do nothing "extra" to assist them.

Each state's response to the imposition of benefit limits will reflect differences in state political culture, political leadership, and fiscal circumstances. Another important factor is the extent to which the state's welfare population is disadvantaged. The more disadvantaged the state's welfare population, the more likely the state will experience a relatively large number of families that reach the limit, and the more likely fiscal pressures will make granting an exemption under the 1996 circuit breaker provision less likely to occur.

The time limit on the receipt of benefits is of special interest to policymakers, practitioners, scholars, and welfare advocacy groups because it is relatively new, and it is unclear how states will respond. To date, most states have elected not to grant many exemptions to their time limit. For example, during the first five years of its implementation of WV WORKS, West Virginia granted only thirty exemptions to the state's sixty-month time limit on the receipt of benefits. In 2002, West Virginia's Department of Health and Human Resources (DHHR) approved only six of 187 requests for an exemption under the federal circuit breaker provision: one out of eighteen requests for domestic violence reasons, five out of thirteen requests for pregnancy, none out of fifteen requests because of the lack of childcare, none out of forty-five requests because of chronic unemployment, and none out of ninety-six requests for living in an area of high unemployment (*State of West Virginia ex rel. K.M, vs. West Virginia Department of Health and Human Resources* 2002).

In 2002, West Virginia's policy of denying families benefits once they reached the state's sixty-month time limit generated a lawsuit that attracted nationwide attention and ended up in the West Virginia Supreme Court of Appeals. The plaintiffs argued that the state's sixty-month time limit violated West Virginia's Constitutional provisions concerning the state's responsibility as overseer of the poor. West Virginia's Supreme Court of Appeals upheld the state's position, noting that former welfare recipients have other government programs available to them. They ruled that the state's denial of benefits was constitutional, so long as former recipients continued to have access to other support programs, such as Medicaid, Food Stamps, and housing assistance (Miller 2002b; *State of West Virginia ex rel. K.M, vs. West Virginia Department of Health and Human Resources* 2002; Wetzstein 2002).

The Most At-Risk, Disadvantaged Populations

The lawsuit concerning West Virginia's sixty-month time limit on the receipt of benefits is indicative of the interest welfare advocates and others have in the issue of time limits and their effect on the state's most disadvantaged recipients. These recipients, by definition, are the ones most likely to exhaust their eligibility for benefits. This chapter adds to the literature concerning those most at risk of not making the transition to self-sufficiency by examining previous research about employment barriers welfare recipients and others face. It then identifies which employment barriers have proved to have the greatest adverse effect on welfare recipients' efforts to transition off welfare and achieve economic self-sufficiency. An index of employment adversity is then constructed from these employment barriers and is applied to the authors' WV WORKS 2000 survey of WV WORKS recipients to identify respondents who are most at risk of being unable to transition off cash assistance and achieve economic self-sufficiency (Dilger et al. 2001). Their survey responses are then compared to the responses from the other recipients. The goal is to (1) develop a better means to identify those who are most at risk of not being able to transition off cash assistance, (2) determine if the current means of identifying those who are most at risk of not being able to transition off cash assistance undercounts or overcounts that population, and (3) discuss the possible effects undercounting or overcounting that population has for national policy and for West Virginia.

DEFINING THE MOST AT-RISK, DISADVANTAGED POPULATIONS

Length of Dependency

The provision in the *Personal Responsibility and Work Opportunity Reconciliation Act of 1996* allowing states to exempt up to 20 percent of their average monthly caseload from the state's time limit on the receipt of benefits was not the first time federal policymakers provided exemptions to sanctions against individuals or families receiving government assistance. For example, in recognition of the employment difficulties Supplemental Security Income (SSI) recipients face (SSI provides financial assistance to the severely disabled), the *Welfare Reform Technical Corrections Act of 1997* specified that states were to treat two-parent families with one disabled parent as a single-parent family when determining compliance with TANF's work participation requirements (which were lower than those for two-parent families). Also, in 1997, the U.S. Department of Labor was authorized to spend up to $3 billion on Welfare-to-Work grants to state and local governments for programs that help the most disadvantaged welfare recipients find and retain employment (Perez-Johnson, Hershey, and Bellotti 2000; Zedlewski and Loprest 2001). States had to spend at least 70 percent of their funds on adult recipients who had 1) received TANF or AFDC for thirty months or more, or were within twelve months of reaching TANF's time limitation on the receipt of benefits; and 2) faced two of three specific employment barriers: (1) the lack of a high school diploma or General Educational Development credential (GED) and low reading or math skills, (2) a substance abuse problem, or (3) a poor work history. Funds spent on non-custodial parents who faced two of the three employment barriers also qualified under the 70 percent criteria, if their child (or children) had received benefits for at least thirty months (Nightingale et al. 1999; Trutko et al. 1999).

As the Welfare-to-Work Program's eligibility criteria demonstrate, policymakers often equate length of dependency on cash assistance with being at risk of not being able to transition from cash assistance to economic self-sufficiency. This assumption is understandable because those who have received cash assistance for relatively long periods of time have, obviously, failed to make the transition from cash assistance to economic self-sufficiency. Moreover, data concerning length of dependency is readily available and incontrovertible, characteristics that often prove helpful during program implementation. Confusion over what constituted a substance abuse problem and a poor work history, for example, impeded the implementation of the Welfare-to-Work program (Trutko et al. 1999). However, although some have argued that the social deprivation (or embarrassment) of being on cash assistance for a relatively long time causes some recipients to lose hope or, worse, embrace a "culture of poverty" lifestyle that can lead to perpetual dependence on cash assistance (Banfield 1970; Murray 1984; Niskanen 1996), length of dependency is not an at-risk factor. It results from at-risk factors. Using length of dependency as a proxy for being at-risk does little to help us understand what causes recipients to remain on welfare for long periods of time, what their special needs are, or how to address those needs. Policymakers have used length of dependency as a proxy for being at-risk primarily because they have not been offered a better alternative.

Structural and Personal Characteristics

The framework for offering a better alternative to using length of dependency as a proxy for being at-risk exists in the literature on employment barriers. These studies are of interest because although there are several means available to leave cash assistance, such as getting married or moving in with parents or others, employment is the primary means adult welfare recipients use to leave cash assistance.

Many studies have documented that structural characteristics, such as local labor market conditions and, especially in rural areas, accessibility to affordable transportation, affect the ability of people to find and retain employment (Bloomquist, Jensen, and Teixeira 1988; Polakow 1993; Bane and Ellwood 1994; Rank 1994; Danziger and Danziger 1995; Jensen and Chitose 1997). It is easier for TANF recipients to find and retain a job in a robust, growing labor market than in a declining one and when an affordable means of transportation is readily available. Other studies have shown that certain personal characteristics, such as low educational attainment, lack of job experience, substance abuse problems, domestic violence situations, the presence of physical or mental disabilities, and the presence of preschool-age children (coupled with unmet childcare needs), hinder people's ability to find and retain employment (Bokemeier and Tickamyer 1985; McLaughlin and Sachs 1988; Deseran et al., 1993; Tickamyer and Latimer 1993; Rank 1994; Olson and Pavetti 1996; Latimer 1998). While several of these personal characteristics or circumstances do not necessarily prevent work, most require special support services to help recipients locate and retain employment (Zedlewski and Loprest 2001).

As a group, adult welfare recipients possess a relatively high incidence of personal employment barriers. For example, in an effort to determine the extent of physical and mental disabilities among welfare recipients, the GAO examined data from the U.S. Bureau of the Census' National Survey of Income and Program Participation. The survey asked respondents questions concerning their TANF status and functional impairments covered by the *Americans With Disability Act of 1990*. GAO discovered that 44 percent of adult TANF recipients reported having physical or mental impairments, a proportion nearly three times higher than non-TANF adults (GAO 2001). In addition, more than one-third (38%) of adult TANF recipients reported that they were unable or needed help to perform one or more activities, such as walking up a flight of stairs or keeping track of money or bills. Also, 29 percent of adult TANF recipients reported a mental impairment, such as frequent depression, anxiety, or trouble concentrating. Most (80%) of those reporting a physical or mental impairment were not working at the time they were surveyed.

In an earlier study, Olson and Pavetti (1996) conducted a comprehensive review of fifteen major studies of employment barriers adult welfare recipients face. Because the studies did not utilize a common framework for analysis, with some focusing on personal barriers to employment and others focusing on structural barriers, such as local labor market conditions, the studies' conclusions were somewhat varied and inconsistent. Olson and Pavetti concluded that these studies indicated that somewhere between 25 and 50 percent of adult welfare recipients needed special assistance to help them transition off of welfare (Olson and Pavetti 1996).

Although Olson and Pavetti's conclusion that from 25 to 50 percent of adult welfare recipients need special assistance to transition off welfare was relatively imprecise, it reinforced the prevailing notion that some recipients were more likely than others to need additional time and/or help to transition off welfare. Federal policymakers took that into consideration when they decided to include a circuit breaker provision in the various welfare reform proposals that were debated in Congress. Olson and Pavetti's work is also useful because the structural and personal employment barriers cited in these studies create a framework for determining which adult

The Most At-Risk, Disadvantaged Populations

TANF recipients are especially disadvantaged and most at risk of not being able to transition off welfare. For example, in 1999, the Urban Institute conducted the National Survey of America's Families. Sheila R. Zedlewski and Pamela Loprest (2001) used that survey data to determine the proportion of adult welfare recipients with specific personal characteristics believed to be significant barriers to finding and retaining employment. They discovered that, nationwide, 44 percent of TANF recipients reported that they lacked a high school or GED degree, 28 percent reported that they had mental health problems, 27 percent reported that they last worked more than three years ago, 17 percent reported that they had a health problem that prevented work, 17 percent reported that they had a child under age one, 5 percent had a child receiving SSI, and 5 percent reported that they did not speak English. Unfortunately, the survey did not include questions concerning domestic violence situations or the incidence of alcohol and other substance abuse issues.

Because previous research had shown that TANF recipients with multiple employment barriers had a very difficult time finding and retaining employment (Olson and Pavetti 1996; Zedlewski 1999; Danziger et. al. 2000), Zedlewski and Loprest also calculated the proportion of adult TANF recipients with multiple personal characteristics believed to be significant employment barriers. They found that 80 percent of adult TANF recipients had at least one of the aforementioned personal employment barrier characteristics, and 40 percent had at least two. As might be expected, despite TANF's work participation requirements, most (68%) of those with at least two personal employment barrier characteristics were not working when they were surveyed. Overall, 32 percent of those facing at least two personal employment barriers were working (20% in a paid job), 25 percent were looking for work, 9 percent were in school, and 34 percent reported no work or educational activity.

Operationalizing (defining) an Index of Employment Adversity

The presence or absence of employment barriers is a useful tool for distinguishing between those who can be expected to transition off cash assistance relatively easily (those with no employment barrier characteristics), and those expected to face more difficulty (those with one or more employment barrier characteristics). Because the literature indicates that adults facing multiple employment barriers have an especially difficult time making the transition off cash assistance, it is possible to create an ordinal index that measures the difficulty in making the transition off cash assistance, ranging from having relatively little difficulty (no employment barriers), moderate difficulty (one employment barrier), severe difficulty (two employment barriers) and acute difficulty (three or more employment barriers). Because there is no consensus on the relative influence of specific employment barriers (e.g., Is the lack of a high school degree more or less important than a physical or mental health problem, or unmet childcare needs?), this index measures relative (ordinal) differences in difficulty, not precise (interval or ratio) differences.

The key to the index's usefulness is in the selection of the employment barriers utilized in the index and how those employment barriers are operationalized (defined). Leaving out important employment barriers weakens the index's usefulness, as does including ones that are not significant or defined improperly.

Although their importance may vary from region-to-region, state-to-state, and even from city-to-city, the literature on employment barriers repeatedly cites the following seven personal employment barriers as being particularly important in influencing the ease or difficulty in finding and retaining employment: the lack of a high school degree or GED; physical or mental health problems that prevent work; lack of job skills/experience; the presence of preschool-age children (coupled with unmet childcare needs); domestic violence situations; substance abuse problems; and the inability to speak English well. The literature also indicates that two structural employment barriers, local labor market conditions and the availability of transportation, also influence the ease or difficulty in finding and retaining employment. Thus, the index of employment adversity presented here utilizes all nine of these personal and structural employment barriers.

States are not required to compile data about employment barriers TANF recipients face. Therefore, scholars have relied primarily on what TANF recipients self-report on surveys, such as the Urban

Institute's National Survey of America's Families, to determine the scope and nature of the employment barriers they face. Some employment barriers are defined relatively easily. For example, recipients are asked to report if they have a high school degree or GED, if they can speak English well, if they have unmet childcare needs that make it difficult to find employment, if they have unmet transportation needs that make it difficult to find employment, if they are involved in a domestic violence situation, or if they have a substance abuse problem. Defining the lack of job skills/experience is more complicated. Although adverse labor market conditions and other employment barriers can also cause a skilled/experienced TANF recipient to be unemployed for relatively long periods of time, scholars typically define the lack of job skills/experience by asking respondents if they have worked during the previous three years.

Defining the presence or absence of a physical or mental health problem that prevents work is also complicated. Although it is tempting to use the receipt of SSI benefits because this information is readily available, it is better to ask respondents to self-report the presence or absence of a physical or mental health problem that prevents work because adult SSI recipients must have a physical disability that is severe enough to prevent them from performing any substantial work for at least one year. This definition is too narrow for this purpose because several studies have found that the presence of disabilities not severe enough to qualify for SSI also adversely influence TANF recipients' ability to find and retain work. Moreover, in 1996, the federal government tightened SSI's definition of disability for children, eliminated the drug addiction and alcoholism diagnosis as a qualification for adults to receive benefits, and eliminated eligibility for most legal immigrants who had not attained citizen status (in 1997, benefits for legal immigrants who entered the United States prior to August 1996, and for some special categories of immigrants who entered the country after that date, were restored). These new restrictions were adopted primarily because it was believed that the expansion of the program's caseload over the previous decade (from 3.8 million in 1985 to 6.7 million in 1995) had caused it to benefit undeserving populations (Karoly, Klerman, and Rogowski 2001). Thus, using receipt of SSI benefits to define the presence or absence of a physical or mental impairment that prevents work would exclude many recipients with lesser disabilities that should be included.

Defining local labor market conditions is, arguably, the most difficult task in constructing an index of employment adversity. Many different economic indices, such as unemployment, poverty, and labor force participation rates, are available for consideration, but none, by itself, fully captures local economic conditions. Fortunately, the Appalachian Regional Commission (ARC) has created a useful measure of local labor market conditions. It has labeled counties as economically distressed if they have a three-year average unemployment rate that is at least 1.5 times higher than the national average, a per capita income that is two-thirds or less than the national average, and a poverty rate that is at least 1.5 times higher than the national average, or has two times the national poverty rate and also qualify on either the unemployment or per capita income indicators (ARC 2002).

West Virginia's Most At-Risk, Disadvantaged Populations

With the assistance of a grant from the West Virginia Department of Health and Human Resources, in 2000 the authors of this book designed and administered a comprehensive, statewide, mailed survey of WV WORKS recipients (Dilger et al. 2001). The ten page, seventy-nine question survey was mailed in July and August 2000 to a scientific random sample of 2,100 WV WORKS recipients. Fifty-seven percent of the mailed surveys (1,206) were completed and returned (see Chapter 1 for information concerning the survey's sampling methodology and tests for representativeness). The survey results provided the respondents' assessment of (1) their WV WORKS' experiences, (2) DHHR personnel and services, and (3) other government assistance programs, including vocation, education, and job training programs. The survey also provided information concerning respondents' (1) work experiences and job readiness, (2) childcare needs and arrangements, (3) current economic and social well-being, (4) knowledge of WV WORKS' rules and regulations, and (5) their assessment of what the state should do to improve their social and economic well-being, including recommended changes to WV WORKS.

As shown on Table 9.1, an analysis of the survey data revealed that more than half (55.9%) of the WV WORKS 2000 survey respondents lived in an economically distressed county, and relatively large numbers reported that they had difficulty finding employment because they could not find transportation (41.1%), lacked a high school degree or GED (37.8%), or had difficulty finding employment because they could not find childcare (31%). Moreover, 19.8 percent reported that they had difficulty finding employment because they have a physical disability, and 17.2 percent reported that they had not worked for at least the past three years. Finally, some respondents reported that they received domestic violence counseling or were in an abusive relationship (2.3%), had difficulty finding employment because they cannot speak English well (1.7%), or received drug/alcohol rehabilitation services or had a drug/alcohol problem (1.5%).

A further examination of the data revealed that the vast majority of WV WORKS recipients (90.5%) faced at least one significant employment barrier in 2000. Specifically, as shown on Table 9.1, 9.5 percent of respondents faced no employment barriers, 24.8 percent faced one employment barrier, 30.5 percent faced two employment barriers, and 35.2 percent faced at least three employment barriers (23.5% faced three, 7.6% faced four, 3.5% faced five, and .6% faced six employment barriers).

These results suggest that many WV WORKS recipients are at risk of not being able to make the transition from cash assistance to economic self-sufficiency. Using the terminology introduced earlier, 9.5 percent can be expected to make the transition relatively easily (no employment barriers), 24.8 percent can be expected to make the transition with moderate difficulty (one employment barrier), 30.5 percent with severe difficulty (two employment barriers), and 35.2 percent with acute difficulty (three or more employment barriers). This finding helps to explain West Virginia's difficulty in obtaining employment for its welfare recipients. Since the adoption of the *Personal Responsibility and Work Opportunity Reconciliation Act of 1996*, West Virginia's work participation rate for welfare recipients has consistently been among the very lowest in the nation (17.1% in

Index of Employment Adversity
WV WORKS 2000 Survey Results

Employment Barrier	Percent of Respondents
Reside in an economically distressed county	55.9%
Had difficulty finding employment because they cannot find transportation	41.1
Lack a high school degree or GED	37.8
Had difficulty finding employment because they cannot find childcare	31.0
Had difficulty finding employment because they have a physical disability	19.8
Had not worked for at least 3 years	17.2
In an abusive relationship or received domestic violence counseling*	2.3
Had difficulty finding employment because they cannot speak English well	1.7
Have a drug or alcohol problem or received drug/alcohol rehabilitation services*	1.5

Number of Employment Barriers	Percent of Respondents
None	9.5%
One	24.8
Two	30.5
Three or more	35.2

*Note: Due to the sensitive nature of questions concerning domestic violence situations and drug and alcohol use, respondents were asked two questions concerning their domestic relationship ("Are you in an abusive relationship?" and "Have you received domestic violence counseling?") and two questions concerning their drug and alcohol use ("Do you have a drug or alcohol problem?" and "Have you received drug or alcohol rehabilitation services?"). Respondents indicating yes to either or both of these questions, respectively, are counted as a yes in the index.

Table 9.1: Index of Employment Adversity WV WORKS 2000 Survey Results (N = 1,206)

2000) (DHHS 2002). It also suggests that unless additional flexibility is added to federal law, West Virginia is going to find it difficult to escape federal sanctions in the future because even if the federal caseload reduction credit were renewed (the Bush Administration has recommended that it be phased out); West Virginia is not likely to qualify for the credit because the state's WV WORKS caseload is no longer falling. Moreover, because West Virginia's caseload includes a relatively high percentage of recipients facing multiple barriers to employment, West Virginia is likely to experience a disproportionally high percentage of recipients that exhaust their time eligibility for benefits. As mentioned previously, West Virginia has, to date, opted not to grant many exemptions to the time limit under the 20 percent federal circuit breaker provision. However, as the number of recipients that exhaust their time eligibility increases, the state is likely to face increased political pressure from welfare advocacy groups and others to reexamine its exemption policy. It will also face increased political pressure to devise programs to help these former recipients find and retain employment.

The Perspectives and Experiences of West Virginia's Most-At-Risk Population

The WV WORKS 2000 survey provided a great deal of useful information concerning the perspectives and experiences of WV WORKS recipients (Dilger et al. 2001). A cross-tabulation and statistical analysis of the survey responses (using the chi-square - χ^2 - statistic) revealed that the perspectives and experiences of those recipients most at risk of not being able to transition off welfare (those facing three or more employment barriers) were statistically different ($\chi^2 < .05$) than those facing fewer employment barriers in several respects. For example, as one might expect, recipients most at risk of not being able to transition off welfare were more likely than other recipients to have been on welfare for more than three years (53% of the most at-risk population compared to 44% of other recipients, $\chi^2 = .043$) and not to be engaged in a work activity (14% of the most at-risk population was engaged in a work activity compared to 33% of other recipients, $\chi^2 = .001$).

Robert Jay Dilger

Less Favorable Program and Departmental Experiences

The WV WORKS 2000 survey asked recipients to indicate their level of satisfaction (very satisfied, satisfied, not sure, dissatisfied, or very dissatisfied) with various aspects of their interaction with DHHR. Specifically, they were asked to indicate their level of satisfaction with:

- The way you are treated at the local DHHR office.
- The way you are treated by your caseworker.
- Where the local DHHR office is located.
- How the local DHHR office looks.
- How long you have to wait before seeing your caseworker.
- The hours your local DHHR office is open.
- WV WORKS' rules and regulations.
- The help you received getting other benefits you might be eligible for (like CHIP, Food Stamps, Medicaid, etc.).
- The help you received in finding a job, job training, or education.
- The help you received in dealing with family problems.
- How quickly your caseworker returned your telephone calls.
- Your overall experience with the local DHHR office, your caseworker, and your job, job training, or educational placement.

Overall, most respondents were either satisfied or very satisfied with where the local DHHR office is located (80.4%), the hours their local DHHR office is open (77.4%), how the local DHHR office looks (74.9%), the way their caseworker treated them (70.6%), the help they received obtaining other benefits (66.6%), their overall experience with their caseworker (65.3%), and the way they were treated at the local DHHR office (61.3%). A majority of respondents

The Most At-Risk, Disadvantaged Populations

were also satisfied or very satisfied with their overall experience with their local DHHR office (56.4%); WV WORKS' rules and regulations (54.2%); how quickly their caseworker returned their telephone calls (53.4%); their job, job training, or educational placement (52.4%); and the help they received dealing with family problems (50.3%). Respondents were either not sure, dissatisfied, or very dissatisfied with how long they had to wait to see their caseworker (54.9%).

A cross tabulation and statistical analysis of the responses to these questions indicated that the experiences of West Virginia's recipients who are most at risk of not being able to transition off welfare were both significantly different and more negative than the experiences of other recipients. For example, the most at-risk recipients expressed significantly less satisfaction than other recipients with the way they were treated at the local DHHR office ($\chi^2 = .006$); the way they were treated by their caseworker ($\chi^2 = .049$); the help they received finding a job, job training, or educational placement ($\chi^2 = .001$); the help they received dealing with family problems ($\chi^2 = .003$); their overall experience with their caseworker ($\chi^2 = .044$); and with their job, job training, or educational placement ($\chi^2 = .009$). These findings suggest that West Virginia's DHHR may have engaged in "creaming" or "triage," a process in which recipients deemed most likely to find and retain employment are given priority over those considered more difficult to place and less likely to retain employment once placed.

Somewhat Less Knowledgeable

The WV WORKS 2000 survey asked recipients six questions testing their level of knowledge about various government assistance program rules and regulations. Specifically, they were asked to respond yes, no, or don't know to the following: You can receive money from the federal earned income tax credit if you work even if you do not make enough money to file a federal income tax form; People will be removed from WV WORKS when they reach their sixty-month time limit; You can appeal decisions made by your caseworker; You cannot receive Medicaid benefits if you leave WV WORKS; You cannot receive Food Stamps if you leave WV WORKS; and Women must cooperate with child support services in order to receive WV

WORKS benefits (unless they are in a domestic violence situation).

Overall, most respondents (75% of those answering the question) provided an incorrect response or did not know that they could receive Medicaid benefits if they left WV WORKS; most (74.6%) provided an incorrect response or did not know that they could receive money from the federal earned income tax credit (EITC) if they worked even if they did not make enough money to file a federal income tax form; and most (70.5%) provided an incorrect response or did not know that they could receive Food Stamps if they left WV WORKS. Also, many respondents (41.8%) provided an incorrect response or did not know that women must cooperate with child support services in order to receive WV WORKS benefits unless they are in a domestic violence situation and approximately one-third of the respondents (36.3%) provided an incorrect response or did not know that people will be removed from WV WORKS when they reach their sixty-month time limit. Finally, approximately one-quarter of the respondents (22.1%) provided an incorrect response or did not know that they can appeal decisions their caseworker make.

The most at-risk respondents were significantly less knowledgeable than other recipients ($\chi^2 < .05$) concerning the federal EITC, their right to appeal decisions made by their caseworker, and their ability to receive Food Stamps after leaving WV WORKS. They were about as knowledgeable as others concerning Medicaid, the sixty-month time limit on the receipt of benefits, and rules concerning child support services.

Somewhat Larger Information Gap

The WV WORKS 2000 survey asked recipients if they had enough information to make an informed decision about the following fourteen programs: the federal EITC; transitional Medicaid benefits; childcare support or subsidies; transportation reimbursements; WV WORKS' dental and vision benefits; job training options; educational options (like GED and vo-tech classes and college); Food Stamp eligibility; emergency assistance; WV WORKS' time limits; WV WORKS' policy (rules and regulations); their personal responsibility contract (PRC); supportive services (clothing for work, car repairs,

The Most At-Risk, Disadvantaged Populations

etc.); and the employer health insurance buy-in program.

Most respondents reported that they had enough information about Food Stamp eligibility (72.2% of those answering the question), and a majority reported that they had enough information about their personal responsibility contract (58%), emergency assistance (56.9%), WV WORKS' rules and regulations (55.8%), and WV WORKS time limits (53.3%). Fewer than half of the respondents reported that they had enough information about education options (48%), transportation reimbursements (37%), job training options (36.9%), supportive services (35.8%), and child care support or subsidies (35.3%). Fewer than one-third of respondents reported that they had enough information about the federal EITC (26.8%), WV WORKS' dental and vision benefits (26.1%), transitional Medicaid benefits (26%), and the employer health insurance buy-in program (15.5%).

The most at-risk recipients were about as knowledgeable as other recipients on ten of the fourteen issues: transitional Medicaid benefits; childcare support or subsidies; transportation reimbursements; WV WORKS' dental and vision benefits; job training options; education options; Food Stamp eligibility; WV WORKS' time limits; WV WORKS' rules and regulations; and the employer health insurance buy-in program. They were significantly less knowledgeable ($\chi^2 < .01$) on the following four issues: the federal EITC, emergency assistance, their PRC, and supportive services.

More Pessimistic and Fatalistic

The WV WORKS 2000 survey asked recipients five questions concerning their outlook on life, their assessment of their future and their children's future, and if they thought they would be on welfare next year. Specifically, they were asked:

- Financially, do you think your future looks... (excellent, good, fair, poor, or very poor).

- Personally, do you think your future looks... (excellent, good, fair, poor, or very poor).

- How do you think your children's future looks? (excellent, good, fair, poor, or very poor).

- I have total confidence in my ability to provide for my family in the future (strongly agree, agree, not sure, disagree, strongly disagree).
- Do you think that you will be on WV WORKS next year? (yes, no).

Overall, respondents were relatively pessimistic concerning their own personal and financial futures (with pluralities indicating fair, poor, or fairly poor), fairly evenly divided concerning their ability to provide for their family in the future, and relatively optimistic concerning their children's future (with 50.4% indicating good or excellent).

West Virginia's most at-risk recipients were significantly more pessimistic and fatalistic than other recipients on all five questions: their financial future, their personal future, their children's future, their ability to provide for their family in the future, and whether they thought that they would be on WV WORKS next year (all $\chi^2 <$ .001). Specifically, 63 percent of the most at-risk population viewed their financial future as either poor or very poor compared to 41.7 percent of other recipients; 46 percent of the most at-risk population viewed their personal future as either poor or very poor compared to 30 percent of other recipients; 24.5 percent of the most at-risk population viewed their children's future as either poor or very poor compared to 15.2 percent of other recipients; 50.1 percent of the most at-risk population agreed or strongly agreed that they had total confidence in their ability to provide for their family in the future compared to 59.9 percent of other recipients; and 58.2 percent of the most at-risk population believed that they would not be on WV WORKS next year compared to 67.1 percent of other recipients.

Conclusion

Most of the previous studies of welfare recipients' employment barriers have focused on personal employment barriers, such as the lack of a high school degree or GED and the presence of physical or mental disabilities. The Urban Institute's Sheila R. Zedlewski and

Pamela Loprest have, over the years, produced the most cited and, arguably, best done studies of this kind (Loprest 1999; Zedlewski 1999; Loprest 2001; Zedlewski and Alderson 2001; Zedlewski and Loprest 2001).

The inclusion of the two structural employment barriers (local labor market conditions and lack of transportation) in the index of employment adversity presented here provides a more comprehensive assessment of the employment barriers welfare recipients face than those provided previously. Unfortunately, respondents to the national survey Zedlewski and Loprest analyzed were not asked questions concerning their childcare and transportation needs, and the wording of other survey questions were not identical to those included in the WV WORKS 2000 survey. As a result, the index of employment adversity cannot be applied to their data source. Comparisons of the findings drawn from the two surveys should be considered suggestive, rather than definitive. Yet, the differences in the results are most interesting and provocative. For example, Zedlewski and Loprest (2001) found that 40 percent of TANF recipients nationwide face at least two personal employment barriers. If they, and others employing personal employment barriers to measure employment adversity, had included structural employment barriers in their analysis, they would have, presumably, found an even higher percentage of TANF recipients facing at least two employment barriers. This is important because these studies affect the perception policymakers and practitioners possess concerning the proportion of welfare recipients that can be expected to have a difficult time transitioning off welfare. This, in turn, affects policy decisions concerning caseload exemptions, mandated work participation rates, sanctions for not meeting work participation rates, etc.

The inclusion of structural employment barriers provides a better measure of employment adversity than relying solely on personal employment barriers. This is especially true for states like West Virginia that have a relatively anemic state economy. West Virginia has one of the lowest median household incomes and per capita incomes in the nation. It also has a relatively high unemployment rate; moderated by population out-migration as opposed to job growth; one of the nation's lowest labor force participation rates;

and one of the highest poverty rates in the nation. It also lacks an extensive public transportation system.

As shown on Table 9.1, nearly two-thirds of WV WORKS recipients (65.7%) face at least two employment barriers, and 35.2 percent face three or more. The relatively large number of recipients facing three or more employment barriers helps to explain why WV WORKS' work participation rate has consistently placed last in the nation. West Virginia, and states like it, face a very difficult, almost daunting task placing its recipients into permanent employment situations. The relatively large number of recipients facing three or more employment barriers also suggests that the federal work participation rate threshold may be too high for rural, impoverished states like West Virginia.

Closer to home, the analysis of the perspectives and experiences reported by West Virginia's most at-risk recipients on the WV WORKS 2000 survey paints a somewhat disturbing portrait. West Virginia's most at-risk recipients report (1) less favorable experiences with both government assistance programs and personnel than other recipients; (2) less knowledge about government assistance programs and policies than other recipients; (3) greater need for information concerning their options and available services than other recipients; and (4) are more pessimistic and fatalistic than other recipients. These findings suggest that West Virginia's most vulnerable citizens are not receiving the help they need to transition off welfare, and many of them have given up hope.

References

Appalachian Regional Commission (ARC). 2002. "ARC-Designated Distressed Counties, FY 2002." Washington, D.C.: Appalachian Regional Commission. http://www.arc.gov/index.do?nodeId=1767.

Bane, Mary Jo and David T. Ellwood. 1994. *Welfare realities: from rhetoric to reform*. Cambridge, MA: Harvard University Press.

Banfield, Edward C. 1970. *The Unheavenly City: the nature and future of our urban crisis*. Boston: Little, Brown Publishers.

Bloomquist, Leonard E., Leif Jensen and Ruy Teixeira. 1988. "Too few jobs for workfare to put many to work." *Rural Development Perspectives* 5:1: 8-12.

Bokemeier, Janet and Ann Tickamyer. 1985. "Labor Force Experiences of Nonmetropolitan Women." *Rural Sociology* 50:1: 51-73.

Boothe, Fred. 2003. West Virginia Bureau for Children and Families. Interviewed by the author. Charleston, West Virginia. January 13.

Danziger, Sandra K. and Sheldon Danziger. 1995. "Will welfare recipients find work when welfare ends?" *Welfare Reform: An Analysis of the Issues*. ed. Isabel V. Sawhill. Washington, D.C.: The Urban Institute.

Danziger, Sandra K, Mary Corcoran, Sheldon Danziger, Colleen Heflin, Ariel Kalil, Judith Levine, Daniel Rosen, Kristen Seefeldt, Kristine Siefert, and Richard Tolman. 2000. "Barriers to the Employment of Welfare Recipients." *Prosperity for All? The Economic Boom and African-Americans*. ed. Robert Cherry and William M.. Rodgers, III, 239-272. New York: Russell Sage Foundation.

Deseran, Forest A, Jiang Hong Li and Roger A. Wojtkiewicz. 1993. "Household Structure, labor market characteristics, and female labor force participation." *Inequalities in labor market areas*. ed. Joachim Singelmann and Forrest A. Deseran. Boulder, CO: Westview Press.

Dilger, Robert Jay, Eleanor Blakely, Melissa Latimer, Barry Locke, Carson Mencken, L. Christopher Plein, Lucinda A. Potter, and David Williams. 2001. *WV WORKS 2000: The Recipients' Perspective*. Morgantown, WV: West Virginia University Institute for Public Affairs. Reprinted in *The West Virginia Public Affairs Reporter* 18:3 (Summer 2001): 2-19. http://www.polsci.wvu.edu/ipa/par/Report18_3.pdf.

Jensen, Leif and Yoshimi Chitose. 1997. "Will Workfare Work?: Job Availability for Welfare Recipients in Rural and Urban America." *Population Research and Policy Review* 16:4: 383-395.

Karoly, Lynn A., Jacob Alex Klerman, and Jeannette A. Rogowski. 2001. "Effects of the 1996 Welfare Reform Changes on the SSI Program." *The New World of Welfare.* ed. Rebecca M. Blank and Ron Haskins, 103-136. Washington, D.C.: The Brookings Institution.

Latimer, Melissa. 1988. "A Multi-Level Analysis of the Barriers to Labor Force Participation Among Welfare Recipients in West Virginia." *Southern Rural Sociology Journal* (14): 67-90.

Loprest, Pamela. 2001. *How Are Families That Left Welfare Doing? A Comparison of Early and Recent Welfare Leavers.* Washington, D.C.: The Urban Institute. http://newfederalism.urban.org/html/series_b/b36/b36.html

_____. 1999. *Families Who Left Welfare: Who Are They and How Are They Doing?* Washington, D.C.: The Urban Institute. http://newfederalism.urban.org/html/discussion99-02.html.

McLaughlin, Diane K. and Carolyn Sachs. 1988. "Poverty in female-headed households: Residential differences." *Rural Sociology* 53:3: 287-306.

Miller, Dawn. 2002a. "Family welfare checks run out: Lifetime limit on cash benefits felt most in McDowell County." *Sunday Gazette-Mail.* January 13. http://www.sundaygazettemail.com/news/News/2002011225/library.cnpapers.com.

_____. 2002b. "Welfare cuts constitutional, court rules." *The Charleston Gazette.* December 10. http://www.wvgazette.com/news/News/2002120938/library.cnpapers.com.

Murray, Charles. 1984. *Losing Ground: American Social Policy 1950-1980.* New York: Basic Books.

Nightingale, Demetra Smith, John Trutko and Burt S. Barnow. 1999. *Status of the Welfare-to-Work (WtW) Grants Program After One Year.* Washington, D.C.: The Urban Institute. http://www.urban.org/welfare/wtw_labor.html.

Niskanen, William A. 1996. "Welfare and the Culture of Poverty." *The Cato Journal* 16:1 (Spring/Summer). http://www.cato.org/pubs/journal/cj16n1-1.html.

Olson, Krista and LaDonna Pavetti. 1996. *Personal and Family Challenges to the Successful Transition from Welfare to Work*. Washington, D.C.: The Urban Institute.

Perez-Johnson, Irma, Alan Hershey, and Jeanne Bellotti. 2000. *Further Progress, Persistent Constraints: Findings from a Second Survey of the Welfare-to-Work Grants Program*. Washington, D.C.: Mathematica.

Polakow, Valerie. 1993. *Lives on the edge: single mothers and their children in the other America*. Chicago: University of Chicago Press.

Rank, Mark R. 1994. *Living on the edge: the realities of welfare in America*. New York: Columbia University Press.

State of West Virginia ex rel. K.M,, vs. West Virginia Department of Health and Human Resources. 2002. 30494.Con. Charleston, WV: West Virginia Supreme Court of Appeals. http://www.state.wv.us/wvsca/docs/fall02/30494.htm.

Tickamyer, Ann and Melissa Latimer. 1993. "A Multilevel Analysis of Income Sources of the Poor and Near Poor." *Inequalities in Labor Market Areas*. ed. Joachim Singelmann and Forrest A. Deseran. Boulder, CO: Westview Press.

Trutko, John, Nancy Pindus, Burt S. Barnow and Demetra Smith Nightingale. 1999. *Early Implementation of the Welfare-to-Work (WtW) Grants Program*. Washington, D.C.: The Urban Institute. http://www.urban.org/url.cfm?ID=410336.

U.S. Department of Health and Human Services (DHHS). 2002. *Temporary Assistance to Needy Families, Fourth Annual Report to Congress*. Washington, D.C.: U.S. Department of Health and Human Services. http://www.acf.dhhs.gov/programs/opre/ar2001/indexar.htm.

_____. 2000. *Temporary Assistance for Needy Families: Third Annual Report to Congress*. Washington, D.C.: U.S. Department of Health and Human Services, Office of Planning, Research and Evaluation. August. http://www.acf.dhhs.gov/programs/opre/annual3.pdf.

U.S. General Accounting Office (GAO). 2001. *Welfare Reform: More Coordinated Federal Effort Could Help States and Localities Move TANF Recipients With Impairments Toward Employment.* GAO-02-37. Washington, D.C.: U.S. Government Printing Office, October.

Vallianatos, Corinna. 2002. "Welfare Limits: Disaster in the Making." *NASW News* 47:2 (February): 3.

Weaver, R. Kent. 2000. *Ending Welfare as We Know It.* Washington, D.C.: The Brookings Institution.

Weaver, R. Kent, and William T. Dickens. 1995. *Looking Before We Leap: Social Science and Welfare Reform.* Washington, D.C.: The Brookings Institution.

Wetzstein, Cheryl. 2002. "Court Upholds Time Limits on Welfare." *The Washington Times.* December 30. http://www.washingtontimes.com/archive.

Zedlewski, Sheila R. 1999. *Work-Related Activities and Limitations of Current Welfare Recipients.* Washington, D.C.: The Urban Institute. http://newfederalism.urban.org/pdf/anf_b2.pdf.

Zedlewski, Sheila R. and Donald W. Alderson. 2001. *Before and After Reform: How Have Families on Welfare Changed?* Washington, D.C.: The Urban Institute. http://newfederalism.urban.org/html/series_b/b32/b32.html.

Zedlewski, Sheila R. and Pamela Loprest. 2001. "Will TANF Work for the Most Disadvantaged Families?" *The New World of Welfare.* ed. Rebecca M. Blank and Ron Haskins, 311-334. Washington, D.C.: The Brookings Institution.

Zedlewski, Sheila, Sandra Clark, Eric Meier, and Keith Watson. 1996. "Potential Effects of Congressional Welfare Reform Legislation on Family Incomes." Washington, D.C.: The Urban Institute. http://www.urban.org/welfare/PEC72696.htm.

Chapter 10

WV WORKS Recipients' Orientations About the Future: Does Place Matter?

F. CARSON MENCKEN

The *Personal Responsibility and Work Opportunity Reconciliation Act of 1996* was landmark legislation. It replaced the Aid to Families with Dependent Children and Job Opportunities and Basic Skills Training programs with the state-centered Temporary Assistance for Needy Families program, eliminated welfare's entitlement status, and imposed mandatory work requirements and lifetime benefit limits on recipients and mandatory work participation rates and maintenance-of-effort requirements on states. Its goal was to end welfare dependency by requiring most able-bodied, adult recipients to work. The programmatic changes brought about by the 1996 welfare reform law also represent a latent change in ideology. Welfare recipients are no longer viewed as victims of circumstances largely beyond their control (e.g. bad economy, personal tragedies, etc.). Instead, they are now viewed as being largely responsible for their circumstances and for changing those circumstances (See Chapter 3; Rural Policy Research Institute [RUPRI] 2001).

This fundamental shift in philosophy suggests that the framework used to study welfare reform should be broadened. Examining the effects of structural conditions (e.g. local economic conditions), household needs (e.g. access to transportation and childcare), and individual capacity (e.g. educational attainment and participation in job training programs) continue to be important.

However, previous research has suggested that recipient orientations (attitudes/beliefs) about the future also affect their behavior and prospects of leaving and staying off welfare (Jessor and Jessor 1977; Goodwin 1983; O'Neill et al. 1987; Dolinsky et al. 1989; Edwards et al. 2001). Given the *Personal Responsibility and Work Opportunity Reconciliation Act of 1996*'s emphasis on personal responsibility and self-help, additional attention to the effect recipient orientations about the future have on recipient behavior is also needed (Goldsmith et al. 1997; Kunz and Kalil 1999; Edwards et al. 2001).

This chapter contributes to the growing literature on welfare recipient orientations by examining how local economic conditions, particularly local economic growth, affect WV WORKS recipients' attitudes and opinions about their ability to control and manage their future (often referred to as their locus of control). This chapter moves beyond conventional models by proposing that the effects of local economic growth on welfare recipients' future orientations is mediated by the recipient's relationship with one of the key gatekeepers in their lives: the organization responsible for managing (and potentially closing) their welfare case.

Literature Review

Some scholars argue that recipients living in areas experiencing economic growth should have more positive attitudes and opinions about their future (and, by inference, should be more capable of altering their life circumstances for the better) than those living in areas not experiencing economic growth. They usually cite what the literature refers to as the individuals' "motivation and opportunity effects." Drawing on economic's basic utility function theories, they argue that behavior is shaped by two interrelated processes: a motivation effect at the individual level and an opportunity effect at the aggregate level (Block and Heineke 1975). They suggest that changes in aggregate levels of wealth (opportunity effect) create positive market behavior for individuals who experience or anticipate an expected payoff at the individual level (motivation effect). In other words, WV WORKS recipients living in a county experiencing economic growth should, on balance, have more positive attitudes and opinions about their future (and, by inference, be more capable of altering their life circumstances for the better) than WV WORKS recipients living in a county not experiencing economic growth because the former anticipate that they may ultimately benefit from this economic growth at some future point in time.

Other scholars argue that recipients living in areas experiencing economic growth should have more positive attitudes and opinions about their future than those living in areas not experiencing economic growth because they are more likely to find a positive role model or "significant other" to emulate (referred to in the literature as status attainment theory) (Blau and Duncan 1967; Wan et al. 1999). Typically, the role model is someone they know (e.g., a teacher, relative, neighbor, or friend) and is not chosen at random or from those who are socially distant (e.g. a movie star).

Some scholars argue that recipients living in areas experiencing economic growth should have less positive attitudes and opinions about their future than those living in areas not experiencing economic growth because they become frustrated by their inability to take advantage of the area's economic opportunities (Matvey 1987; Duncan 1992, 1999; Lobao 1996; Haynes 1997; Billings and Blee 2000). They argue that welfare recipients often feel trapped by both the welfare system and the overall economic system and, over time, become less and less optimistic about their future. This is especially true when economic growth does not create actual or perceived payoffs. When that happens, the individual is less likely to have positive attitudes and opinions about their future (sociologists referred to this as macrostructural theory and economists refer to this as interdependent utility theory) (Danziger and Wheeler 1975; Blau and Blau 1982).

Gatekeepers

Self-esteem and self-worth depend largely on how people perceive significant others in their lives treat/respond to them (Coser 1977; Judge and Bono 2001). For example, if they perceive that their significant others treat them as a worthless person, they tend to view themselves as worthless. The Department of Health and Human Resources (DHHR), and particularly the recipient's caseworker, serve as one of the most important significant others in the lives of WV WORKS recipients. Their caseworker are key gatekeepers in their life. They make certain that the WV WORKS recipient is complying with the Personal Responsibility Contract and have the power to make work assignments and terminate benefits if they feel the recipient is not living up to the contract. In short, the caseworker has considerable control over WV WORKS recipients' lives. Furthermore, an emerging volume of research underscores the importance of the recipient and caseworker relationship in the recipient's compliance with government expectations (Brodkin 1997; Anderson 2002). This suggests that the experiences WV WORKS recipients have with their caseworker and DHHR should shape how they perceive their future well-being. Responses to the authors' 2000 survey of WV WORKS recipients suggest that most WV WORKS recipients (70.6%) are pleased with the way they are treated by their caseworker and with their overall experience with their caseworker (61.3%) (Dilger et al. 2001). However, some recipients were very displeased. For example, here are some responses to the open-ended question, "Is there anything that the Department of Health and Human Resources can do, or do differently, to help you overcome these challenges to working?":

> "They could treat us like human beings instead of leeches. They could understand that not everyone has a job that pays as well as their jobs do."
>
> "Be more compassionate and look at us as people trying to do for ourselves. Not a low life, or a *customer*! I have been referred to as a customer other than a 'client.'"
>
> "There are too many rules. And the people at the welfare office could stop acting like my check is coming straight out of their pocket."
>
> "They could be more caring and helpful instead of making you feel less important than they are. They try to make you feel inferior!! They should try to be more helpful and considerate. Most are very rude and sarcastic."
>
> "That the workers would care about the people that are there. Some of them have to swallow a lot of pride to be there."

WV WORKS Recipients' Orientations About the Future

"The degradation you are made to feel and to find a place for people like me without the threats that are constantly made to you about being cut off."

"To be treated with respect and like a person not as a dirt or slave."

"They could be way more helpful and a lot less rude! Even the family specialists cannot help you find a job. My background and training is in secretarial but yet I have to be cleaning everywhere they hire me for WV WORKS. As long as I am working for my check and my worker's supervisor is happy they don't care about you."

The Research Design

This chapter presents the results of a regression analysis of data from the authors' 2000 survey of 1,206 WV WORKS recipients (see Chapter 1 for a description of the data gathering process and tests of the sample's representativeness). Specifically, the analysis determines (1) the relationship between place (the economic conditions of the recipient's county of residence) and recipient attitudes and beliefs concerning their future, (2) the relationship between the recipient's assessment of their caseworker and DHHR and their attitudes and beliefs concerning their future, and (3) the interactive effects of place and their assessment of their caseworker and DHHR on recipient attitudes and beliefs concerning their future.

The Dependent Variable

A Future Orientation Index was created to measure recipient attitudes and orientations concerning their future (the dependent variable). The Future Orientation Index is based on the responses to the following four questions on the authors' survey of WV WORKS recipients:

- Financially, do you think that your future looks: excellent, good, fair, poor, or very poor?
- Personally, do you think that your future looks: excellent, good, fair, poor, or very poor?

- How do you think that your children's future looks: excellent, good, fair, poor, or very poor?
- I have total confidence in my ability to provide for my family in the future: strongly agree, agree, not sure, disagree, and strongly disagree.

A high value of the Future Orientation Index represents a high level of negative orientation about the future.[1]

There was considerable variation among WV WORKS recipients concerning their future orientation. For example, relatively few recipients viewed their financial future as either excellent (2.8%) or good (12.8%). Most reported that their financial future was either fair (35.2%), poor (31.3%) or very poor (17.9%). Recipients also had relatively negative views concerning their personal future. Relatively few recipients reported that they viewed their personal future as either excellent (6.4%) or good (19.2%). Most reported that they viewed their personal future as either fair (38.8%), poor (23.7%), or very poor (12%). Recipients were somewhat more optimistic concerning their children's future. Approximately half (50.1%) reported that they viewed their children's future as either excellent (14.5%) or good (35.6%), and about half (49.9%) reported that they viewed their children's future as either fair (35.6%), poor (13.7%), or very poor (4.8%). Finally, recipients had somewhat more positive views concerning their confidence in their ability to provide for their family in the future. Most recipients either strongly agreed (27.6%) or agreed (28.9%) with the statement "I have total confidence in my ability to provide for my family in the future." One-third of them (33 percent) were not sure, 6.4 percent disagreed, and 4.1 percent strongly disagreed (Dilger et al. 2001).

Independent Variables

Two measures of economic growth are used to predict WV WORKS recipient attitudes and opinions about the future. The first is the county's inflation-adjusted earnings growth rate for 1994-1999. Earnings were used instead of income because earnings come from paid employment while income includes all sources of income, such as Social Security, retirement funds, and disability payments. As a result, earnings are more directly related to employment opportunities.[2] The second measure of economic growth is the county's 1999 per capita non-farm earnings (this includes earnings from both private non-farm and government employment). It captures county differences in the level of employment-related earnings.

The DHHR/Caseworker Experience Index was created to measure the nature of WV WORKS recipient's experiences with their caseworker and DHHR. It is based on the responses to the following four questions on the authors' survey of WV WORKS recipients:

- How satisfied are you with the way that you are treated at the local DHHR office: very satisfied, satisfied, not sure, dissatisfied, or very dissatisfied?

- How satisfied are you with the way that you are treated by your caseworker: very satisfied, satisfied, not sure, dissatisfied, or very dissatisfied?

- How satisfied are you with your overall experience with the local DHHR office: very satisfied, satisfied, not sure, dissatisfied, or very dissatisfied?

- How satisfied are you with your overall experience with your caseworker: very satisfied, satisfied, not sure, dissatisfied, or very dissatisfied?

A high value on the DHHR/Caseworker Experience Index represents high levels of dissatisfaction. Approximately 60 percent of WV WORKS recipients reported that they were either very satisfied or satisfied with their experiences with their caseworker and DHHR.

Previous research has indicated that the following variables may affect welfare recipient's ability to leave and stay off welfare: their age, education, household structure (number of children, adults, and relationships), how long they have been on welfare, whether or not they are currently enrolled in a job training program, have difficulty meeting childcare needs, if they have been off and back on welfare in the past twelve months, if they are currently receiving Supplemental Security Income, if they are currently receiving child support, and their gender. Each of these variables are included in the analysis as control variables.

FUTURE ORIENTATION REGRESSION		
CONTROL VARIABLES	B	Beta
Childcare difficulties (1 =yes)	0.691	0.091**
Back on welfare (l=yes)	0.074	-0.01
No high school diploma/GED (1=do not have)	0.553	0.076*
3 or more kids in household (l=yes)	0.072	0.009
In job training program (l=yes)	-0.027	-0.003
On welfare 3 or more years (1 =yes)	0.414	0.056
SSI in household (1 =yes)	0.086	0.009
Age	0.185	0.418***
Age sq	-0.001	-0.215*
Currently receiving child support (l=yes)	-0.107	-0.012
Female (1 =yes)	-0.054	-0.005
MARITAL STATUS DUMMY VARIABLES		
Divorced/separated (l=yes)	0.516	0.071
Single (l=yes)	-0.321	-0.039
Cohabitating (l=yes)	-0.145	-0.01
LABOR MARKET CONDITIONS		
County earnings change 1994-99	-1.206	-0.0422
County per capita earnings 1999	0.00006	0.005
DHHR/CASEWORKER EXPERIENCES		
DHHR/caseworker experience index	0.16	0.244***
Earnings change/DHHR/caseworker index	-0.621	-0.112 ***
Intercept	6.432	n/a***
Adj. Rsq		0.156 ***

*p<.05   **p<.01   ***p<.001

Table 10.1: Future Orientation Regressed on Individual, Household, and West Virginia County Characteristics (N=871)

The Data Analysis

As shown on Table 10.1, the regression results indicate that the existing literature about the affect of economic growth on recipient attitudes and opinions about their future needs to take into account the important role gatekeepers play in recipients' lives. Neither of the economic variables, by themselves, are related, either positively or negatively, to WV WORKS recipients' future orientations. However, WV WORKS recipient orientations about the future are related to the recipient's level of satisfaction with their caseworker and DHHR. Also, WV WORKS recipient satisfaction with their caseworker and DHHR interacts negatively with county earnings growth and are, together, related to recipient orientations about the future. This helps to explain the lack of consensus in the literature concerning economic growth's affect on future orientations. There is a relationship between economic growth and orientations about the future, but that relationship is mediated by the recipient's gatekeeper.

As Table 10.2 demonstrates, the regression analysis indicates that economic growth can have either a positive or negative influence on recipients' future orientations, depending on the nature of the recipient's relationship with their caseworker/welfare agency. WV WORKS recipients who are satisfied with their DHHR/caseworker experiences and live in a county experiencing economic growth (top left on the table) have relatively poor (negative) future orientations. It is likely that their more negative orientations result from their still being on welfare. The more economic growth they see around them, the less optimistic they feel because they are still "stuck" on welfare. In addition, unlike those who are dissatisfied with their DHHR/caseworker experiences, they do not have an outlet (bad economy or bad caseworker) to attribute at least part of the blame for their situation.

WV WORKS recipients who are dissatisfied with their DHHR/caseworker experiences and live in a county experiencing economic growth (bottom left on the table) have relatively positive future orientations. This finding suggests that recipients who are dissatisfied with their DHHR/caseworker experiences blame the gatekeeper for their plight (i.e., for their still being on WV WORKS), but their county's economic growth gives them some hope for the future.

WV WORKS recipients who are satisfied with their DHHR/caseworker experiences and live in a county experiencing economic decline (top right on the table) have the most positive future orientations. Although they are still on welfare, they blame their plight on the bad economy and, with the help and encouragement of their gatekeeper, are hopeful that economic conditions, and their opportunity to improve their own economic condition, will improve in the future.

WV WORKS recipients who have both an unsatisfactory experience with their gatekeeper (DHHR/caseworker) and live in a county experiencing economic decline (bottom right on the table) have poor future orientations. This is expected because there are not enough positive events in their lives to give them hope (i.e., bad economy and a poor relationship with gatekeeper).

	COUNTY EARNINGS INCREASED 1994-1999	COUNTY EARNINGS DECLINED 1994-1999
Satisfied with DHHR/Caseworker	Poor	Best
Dissatisfied with DHHR/Caseworker	Good	Poorest

Table 10.2: Predicted Future Orientations of WV WORKS Recipients

Conclusion

The oftentimes acrimonious debate over poverty's causes and solutions, for the most part, has been limited to a 'horizontal' debate concerning the extent of individual responsibility for their current circumstances and their capacity to help themselves change those circumstances (See Chapter 3). This research suggests that the debate ought to be more "vertical" in nature. Macro-level opportunity structures at the community level (i.e. a growing economy) are important determinants of recipient life aspirations and expectations, but this relationship is mediated by other social processes, particularly the recipients' experiences with the gatekeepers in their lives. Therefore, in order to understand fully welfare reform's effect on those in the system, it is important to document and understand these mediating roles. This research has shown that DHHR and the recipients' caseworker mediate how local economic conditions shape recipient future orientations. The question left unexplored here is what other mediating functions also serve similar intervening roles in WV WORKS recipients' lives? The answer to this and related questions will help to develop a more inclusive framework for assessing welfare reform's impact.

The analysis also addresses another important issue concerning poverty and welfare in Appalachia: the stereotype that Appalachia's economic difficulties creates a culture of "fatalism" (Haynes 1997). Writing about how economic conditions have broken the spirit of the Appalachian mountaineer, Caudill (1962, 235) writes:

> The present crisis is compounded of many elements, human and material. They have produced what is probably the most seriously depressed region in the nation, and the adjective applies in much more than an economic sense. They have brought economic depression, to be sure, and it lies like a gray pall over the whole land. But a deeper tragedy lies in the depression of the spirit which has fallen upon so many of the people, making them, for the moment at least, listless, hopeless, and without ambition.

This quotation is more than forty years old, yet this perception of poor people in Appalachia persists (Van Atta 1993; Haynes 1997). However, the data from this analysis suggest that "fatalism" is not widespread among WV WORKS recipients. Many recipients have relatively positive outlooks about their future, their children's future, and they express confidence in their ability to provide for their family in the future.

Finally, the analysis highlights the very important role caseworkers play in the welfare system. Caseworkers have a demanding job and are among the lowest paid professionals in government. Yet, this research shows that they play a key role in mediating recipient orientations about the future. Their role is especially important in areas experiencing economic decline. Recipients who have both a poor relationship with their caseworker/DHHR and live in a county experiencing economic decline have relatively poor future orientations. Previous research indicates that self-confidence and an orientation toward believing that they can provide for their future is an important predictor of leaving and staying off welfare (Goodwin 1983; O'Neill et al. 1987; Dolinsky et al. 1989; Edwards et al. 2001). As a result, any actions the gatekeeper (DHHR/caseworker) can make for a positive intervention (e.g, increased training for caseworkers and additional opportunities for recipient input) are warranted.

Notes

1. The four questions were factor analyzed with principle components factor analysis and varimax rotation. The responses to the four questions are added together to form a standardized index with a Cronbach alpha of .85. The Index is centered around its mean, with a high value representing a high level of negative orientation.

2. This variable is a centered, first difference growth rate. Centering is the practice of deviating each observation from the mean. It is necessary when using interaction terms in a regression analysis (Aiken and West 1990; Jackman 1980).

3. The four questions were factor analyzed with principle components factor analysis and varimax rotation. The DHHR Experience Index has a Cronbach's alpha of greater than .9. The index is centered about its mean.

References

Aiken, Leona and Stephen West. 1990. *Multiple Regression: Testing and Interpreting Interactions*. Newbury Park, CA: Sage Publications.

Anderson, Stephen G. 2002. "Ensuring the Stability of Welfare-to-Work Exits: The Importance of Recipient Knowledge about

Work Incentives." *Social Work* 47(2): 162-170.

Billings, Dwight B. and Kathleen M. Blee. 2000. *The Road to Poverty: The Making of Wealth and Hardship in Appalachia*. New York: Cambridge University Press.

Blau, Judith R. and Peter M. Blau. 1982. "The Cost of Inequality: Metropolitan Structure and Violent Crime." *American Sociological Review* 47(1): 114-129.

Blau, Peter M. and Otis Duncan. 1967. *The American Occupational Structure*. New York: Wiley.

Block, Michael K. and John M. Heineke. 1975. "A Labor Theoretic Analysis of Criminal Choice." *The American Economic Review* 65(3): 314-325.

Brodkin, Evelyn Z. 1997. "Inside the Welfare Contract: Discretion and Accountability in State Welfare Administration." *Social Service Review* 71(1): 1-33.

Caudill., Harry. 1962. *Night Comes to the Cumberlands*. Boston, MA: Little, Brown and Co.

Coser, Lewis A. 1977. *Master's of Sociological Thought*. New York: Harcourt, Brace, Jovanovich.

Danziger, Sheldon and D. Wheeler. 1975. "The Economics of Crime: Punishment or Income Redistribution." *Review of Social Economy* (October):113-131.

Dilger, Robert Jay, Eleanor Blakely, Melissa Latimer, Barry Locke, Carson Mencken, L. Christopher Plein, Lucinda A. Potter, and David Williams. 2001. *WV WORKS 2000: The Recipients' Perspective*. Morgantown, WV: West Virginia University Institute for Public Affairs. Reprinted in *The West Virginia Public Affairs Reporter* 18:3 (Summer 2001): 2-19.

Dolinsky, Arthur, Richard Caputo, and Patrick O'Kane. 1989. "Competing Effects of Culture and Situation on Welfare Receipt." *Social Service Review* 63 (September): 359-371.

Duncan, Cynthia M. 1992. "Persistent Poverty in Appalachia: Scarce Work and Rigid Stratification." *Rural Poverty in America*. ed. Cynthia M. Duncan, 111-133. New York: Auburn House.

_____. 1999. *Worlds Apart: Why Poverty Persists in Rural America.* New Haven, CT: Yale University Press.

Edwards, Mark E., Robert Plotnick, and Marieka Klawitter. 2001. "Do Attitudes and Personality Characteristics Affect Socioeconomic Outcomes? The Case of Welfare Use by Young Women." *Social Science Quarterly* (82): 827–843.

Goldsmith, Arthur, Jonathan Veum, and William Darity. 1997. "The Impact of Psychological and Human Capital on Wages." *Economic Inquiry* (35): 815-829.

Goodwin, Leonard. 1983. *Causes and Cures of Welfare: New Evidence on the Social Psychology of the Poor.* Lexington, MA: Lexington.

Haynes, Ada F. 1997. *Poverty in Central Appalachia.* New York: Garland Publishing.

Jackman, Robert W. 1980. "A Note on the Measurement of Growth Rates in Cross-National Research." *American Journal of Sociology* (86): 604-617.

Jessor, Richard. and Shirley Jessor. 1977. *Problem Behavior and Psychosocial Development: A Longitudinal Study of Youth.* New York: Academic.

Judge, Timothy and Joyce Bono. 2001. "Relationship of Core Self-Evaluations Traits - Self-Esteem, Generalized Self-efficacy, Locus of Control, and Emotional Stability– with Job Satisfaction and Job Performance: A Meta-Analysis." *Journal of Applied Psychology* (86): 80-92.

Kunz, James and Ariel Kalil. 1999. "Self-Esteem, Self-Efficacy, and Welfare Use." *Social Work Research* 23(2): 119-126.

Lobao, Linda. 1996. "A Sociology of the Periphery vs a Peripheral Sociology." *Rural Sociology* 61(1): 77-102.

Matvey, Joseph. J. 1987. *Central Appalachia: Distortions in Development, 1750-1986.* Dissertation. Pittsburgh, PA: University of Pittsburgh.

O'Neill, June, Lauri Bassi, and Douglas Wolf. 1987. "The Duration of Welfare Spells." *Review of Economics and Statistics* (69): 241-248.

Rural Policy Research Institute (RUPRI). 2001. "Welfare Reform in Rural America: A Review of Current Research." P2001-5. Columbia, MO: University of Missouri.

Van Atta, D. 1993. "You Can't Kill a Good Giveaway." *Reader's Digest* 143 (August): 55-59.

Wan, Li-Ya, Edward Kick, James Fraser, and Thomas Burns. 1999. "Status Attainment in America: The Roles of Locus of Control and Self-Esteem in Education and Occupation Outcomes." *Sociological Spectrum* 19(3): 281-298.

Chapter 11

Lessons from the Mountain State

ELEANOR H. BLAKELY, ROBERT JAY DILGER, AND BARRY L. LOCKE

Welfare has been one of the most talked about, argued about, and studied intergovernmental programs in American political history. Most of the research that has taken place concerning the program's effect on welfare recipients' ability to leave and stay off welfare has focused on the experiences of welfare recipients residing in urban areas. However, there is a growing body of research about welfare's effect on recipients residing in rural areas. It suggests that rural recipients face several distinct challenges in making the transition from welfare to employment and economic self-sufficiency. Rural residents, for example, often face a more challenging labor market and a longer daily commute to work. They generally have fewer support programs available (such as public transportation, childcare facilities, job training programs, health care facilities, and affordable housing), and they tend to be less educated and less likely to pursue a college degree than their urban counterparts (Cook and Dagata 1997; Parker and Whitener 1997; Besser 1998; Findeis and Jensen 1998; Gibbs et al. 1998; RUPRI 1998; JCPR 2000; Weber and Duncan 2000).

Several organizations, including the Joint Center on Poverty Research (JCPR) and the Rural Policy Research Institute (RUPRI), have argued that some provisions in the *Personal Responsibility and Work Opportunity Reconciliation Act of 1996* are inappropriate because they do not take into account the special circumstances welfare recipients residing in rural areas face. For example, the Joint Center on Poverty Research has argued that rural states should be provided additional flexibility concerning the federally imposed, maximum time limit on the receipt of benefits because rural recipients are more likely to reach the limit than their urban counterparts (JCPR 2000).

This book contributes to the ongoing debate over the efficacy of the *Personal Responsibility and Work Opportunity Reconciliation Act of 1996* in addressing poverty and reducing welfare dependency in rural areas by examining West Virginia's experiences with welfare reform. However, before proceeding, it is important to note that West Virginia is a "post industrial" rural state, largely comprised of small towns and sparsely populated areas that do not depend on agriculture as their primary source of employment and earnings. As a result, while it is appropriate to apply lessons learned from West Virginia's experiences with welfare reform to much of rural America, those lessons should be applied to rural areas that rely primarily on agriculture for employment and earnings with an appropriate measure of caution.

The Efficacy of the Personal Responsibility and Work Opportunity Reconciliation Act of 1996

Nationally, welfare reform proponents have proclaimed the *Personal Responsibility and Work Opportunity Reconciliation Act of 1996* a huge success. In February 2002, President George W. Bush claimed that the program's results were "nothing short of spectacular" (Bush 2002, 5). He, and other advocates, pointed out that since welfare reform was enacted, welfare caseloads have fallen dramatically across the nation (down 56% since 1996); the proportion of welfare recipients engaged in a work-related activity has more than tripled (to 34% in FY 2000); and states did not, as some argued they would, get caught up in a "race to the bottom" by lowering cash payments and reducing funding for support services (U.S. Department of Health and Human Services [DHHS] 2002). In fact, most states, including West Virginia, increased both cash payments and funding for support services. Moreover, child poverty rates, which some had predicted would increase, have declined since the 1996 welfare reform law was adopted (Bush 2002).

Opponents of welfare reform admit that the 1996 law's increased emphasis on the workforce attachment strategy has reduced welfare rolls. However, they argue that welfare reform has failed to improve the lives of most recipients because it has not addressed the more fundamental, underlying problem of poverty in the United States. They point out that nearly half of those who have left welfare are not working, and the vast majority of those who have left welfare remain in poverty. For example, nearly 80 percent of West Virginia's welfare leavers reported that they had annual household incomes of $10,000 or less in 1999. This is well below federal poverty levels and below the state's self-sufficiency standard (a measure of income needed to meet basic needs without government assistance) (Dilger et al. 2000; Pearce and Brooks 2002). They also point out that although the percentage of welfare recipients engaged in a work-related activity has more than tripled, nearly two-thirds of all recipients continue to receive benefits without engaging in a work-related activity (DHHS 2002). Moreover, many of those engaged in a work-related activity were in unpaid, community service positions, not paid employment positions. Finally, states did not race to the bottom, but that was in spite of, not because of, welfare reform. The race to the bottom was avoided because (1) national economic growth provided states with additional revenue that mitigated pressure to use state welfare funds for other programmatic uses and (2) the unanticipated drop in welfare enrollment, coupled with the introduction of state-by-state funding that is not tied to the number of recipients served, provided states an unprecedented "windfall" that had to be spent. Now that the national economy is no longer expanding at a record pace and states have spent the unanticipated windfall, welfare reform opponents argue that it is only a matter of time before states race to the bottom.

West Virginia's Experience with Welfare Reform

West Virginia's experience with welfare reform provides evidence for both sides of this on-going and often acrimonious debate

Eleanor H. Blakely, Robert Jay Dilger, and Barry L. Locke

over the efficacy of the *Personal Responsibility and Work Opportunity Reconciliation Act of 1996* in addressing poverty and reducing welfare dependency. Since the law's enactment, West Virginia's caseload has dropped dramatically, from 36,691 cases in 1997 to 13,142 cases in 2002 (a 64% reduction) (W.V. Department of Health and Human Resources [DHHR] 2001, 2002). The percentage of WV WORKS recipients engaged in a work-related activity has also increased, reaching a record high of 25.6 percent in FY 1998 before falling to 17 percent in FY 2000 (DHHR 2000, DHHS 2002). In addition, the state did not race to the bottom. West Virginia increased recipient cash payments (the average payment increased from $231 in 1997 to $271 in 2000) and increased funding for childcare and other support services (DHHR 2001). However, although West Virginia's caseload dropped dramatically, the authors' 1999 WV WORKS leaver study revealed that nearly half of those who had left WV WORKS were not working, and nearly all of those who left WV WORKS were living in poverty (Dilger et al. 2000). Also, although the percentage of WV WORKS recipients engaged in a work-related activity increased to record levels, West Virginia's work participation rate of 17 percent in FY 2000 was the lowest in the nation (DHHS 2002). Moreover, many of those placements were in unpaid, community service positions. West Virginia escaped federal sanctions for failing to meet the required overall work participation rate because, like other states, it utilized the federal caseload reduction credit. However, even the receipt of that credit has not been enough to prevent West Virginia from failing to meet the work participation requirement for two-parent families every year since the welfare reform law's enactment. Finally, cash payments and funding for support services were increased, but, faced with a projected budget shortfall of nearly $90 million annually, in 2002 West Virginia reduced (1) recipient cash payments, (2) the income disregard used to determine program eligibility (from 60% to its former level of 40%), and (3) funding for many support services. The state scaled back much of its additional spending on welfare because the state's TANF "windfall" was exhausted and the state's continuing economic difficulties precluded it from using its own resources to maintain the higher level of services. However, West

Virginia did increase the state's contribution to the program in 2002 by $20 million to soften the budget cuts' adverse effect on the provision of support services.

West Virginia's welfare reform experiences suggest that the *Personal Responsibility and Work Opportunity Reconciliation Act of 1996* was, at best, only a partial success in West Virginia. WV WORKS enrollment is down, recipient work activity is up, and, even taking the recent budgetary reductions into account, recipient cash payments and funding for childcare and other support services is up. However, most of those who have left WV WORKS continue to experience severe economic hardship, most of those enrolled in WV WORKS are not in a work-related activity, many WV WORKS recipients who have been placed in a work-related activity are not in paid employment, and the state's continuing economic difficulties suggest that the state's efforts in 1999 and 2000 to increase funding to support higher recipient cash payments and more extensive support services is unlikely to be sustained.

Implementing Welfare Reform in a Rural, Impoverished State

As mentioned previously, several organizations have argued that rural states should be provided additional flexibility in meeting specific requirements contained in the *Personal Responsibility and Work Opportunity Reconciliation Act of 1996* because welfare recipients residing in rural areas face several unique challenges in making the transition from welfare to employment and economic self-sufficiency. The three specific provisions in the law that are discussed most are the maximum, sixty-month time limit on the receipt of benefits; the mandated, statewide work participation rates; and the fiscal sanctions for failing to achieve the statewide work participation rates.

West Virginia's experiences with welfare reform support their argument. For example, when examining the efficacy of West Virginia's educational, vocational, and job training programs in helping WV WORKS recipients to leave welfare and move toward economic self-sufficiency, Melissa Latimer discovered that participation in and completion of an educational, vocational, or job training program has a positive effect on employment outcomes. However, only 28 percent of the respondents to the 1999 WV WORKS survey reported that they had completed a training program when they were on welfare. In addition, the three skills recipients most frequently learned in their training programs were: job readiness skills (26.3%), office skills (15.7%), and no skills (14.8%). As Latimer explains, "...These 'skills' do little to help recipients leave and stay off welfare, and they do relatively little to reduce poverty." Moreover, her analysis revealed that access to West Virginia's educational, vocational and job training programs was uneven. Importantly, she discovered that recipients who reported that they lived in a rural area were 1.46 times less likely to participate in a training program than recipients who reported that they lived in a city/suburb or a small town (i.e., "urban areas").

This finding reinforces the argument that recipients residing in rural areas face unique challenges in making the transition from welfare to economic self-sufficiency. Also, Lucinda Potter discovered that paid employment had a positive effect on WV WORKS recipients' ability to leave and stay off welfare, household income, expectations of future household income, and their self-assessment of their personal well-being.

However, finding paid employment in West Virginia, especially in the state's more rural counties, is a daunting task for welfare recipients. This helps to explain why West Virginia's work participation rate has consistently been last or near the bottom nationally every year since the 1996 welfare reform law was passed. Finally, Robert Dilger discovered that West Virginia's welfare recipients face multiple personal and structural barriers to employment and economic self-sufficiency. He found that just 9.5 percent of WV WORKS recipients can be expected to make the transition off welfare with relative ease (no employment barriers); 24.8 percent can be expected to make the transition with moderate difficulty (one employment barrier); 30.5 percent with severe difficulty (two employment barriers); and 35.2 percent with acute difficulty (three or more employment barriers). His findings indicate that it is extremely difficult, if not impossible, for states like West Virginia to meet the mandated work participation rates.

Lessons from DHHR's Implementation of WV WORKS

The analysis of West Virginia's experience with welfare reform also indicates that some states should be provided additional flexibility in meeting specific requirements contained in the *Personal Responsibility and Work Opportunity Reconciliation Act of 1996* because they lack the administrative capacity necessary to fully implement the sweeping changes the legislation required. Although West Virginia's adverse economic circumstances played a key role in helping to explain why welfare reform in West Virginia was not very successful in assisting WV WORKS recipients to achieve economic self-sufficiency or to escape poverty, the state welfare agency's relative lack of administrative capacity was also a factor.

As L. Christopher Plein and David Williams discuss in Chapters 4, 5, and 6, welfare reform created new challenges for state welfare agencies throughout the nation. The *Personal Responsibility and Work Opportunity Reconciliation Act of 1996* required state welfare agencies to reinvent themselves into job placement and career counseling centers, but failed to provide clear directions for how to proceed. Moreover, federal bureaucrats took several years to issue regulations clarifying ambiguities in the law, including specific guidelines concerning what constituted a work activity. Facing the threat of federal sanctions, West Virginia's welfare bureaucracy decided to proceed cautiously. Ironically, the *Personal Responsibility and Work Opportunity Reconciliation Act of 1996* was designed to encourage states to be bold, innovative, and to take risks. Instead, it had the opposite effect. West Virginia Department of Health and Human Resources (DHHR) officials recognized that finding and placing recipients in a work activity, especially paid employment, is a difficult, labor-intensive task, especially in areas of the state experiencing economic decline. Because they lacked the time and resources necessary to retrain existing personnel or to hire additional personnel, DHHR focused on clearing cases (providing diversion payments for new applicants, not providing many exemptions to the sixty-month limitation on the receipt of benefits, and, for a while, counting Supplemental Security Income when determining eligibility, etc.). Clearing cases was the most cost effective and efficient way to avoid federal sanctions, especially given the ambiguities concerning what counted as a work activity and the state's ability to apply the federal caseload reduction credit against the mandated work participation rates. The lesson to be learned from West Virginia's experiences implementing welfare reform is that the implementation of major policy change requires clarity of rules and regulations, clear lines of administrative autonomy, and adequate time and resources to hire new and retrain existing agency personnel. None of these conditions were present during West Virginia's implementation of welfare reform. As Plein and Williams put it:

> ...The clearest lesson that can be learned from West Virginia's welfare reform experience is that implementing change in an environment marked by the lack of time, resources, and clarity is not conducive to the formation of a coherent and broad-based strategy of change. Instead, the institutional response is likely to be reactive, cautious, crisis-driven, and piecemeal, and the programmatic outcomes are likely to be less than hoped for, and often at the expense of those among us who can least afford to be ill-served.

F. Carson Mencken also demonstrated the importance of administrative capacity in his study of the effect place (local labor market conditions) and recipients' relationship with their caseworker and administrative agency have on dependency. He found that the local labor market is an important factor in determining recipient orientations about the future and success in leaving and staying off welfare. He also found that recipients' relationship with their caseworker was an important mediating factor in determining recipient orientations about the future and success in leaving and staying off welfare. His work suggests that state welfare agencies, like West Virginia's, that suffer from high turnover, primarily because they can not afford to provide salaries, benefits, and work conditions sufficient to retain their better employees, are at a real disadvantage when attempting to implement the many changes required to meet the new federal welfare guidelines, especially the need to reinvent themselves into employment centers.

The Fallacy of "One Size Fits All"

Two of the key lessons to be learned from West Virginia's experience with welfare reform are (1) place matters and (2) the "one-size-fits-all" mentality that underlies much of the 1996 welfare reform law is inappropriate for states, like West Virginia, which are at a comparative disadvantage in helping its welfare recipients achieve economic self-sufficiency. Although the *Personal Responsibility and Work Opportunity Reconciliation Act of 1996* was hailed by its authors for providing states greater programmatic flexibility, many of its key features, such as its mandatory work participation rates and its maximum, sixty-month time limit on the receipt of benefits, apply equally to all states, regardless of their economic circumstances, administrative capacity, and the employment barriers their welfare recipients face. States like West Virginia, which have a relatively weak economy, limited administrative capacity to enact sweeping change, and a relatively high proportion of welfare recipients facing multiple employment barriers, are at a real disadvantage. National policy should take these variations in circumstances into account by providing states experiencing economic difficulty, lacking administrative capacity, or with especially disadvantaged welfare populations additional flexibility concerning the sixty-month time limit on the receipt of benefits, the mandated work participation thresholds, and the fiscal sanctions associated with those work participation thresholds.

Conclusion

Everyone—elected officials, practitioners, scholars, and advocacy groups—agrees that the *Personal Responsibility and Work Opportunity Reconciliation Act of 1996* was landmark legislation. However, there is little agreement concerning its effectiveness. Some claim that it is a huge policy success. Others claim that it is a huge policy failure. Part of the reason for this lack of consensus about the law's efficacy is that there is no consensus about what constitutes success. Some argue that success is getting people off welfare. Others argue that success is getting people off welfare and keeping them off welfare. Still others argue that success is getting people off welfare, keeping them off welfare, and moving them out of poverty.

The *Personal Responsibility and Work Opportunity Reconciliation Act of 1996* resulted in a dramatic decline in the number of people on welfare, both nationally and in West Virginia. Although the number of welfare recipients, both nationally and in West Virginia, has increased marginally in recent years, there are far fewer welfare recipients today than there were in 1996. For those who define success as getting people off welfare and keeping them off, the 1996 welfare reform law is a success. However, others argue that, at least nationally, the caseload reduction was largely a function of national economic growth, not welfare reform. They also note that, both nationally and in West Virginia, most welfare leavers continue to live in poverty. As a result, those defining success as getting people off welfare, keeping them off welfare, and moving them out of poverty argue that the 1996 welfare reform law is a failure.

It is natural for policymakers, scholars, and others to want to reach a definitive conclusion concerning the overall success or failure of the *Personal Responsibility and Work Opportunity Reconciliation Act of 1996*. However, generally speaking, welfare recipients have little or no interest in this issue. They are more interested in knowing how the system affects them and their family. This research indicates that much remains to be done in West Virginia. Too many of West Virginia's most vulnerable citizens are being left behind. For example, most WV WORKS recipients have not had the opportunity to test the efficacy of the *Personal Responsibility and Work Opportunity Reconciliation Act of 1996's* emphasis on the work-first strategy because jobs in West Virginia are scarce and DHHR has not been able to place them in a work-related activity. Also, access to educational, vocational, and job-training programs in West Virginia is uneven, and those who need training the most have not been provided an opportunity to get it. Moreover, as Plein and Williams demonstrated, federal rules and regulations often have the unintended consequence of discouraging agency innovation and risk-taking, two traits that are absolutely essential in a state like West Virginia that suffers from both an anemic economy and a recipient population facing multiple employment barriers.

Another lesson that can be drawn from West Virginia's

experiences with welfare reform is that education is important. In nearly all of the statistical tests performed on the survey data, education was, time and time again, a significant predictor of a positive outcome for the recipient (more likely to have paid employment, more likely to leave and stay off welfare, more likely to participate in and complete a job training program, more likely to have a positive assessment of well-being, etc.).

Finally, returning to the "one size does not fit all" theme, the survey data from the WV WORKS leaver and WV WORKS recipient studies suggest that each family has a unique circumstance that needs to be addressed. Some families report that in order to leave and stay off welfare they need childcare, others need transportation (an especially acute problem for those residing in rural areas), some need education, others need vocational training, some need job training, others need job readiness skills, some need job referral services, some just need a job, and others need multiple support services. Therefore, it is important for the policymaking community to recognize that focusing on the work-first strategy may be appropriate for some families and for some places, but, for the most part, it is inappropriate for many families residing in places like West Virginia, which suffer from persistent poverty, weak labor markets, and underfunded and understaffed public and private support organizations.

References

Besser, Terry. 1998. "Employment in Small Towns." *Rural Development Perspectives* 3(2):31-39.

Bush, George W. 2002. *Working Toward Independence*. Washington, D.C.: U.S. Government Printing Office. http://www.whitehouse.gov/news/releases/2002/02/welfare-reform-announcement-book.pdf.

Cook, Peggy and Elizabeth Dagata. 1997. "Welfare Reform Legislation Poses Opportunities and Challenges for Rural America." *Rural Conditions and Trends* 8(1): 32-41.

Dilger, Robert Jay, Eleanor Blakely, Karen V. H. Dorton, Melissa Latimer, Barry Locke, Carson Mencken, L. Christopher

Plein, Lucinda A. Potter, David Williams, and Dong Pil Yoon. 2000. "WV WORKS Case Closure Study." *The West Virginia Public Affairs Reporter* 17:1 (Winter):1-15.

Findeis, Jill and Leif Jensen. 1998. "Employment Opportunities in Rural Areas: Implications for Poverty in a Changing Policy Environment." Paper presented at the Annual Meeting of the American Agricultural Economics Association. Salt Lake City, Utah.

Gibbs, Robert M., Paul L. Swaim, and Ruy Teixeira. 1998. *Rural Education and Training in the New Economy: The Myth of the Rural Skills Gap.* Ames, IA: Iowa State University Press.

Joint Center on Poverty Research (JCPR). 2000. "Rural Dimensions of Welfare Reform." Conference. Washington, D.C., May 4-5. Program Findings. http://www.jcpr.org/conferences/ruralbriefing.html#selectfindings.

Parker, Timothy and Leslie Whitener. 1997. "Minimum Wage Legislation: Rural Workers Will Benefit More Than Urban Workers From Increase in Minimum Wage." *Rural Conditions and Trends* 8(1): 48-52.

Pearce, Diana and Jennifer Brooks. 2002. *The Self-Sufficiency Standard for West Virginia.* Washington, D.C.: Wider Opportunities for Women.

Rural Policy Research Institute (RUPRI). 1998. *Welfare Reform in Rural Areas.* Washington, D.C.: Rural Policy Research Institute.

U.S. Department of Health and Human Services (DHHS). 2002. *Temporary Assistance for Needy Families Program (TANF): Fourth Annual Report to Congress.* Washington, D.C.: U.S. Department of Health and Human Services, Office of Planning, Research and Evaluation. May. http://www.acf.dhhs.gov/programs/opre/ar2001/indexar.htm.

Weber, Bruce and Greg Duncan. 2000. "Welfare Reform and Food Assistance in Rural America." Congressional Research Briefing on Welfare Reform and Rural Poverty. Washington,

D.C., June 21. http://www.jcpr.org/conferences/rural-summary.pdf.

West Virginia Department of Health and Human Resources (DHHR). 2001. *WV WORKS: West Virginia's Welfare Program, 2000 Annual Report*. Charleston, WV: West Virginia Department of Health and Human Resources. http://www.wvdhhr.org/ofs/2000%20Annual%20Report/2000AnnualReport.PDF.

———. 2002. "WV WORKS Caseload Statistics 2002." Charleston, WV: West Virginia

About the Authors

Dr. Eleanor H. Blakely is an Associate Professor in the Division of Social Work in West Virginia University's School of Applied Social Sciences. She has authored a dozen articles in the leading journals of social work and coauthored *Gatekeeping in BSW Programs*, published by Columbia University Press. Dr. Blakely also has extensive experience working with West Virginia's welfare policymaking community.

Dr. Robert Jay Dilger is Assistant Director for Government and Finance and Senior Specialist in American National Government for the Library of Congress' Congressional Research Service. Previously, Dr. Dilger served as Director of West Virginia University's Institute for Public Affairs and as a Professor of Political Science. He has published eight books and more than 50 articles and book chapters on a variety of topics, including poverty and welfare reform, environmental policy, transportation infrastructure, American federalism, intergovernmental relations, and state and local governance. Dr. Dilger's work has appeared in the leading journals of both Political Science and Public Administration. He has also authored several peer-reviewed monographs for the National League of Cities, the U.S. Advisory Commission on Intergovernmental Relations, and West Virginia University's Institute for Public Affairs. Dr. Dilger is a recipient of the outstanding researcher award from West Virginia University's Eberly College of Arts and Sciences.

DR. MELISSA LATIMER is an Associate Professor in the Division of Sociology and Anthropology, in West Virginia University's School of Applied Social Sciences. Dr. Latimer's research focuses on the major ways in which gender, race, and class inequality are constructed and reconstructed through labor market processes and welfare policies. Much of her published work involves understanding individual experiences with social insurance (i.e., unemployment insurance) and social assistance programs (i.e., AFDC/TANF) and how these experiences vary by gender, race, ethnicity, socioeconomic status, age, and place. More recently, her research has concentrated on welfare reform's short-term and long-term effects on individuals in economically disadvantaged areas. Dr. Latimer's research has appeared in many nationally respected journals, including *Sociological Spectrum, Sociological Focus, Southern Rural Sociology Journal, The Journal of Sociology and Social Welfare,* and *The West Virginia Public Affairs Reporter.*

DR. BARRY L. LOCKE is an Associate Professor and former Chair of the Division of Social Work in West Virginia University's School of Applied Social Sciences. He has authored a dozen articles in the leading journals of social work and has extensive experience working with West Virginia's welfare policymaking community, where he has been an active leader of three statewide policy organizations and member of several boards of directors in the public and non-profit sectors. Dr. Locke is co-author of an important text on social work practice, as well as a recognized leader in the areas of rural social welfare policy and human services at the state and national levels.

DR. F. CARSON MENCKEN is an Associate Professor of Sociology in the Department of Sociology and Anthropology at Baylor University. Previously, Dr. Mencken served as Associate Professor and Chair of the Division of Sociology and Anthropology in West Virginia University's School of Applied Social Sciences. Dr. Mencken's research focuses on the macroeconomic forces that affect the quality of life across geographic places and how those forces effect local firms, governments, households, and individuals. He has authored more

About the Authors

than a dozen articles in the leading journals of sociology, including *Sociological Focus, Rural Sociology, Journal of Appalachian Studies, American Journal of Economics and Sociology, Sociological Quarterly* and *Growth and Change.* He is also a nationally recognized expert on statistical analysis and advanced methodology and a recipient of the outstanding researcher award from West Virginia University's Eberly College of Arts and Sciences.

DR. L. CHRISTOPHER PLEIN is an Associate Professor and Chair of the Division of Public Administration in West Virginia University's School of Applied Social Sciences. Dr. Plein's research focuses on public policy formation and implementation. Recently, his research has concentrated on the study of Medicaid and welfare reform. For the past seven years, he has served as a field research associate with the Rockefeller Institute of Government's State Capacity Study investigating state responses to reforms in Medicaid, food stamps, and welfare policy. Dr. Plein's publications have appeared in several leading journals, including *Comparative Politics, International Journal of Public Administration, Policy Studies Journal, Health Affairs* and the *Journal of Public Affairs Education,* as well as in several book chapters and monographs. Dr. Plein's "Welfare Reform in a Hard Place: The West Virginia Experience,"*Rockefeller Report* No. 13 (November 2001), has gained wide-spread distribution in the policy community.

DR. LUCINDA A. POTTER served as a Graduate Research Assistant with the Institute for Public Affairs at West Virginia University. She recently received her Ph.D. in Political Science from West Virginia University's Department of Political Science. Dr. Potter's research interests focus on welfare reform and the role of work in addressing poverty.

DR. DAVID WILLIAMS is the Assistant Dean of the West Virginia University School of Applied Social Sciences and formerly served as Chair of the Division of Public Administration in the School of Applied Social Sciences. Dr. Williams's research interests include public management, public policy, participative governance, local government, outcome measurement, public decision making and public affairs education. His research has appeared in many leading journals including *Public Administration Review, PM: Public Management, State and Local Government Review, Social Science Journal,* and the *Journal of Public Affairs Education.* Dr. Williams's books include one on a macro-policy approach to improve public policy processes and one on cooperative federalism. Dr. Williams has served on the Commission on Peer Review and Accreditation (the accrediting body in public administration) and twice was a member of the National Executive Council of the National Association of Schools of Public Affairs and Administration. He has consulted widely with various state agencies and has conducted numerous workshops on public management at all levels of government and for nonprofit organizations.

Index

SUBJECT INDEX

9/11, 125
  Economic fallout, 98-99
Act for the Punishment of Vagabonds and Beggars, 238
Adams, Jane, 61
ADC (Aid to Dependent Children), 2; 64; 66-67; 68; 70
AFDC (Aid to Families with Dependent Children), 2; 56; 70; 72; 75; 140; 154; 179; 186-185; 215
  Attempts to reform, 77-79
  Family Support Act, 82-85
  Replacing with TANF, 88; 109-110; 113-114; 138; 142-144; 147; 163; 172
  WV Reforms 81
Aging Population
  See Demographics
Americans with Disabilities Act of 1990, 268
At-risk populations, 261-265
  Defining, 265-269
  TANF Recipients, 268-279
  West Virginia, 272-275
  WV WORKS 2000 survey results, 275-282
  WV Works recipients 272-273
Appalachia
  Central Appalachia, 25-26
  Definition, 24-26
  Poverty, 67; 296-298
  Welfare enrollment, 195-196

Balanced Budget Act of 1997, 87; 91; 115-116; 178; 184
Bush, George W., 192; 304

Caperton, Gaston, 109-110
Carter, Jimmy, 77
Caseworker
  See DHHR
CETA (Comprehensive Employment Training Act) 80; 209
Child Care, 40; 219; 225; 228-229
Child Care and Development Block Grant, 88
CHIP, 87; 91; 116; 120; 123; 151; 153-154; 176; 180-181; 191; 193-194
Clinton, Bill, 85; 113

Coal mining, 33-35
  Economic effects, 33-35; 230-231
CSP (Community Services Program), 148-149
CWEP (Community Work Experience), 80; 81-82; 145; 148-149

Demographics (welfare), 30-32
Department of Public Assistance (WV), 65
DHHR, 177; 193; 210; 309-310
DHHR (*continued*)
  Caseworkers 146-156
    Recipient satisfaction with, 276-277; 290-291; 293-298
  Federal Influence 117-120
  Funding, 112-114
  Implementing Welfare change, 107-110; 128-130; 145-147
  Budget Deficits, 124-126
  Budget Surplus, 121-123
  Organizational Changes, 139-141; 143
  Responsibilities, 115-117
  SSI, 186; 188
  See also WV WORKS
Dix, Dorothea, 59
Dole, Robert, 262

Economy, WV, rural nature of, 26-30; 222; 225; 227; 303-304
  Childcare, 40
  Coal mining, 33-35
  Deindustrialization, 42-43
  Education, 43-45
  Effect of Geography on, 23-26
  Farming, 32-33
  Health care, 39

Housing, 40-42
Public Services, 37-38
Transportation, 38-39; 231; 251; 270; 273
Economic Opportunity Act of 1964, 71
Education and welfare, 44-45; 221-223
  And Employment, 230-232
  Participation in Job Training, 227-228
  Staying off Welfare, 248; 254-255
EIC (Earned Income Tax Credit), 77; 240
Elizabethan Poor Law of 1601, 56; 58; 239

Family Assistance Plan, 76 –78; 241
Family Support Act of 1988, 83; 84-85; 209; 241-242
Federal Relief Administration, 64
Fiscal conservatives, 72
Food Stamp Act of 1964, 166
Food Stamp Program, 71; 73; 77; 82; 87; 94; 120; 153; 186; 240
  And other welfare reforms, 114-115; 117; 163-164; 169-172; 189-197
  Case management, 109; 140; 146; 172-174
  Enrollment requirements, 166-168
  History 165-166
  At-risk population, 277-279
Friedman, Milton, 72-73

Galbraith, John Kenneth, 67
Gender
  Education and job training, 214; 215; 222; 224

Index

Employment, 28; 32; 82-83; 241
Income, 28-29; 248; 251
Married, 228-229

Harrington, Michael, 67-68; 165
Henrican Poor Law, 238,
History of welfare, 1-5
   United Kingdom, 56–57; 238-239
   United States, 57–99; 62; 239-241
      Charities, 60-62
      Great Depression, 62-65; 239
   West Va., 59; 63; 65; 71; 81-82
Hoover, Herbert, 63
Hull House, 61
Human capital development theory, 4-5; 67-69; 68-70; 73-74; 83; 242-243
   Defined, 55
Humphrey, Hubert, 67

Income and welfare, 28-29
Index of Employment Adversity, 269-272

JOBS (Job Opportunities and Basic Skills Programs), 83-84; 88; 209; 212-213; 215; 222; 229; 241
Johnson, Lyndon Baines, 71; 240
JTPA (Job Training and Partnership Act), 80; 220; 222; 228

Kennedy, John, 67; 71; 165

Labor market and welfare, 27-28; 272-273; 310-311
Leavers, 93-95
   See also WV WORKS (survey)

Medicaid, 77; 82; 87; 88; 94; 109; 167; 186; 240
   And welfare reform, 163-164; 178-182; 189-197
   Case management, 114; 116; 120; 140; 146-147; 153
   Funding Formula, 71-73
   History, 175-178
   At-risk population, 277-279

Negative income tax, 72-74; 76
Neighborhood Guild, 61
Nixon, Richard, 76; 241

Omnibus Budget Reconciliation Act of 1981, 78-80
Other America, The, 67-68; 165; 240

Personal Responsibility and Work Opportunity Reconciliation Act of 1996, 23; 24; 55; 87; 93-97; 142-146; 209; 212
   And job training, 209-212
   Budget deficits, 123-126
   Budget surplus, 120-123.
   Effect in West Virginia, 95-97; 108-115; 305-313
   Efficacy, 304-305
   Federal influence on states, 117-120.
   Food Stamp Program, 165-169
   Goals, 88-89
   Limits, 126-128
   Local implementation, 139-142
   Problems and corrections, 146-150; 150-155
   Participation, 213
      At-risk populations, 261-265
   Requirements, 89-90; 237-238;

Welfare Reform in West Virginia

262-264
Reforms, 115-117
SSI, 183-184
Picket fence federalism, 117-118
Pierce, Franklin, 59
Program for Better Jobs and Income, 77
Progressives, 61
Poverty,
   in Appalachia, 67
   Structuralist view, 68

Race,
   See Demographics
RAPIDS, 149-150; 181
Reagan, Ronald, 79; 82
Resource extraction industry
   See Coal mining
Roosevelt, Franklin Delano, 64

Social Security Act of 1935, 64-65; 239
Social Security Act, 1962, 70; 240
SSI (Supplemental Security Income),
   77; 86; 91; 115; 144; 163-164;
   174; 176; 271; 293
   And welfare reform, 182-185;
   189-197
   Problems, 185-188
State Children's Health Insurance
   Program
   See CHIP
Statute of Laborers, 238
Starr, Ellen Gates, 61

TANF (Temporary Assistance for
   Needy Families), 2; 56; 111; 115;
   118; 281
   And Safety Net Programs, 163-
   164; 190-197

Food Stamps Program, 167-
174
Medicaid, 177-182
SSI, 185-188
Budget Deficit, 124-126; 156
Budget Surplus, 121; 151; 153
Extending Welfare Time Limit,
264-265
Initial Lack of Guidelines, 118-
119
Leavers, 92-95
Requirements, 88-90; 266
Reorganizing State Agencies,
128-130; 138-144; 147
See also At Risk Populations
See also WV WORKS
Taxpayer Relief Act of 1997, 91-92
Thompson Tommy, 126

Underwood, Cecil, 126; 156
Unemployed Parent program
   See AFDC-UP

War on Poverty, 71; 240
Welfare Ideology, 2-4
   Fiscal conservatives, 63; 72; 74; 79
Welfare-to-Work Program, 91; 266-
267
Welfare-to-Work Tax Credit, 91
Welfare Reform Act, The, 86
*Welfare Reform Technical Corrections
Act of 1997*, 90-92; 265-266
West Virginia Department of Health
   and Human Services
   See DHHR
WIN (Work Incentive Program), 74-
75; 80-81; 209; 240
Wisconsin WORKS, 126-127

324

Index

Wise, Robert, 124; 156; 181
Work Opportunity Tax Credit, 91
Workfare
   See CWEP
Workforce Attachment Strategy, 55, 70, 74, 80-83
   Defined, 55
   Success of 97-99
Workforce Investment Act of 1998, 91; 116; 229-230
WV WORKS, 92; 112; 167-168; 264-265
   And Safety Net Programs, 190-194
      Food Stamp Program, 169-174
      Medicaid, 179-182
      SSI, 185-186
   Background, 210-212
   Designing Program, 109-110
   DHHR and statewide implementation, 139-140
      Budget Surplus, 122-123; 151-155
      Budget Deficits, 125-126; 156-158; 195-196
      Demonstration Program, 142-145
      Federal Influence on, 116-119
      Limiting enrollment, 146-150
   Effect of Good Economy, 96-97
   Extending Welfare Time Limit, 264-265
   Leavers, 94-95; 148; 210; 219-220; 225; 230-232; 306
   Recipient attitudes, 287-291
   Success of, 306-313
   Survey of Participants, 7-12
   See also At-risk populations
WV WORKS 2000 (survey), 272-275
   Analysis, 218-226; 248-254; 295-296
   Design, 215-217; 244-245; 291
   Discussion, 227-232; 254-256
   Variables, 217-218; 245-248; 291-294
   See also At-Risk

CHARTS AND TABLES

ADC / TANF Recipients 1936 – 2002, 75
Future Orientation Regressed on Individual, Household, and West Virginia County Characteristics, 294
Key West Virginia Office of Family Support Positions, 141
Index of Employment Adversity WV WORKS 2000 Survey, 274
Logistic Regression of EMPLOYED on Labor Market, Household, and Individual Variables, 226
Logistic Regression of FEELING BETTER OFF NOW on Labor and Individual Variables, 253
Logistic Regression of HELPFUL on Labor Market, Household, and Individual Variables, 224
Logistic Regression of JOBS READY, OFFICE SKILLS, and NO SKILLS on Labor Market, Household, and Individual Variables, 223
Logistic Regression of LEFT AND STAYED OFF WV WORKS on Labor and Individual Variables, 249
Logistic Regression of RECEIVED

TRAINING on Labor Market, Household, and Individual Variables, 220

Logistic Regression of TOTAL EXPECTED HOUSEHOLD INCOME on Labor and Individual Variables, 252

Logistic Regression of TOTAL HOUSEHOLD INCOME on Labor and Individual Variables, 250

Logistic Regression of TRAINING COMPLETION on Labor Market, Household, and Individual Variables, 221

Predicted Future Orientations of WV WORKS Recipients, 296

Regional Caseloads, 155